Software Estimation:
Demystifying the Black Art

Steve McConnell

PUBLISHED BY
Microsoft Press
A Division of Microsoft Corporation
One Microsoft Way
Redmond, Washington 98052-6399

Library of Congress Control Number 2005936847

Printed and bound in the United States of America.

1 2 3 4 5 6 7 8 9 QWT 0 9 8 7 6

Distributed in Canada by H.B. Fenn and Company Ltd..

A CIP catalogue record for this book is available from the British Library

Microsoft Press books are available through booksellers and distributors worldwide. For further information about international editions, contact your local Microsoft Corporation office or contact Microsoft Press International directly at fax (425) 936-7329. Visit our Web site at www.microsoft.com/mspress. Send comments to mspinput@microsoft.com.

Acquisitions Editor: Ben Ryan
Project Editor: Devon Musgrave
Copy Editor: Becka McKay
Indexer: Seth Maislin

Body Part No. X11-82276

Contents at a Glance

Table of Contents

Part I Critical Estimation Concepts

What do you think of this book?
We want to hear from you!

Microsoft is interested in hearing your feedback about this publication so we can continually improve our books and learning resources for you. To participate in a brief online survey, please visit: *www.microsoft.com/learning/booksurvey/*

Part II Fundamental Estimation Techniques

Welcome

> *The most unsuccessful three years in the education of cost estimators appears to be fifth-grade arithmetic.*
>
> —Norman R. Augustine

Software estimation is not hard. Experts have been researching and writing about software estimation for four decades, and they have developed numerous techniques that support accurate software estimates. Creating accurate estimates is straightforward—once you understand how to create them. But not all estimation practices are intuitively obvious, and even smart people won't discover all the good practices on their own. The fact that someone is an expert developer doesn't make that person an expert estimator.

Numerous aspects of estimation are not what they seem. Many so-called estimation problems arise from misunderstanding what an "estimate" is or blurring other similar-but-not-identical concepts with estimation. Some estimation practices that seem intuitively useful don't produce accurate results. Complex formulas sometimes do more harm than good, and some deceptively simple practices produce surprisingly accurate results.

This book distills four decades of research and even more decades of hands-on experience to help developers, leads, testers, and managers become effective estimators. Learning about software estimation turns out to be generally useful because the influences that affect software estimates are the influences that affect software development itself.

Art vs. Science of Software Estimation

Software estimation research is currently focused on improving estimation techniques so that sophisticated organizations can achieve project results within ±5% of estimated results instead of within ±10%. These techniques are mathematically intensive. Understanding them requires a strong math background and concentrated study. Using them requires number crunching well beyond what you can do on your hand calculator. These techniques work best when embodied in commercial software estimation tools. I refer to this set of practices as the *science of estimation*.

Meanwhile, the typical software organization is not struggling to improve its estimates from ±10% to ±5% accuracy. The typical software organization is struggling to avoid estimates that are incorrect by 100% or more. (The reasons for this are manifold and will be discussed in detail in Chapters 3 and 4.)

Our natural tendency is to believe that complex formulas like this:

$$\text{Effort} = 2.94 * (\text{KSLOC})^{[0.91 + 0.01 * \Sigma_{j=1}^{5} SF_j]} * \prod_{i=1}^{17} EM_i$$

will always produce more accurate results than simple formulas like this:

Effort = NumberOfRequirements * AverageEffortPerRequirement

But complex formulas aren't necessarily better. Software projects are influenced by numerous factors that undermine many of the assumptions contained in the complex formulas of the science of estimation. Those dynamics will be explained later in this book. Moreover, most software practitioners have neither the time nor the inclination to learn the intensive math required to understand the science of estimation.

Consequently, this book emphasizes rules of thumb, procedures, and simple formulas that are highly effective and understandable to practicing software professionals. These techniques will not produce estimates that are accurate to within ±5%, but they will reduce estimation error to about 25% or less, which turns out to be about as useful as most projects need, anyway. I call this set of techniques the *art of estimation*.

This book draws from both the art and science of software estimation, but its focus is on software estimation as an art.

Why This Book Was Written and Who It Is For

The literature on software estimation is widely scattered. Researchers have published hundreds of articles, and many of them are useful. But the typical practitioner doesn't have time to track down dozens of papers from obscure technical journals. A few previous books have described the science of estimation. Those books are 800–1000 pages long, require a good math background, and are targeted mainly at professional estimators—consultants or specialists who estimate large projects and do so frequently.

I wrote this book for developers, leads, testers, and managers who need to create estimates occasionally as one of their many job responsibilities. I believe that most practitioners want to improve the accuracy of their estimates but don't have the time to obtain a Ph.D. in software estimation. These practitioners struggle with practical issues like how to deal with the politics that surround the estimate, how to present an estimate so that it will actually be accepted, and how to avoid having someone change your estimate arbitrarily. If you are in this category, this book was written for you.

The techniques in this book apply to Internet and intranet development, embedded software, shrink-wrapped software, business systems, new development, legacy systems, large projects, small projects—essentially, to estimates for all kinds of software.

Key Benefits Of This Book

By focusing on the art of estimation, this book provides numerous important estimation insights:

- What an "estimate" is. (You might think you already know what an estimate is, but common usages of the term are inaccurate in ways that undermine effective estimation.)

- The specific factors that have made your past estimates less accurate than they could have been.

- Ways to distinguish a good estimate from a poor one.

- Numerous techniques that will allow *you personally* to create good estimates.

- Several techniques you can use to help *other people on your team* create good estimates.

- Ways that *your organization* can create good estimates. (There are important differences between personal techniques, group techniques, and organizational techniques.)

- Estimation approaches that work on agile projects, and approaches that work on traditional, sequential (plan-driven) projects.

- Estimation approaches that work on small projects and approaches that work on large projects.

- How to navigate the shark-infested political waters that often surround software estimation.

In addition to gaining a better understanding of estimation concepts, the practices in this book will help you estimate numerous specific attributes of software projects, including:

- New development work, including schedule, effort, and cost

- Schedule, effort, and cost of legacy systems work

- How many features you can deliver within a specific development iteration

- The amount of functionality you can deliver for a whole project when schedule and team size are fixed

- Proportions of different software development activities needed, including how much management work, requirements, construction, testing, and defect correction will be needed

- Planning parameters, such as tradeoffs between cost and schedule, best team size, amount of contingency buffer, ratio of developers to testers, and so on

- Quality parameters, including time needed for defect correction work, defects that will remain in your software at release time, and other factors

- Practically anything else you want to estimate

In many cases, you'll be able to put this book's practices to use right away.

Most practitioners will not need to go any further than the concepts described in this book. But understanding the concepts in this book will lay enough groundwork that you'll be able to graduate to more mathematically intensive approaches later on, if you want to.

What This Book Is Not About

This book is not about how to estimate the very largest projects—more than 1 million lines of code, or more than 100 staff years. Very large projects should be estimated by professional estimators who have read the dozens of obscure journal articles, who have studied the 800–1000-page books, who are familiar with commercial estimation software, and who are as skilled in both the art and science of estimation.

Where to Start

Where you start will depend on what you want to get out of the book.

If you bought this book because you need to create an estimate right now...   Begin with Chapter 1 ("What Is an "Estimate"?), and then move to Chapter 7 ("Count, Compute, Judge") and Chapter 8 ("Calibration and Historical Data"). After that, skim the tips in Chapters 10–20 to find the techniques that will be the most immediately useful to you. By the way, this book's tips are highlighted in the text and numbered, and all of the tips—118 total—are also collected in Appendix C, "Software Estimation Tips."

If you want to improve your personal estimation skills, if you want to improve your organization's estimation track record, or if you're looking for a better understanding of software estimation in general...   You can read the whole book. If you like to understand general principles before you dive into the details, read the book in order. If you like to see the details first and then draw general conclusions from the details, you can start with Chapter 1, read Chapters 7 through 23, and then go back and read the earlier chapters that you skipped.

Bellevue, Washington
New Year's Day, 2006

Microsoft Press Support

Every effort has been made to ensure the accuracy of this book. Microsoft Press provides corrections for books through the World Wide Web at the following address:

http://www.microsoft.com/learning/support/books/

To connect directly to the Microsoft Press Knowledge Base and enter a query regarding a question or issue that you may have, go to:

http://www.microsoft.com/mspress/support/search.asp

If you have comments, questions, or ideas regarding this book, please send them to Microsoft Press using either of the following methods:

Postal Mail:

Microsoft Press
Attn: Software Estimation *Editor*
One Microsoft Way
Redmond, WA 98052-6399

E-Mail:

mspinput@microsoft.com

Acknowledgments

I continue to be amazed at the many ways the Internet supports high-quality work. My first book's manuscript was reviewed almost entirely by people who lived within 50 miles of me. This book's manuscript included reviewers from Argentina, Australia, Canada, Denmark, England, Germany, Iceland, The Netherlands, Northern Ireland, Japan, Scotland, Spain, and the United States. The book has benefited enormously from these reviews.

Thanks first to the people who contributed review comments on significant portions of the book: Fernando Berzal, Steven Black, David E. Burgess, Stella M. Burns, Gavin Burrows, Dale Campbell, Robert A. Clinkenbeard, Bob Corrick, Brian Donaldson, Jason Hills, William Horn, Carl J Krzystofczyk, Jeffrey D. Moser, Thomas Oswald, Alan M. Pinder, Jon Price, Kathy Rhode, Simon Robbie, Edmund Schweppe, Gerald Simon, Creig R. Smith, Linda Taylor, and Bernd Viefhues.

Thanks also to the people who reviewed selected portions of the book: Lisa M. Adams, Hákon Ágústsson, Bryon Baker, Tina Coleman, Chris Crawford, Dominic Cronin, Jerry Deville, Conrado Estol, Eric Freeman, Hideo Fukumori, C. Dale Hildebrandt, Barbara Hitchings, Jim Holmes, Rick Hower, Kevin Hutchison, Finnur Hrafn Jonsson, Aaron Kiander, Mehmet Kerem Kızıltunç, Selimir Kustudic, Molly J. Mahai, Steve Mattingly, Joe Nicholas, Al Noel, David O'Donoghue, Sheldon Porcina, David J. Preston, Daniel Read, David Spokane, Janco Tanis, Ben Tilly, and Wendy Wilhelm.

I'd especially like to acknowledge Construx's estimation seminar instructors. After years of stimulating discussions, it's often impossible to tell which ideas originated with me and which originated with them. Thanks to Earl Beede, Gregg Boer, Matt Peloquin, Pamela Perrott, and Steve Tockey.

This book focuses on estimation as an art, and this book's simplifications were made possible by researchers who have spent decades clarifying estimation as a science. My heartfelt appreciation to three of the giants of estimation science: Barry Boehm, Capers Jones, and Lawrence Putnam.

Working with Devon Musgrave, project editor for this book, has once again been a privilege. Thanks, Devon! Becka McKay, assistant editor, also improved my original manuscript in countless ways. Thanks also to the rest of the Microsoft Press staff, including Patricia Bradbury, Carl Diltz, Tracey Freel, Jessie Good, Patricia Masserman, Joel Panchot, and Sandi Resnick. And thanks to indexer Seth Maislin.

Thanks finally to my wife, Ashlie, who is—in my estimation—the best life partner I could ever hope for.

Equations

Figures

Part I
Critical Estimation Concepts

Chapter 1
What Is an "Estimate"?

It is very difficult to make a vigorous, plausible, and job-risking defense of an estimate that is derived by no quantitative method, supported by little data, and certified chiefly by the hunches of the managers.

–Fred Brooks

You might think you already know what an estimate is. My goal by the end of this chapter is to convince you that an estimate is different from what most people think. A *good* estimate is even more different.

Here is a dictionary definition of *estimate*: 1. A tentative evaluation or rough calculation. 2. A preliminary calculation of the cost of a project. 3. A judgment based upon one's impressions; opinion. (Source: *The American Heritage Dictionary*, Second College Edition, 1985.)

Does this sound like what you are asked for when you're asked for an estimate? Are you asked for a *tentative* or *preliminary* calculation–that is, do you expect that you can change your mind later?

Probably not. When executives ask for an "estimate," they're often asking for a commitment or for a plan to meet a target. The distinctions between estimates, targets, and commitments are critical to understanding what an estimate is, what an estimate is not, and how to make your estimates better.

1.1 Estimates, Targets, and Commitments

Strictly speaking, the dictionary definition of *estimate* is correct: an estimate is a prediction of how long a project will take or how much it will cost. But estimation on software projects interplays with business targets, commitments, and control.

A *target* is a statement of a desirable business objective. Examples include the following:

- "We need to have Version 2.1 ready to demonstrate at a trade show in May."
- "We need to have this release stabilized in time for the holiday sales cycle."
- "These functions need to be completed by July 1 so that we'll be in compliance with government regulations."
- "We must limit the cost of the next release to $2 million, because that's the maximum budget we have for that release."

Businesses have important reasons to establish targets independent of software estimates. But the fact that a target is desirable or even mandatory does not necessarily mean that it is achievable.

While a target is a description of a desirable business objective, a *commitment* is a promise to deliver defined functionality at a specific level of quality by a certain date. A commitment can be the same as the estimate, or it can be more aggressive or more conservative than the estimate. In other words, do not assume that the commitment has to be the same as the estimate; it doesn't.

Tip #1	Distinguish between estimates, targets, and commitments.

1.2 Relationship Between Estimates and Plans

Estimation and planning are related topics, but estimation is not planning, and planning is not estimation. Estimation should be treated as an unbiased, analytical process; planning should be treated as a biased, goal-seeking process. With estimation, it's hazardous to want the estimate to come out to any particular answer. The goal is accuracy; the goal is not to seek a particular result. But the goal of planning is to seek a particular result. We deliberately (and appropriately) bias our plans to achieve specific outcomes. We plan specific means to reach a specific end.

Estimates form the foundation for the plans, but the plans don't have to be the same as the estimates. If the estimates are dramatically different from the targets, the project plans will need to recognize that gap and account for a high level of risk. If the estimates are close to the targets, then the plans can assume less risk.

Both estimation and planning are important, but the fundamental differences between the two activities mean that combining the two tends to lead to poor estimates *and* poor plans. The presence of a strong planning target can lead to substitution of the target for an analytically derived estimate; project members might even refer to the target as an "estimate," giving it a halo of objectivity that it doesn't deserve.

Here are examples of planning considerations that depend in part on accurate estimates:

- Creating a detailed schedule
- Identifying a project's critical path
- Creating a complete work breakdown structure
- Prioritizing functionality for delivery
- Breaking a project into iterations

Accurate estimates support better work in each of these areas (and Chapter 21, "Estimating Planning Parameters," goes into more detail on these topics).

1.3 Communicating about Estimates, Targets, and Commitments

One implication of the close and sometimes confusing relationship between estimation and planning is that project stakeholders sometimes miscommunicate about these activities. Here's an example of a typical miscommunication:

> EXECUTIVE: *How long do you think this project will take? We need to have this software ready in 3 months for a trade show. I can't give you any more team members, so you'll have to do the work with your current staff. Here's a list of the features we'll need.*

> PROJECT LEAD: *OK, let me crunch some numbers, and get back to you.*

Later...

> PROJECT LEAD: *We've estimated the project will take 5 months.*

> EXECUTIVE: *Five months!? Didn't you hear me? I said we needed to have this software ready in 3 months for a trade show!*

In this interaction, the project lead will probably walk away thinking that the executive is irrational, because he is asking for the team to deliver 5 months' worth of functionality in 3 months. The executive will walk away thinking that the project lead doesn't "get" the business reality, because he doesn't understand how important it is to be ready for the trade show in 3 months.

Note in this example that the executive was not really asking for an estimate; he was asking the project lead to come up with a *plan* to hit a *target*. Most executives don't have the technical background that would allow them to make fine distinctions between estimates, targets, commitments, and plans. So it becomes the technical leader's responsibility to translate the executive's request into more specific technical terms.

Here's a more productive way that the interaction could go:

> EXECUTIVE: *How long do you think this project will take? We need to have this software ready in 3 months for a trade show. I can't give you any more team members, so you'll have to do the work with your current staff. Here's a list of the features we'll need.*

> PROJECT LEAD: *Let me make sure I understand what you're asking for. Is it more important for us to deliver 100% of these features, or is it more important to have something ready for the trade show?*

EXECUTIVE: *We have to have something ready for the trade show. We'd like to have 100% of those features if possible.*

PROJECT LEAD: *I want to be sure I follow through on your priorities as best I can. If it turns out that we can't deliver 100% of the features by the trade show, should we be ready to ship what we've got at trade show time, or should we plan to slip the ship date beyond the trade show?*

EXECUTIVE: *We have to have something for the trade show, so if push comes to shove, we have to ship something, even if it isn't 100% of what we want.*

PROJECT LEAD: *OK, I'll come up with a plan for delivering as many features as we can in the next 3 months.*

Tip #2	When you're asked to provide an estimate, determine whether you're supposed to be estimating or figuring out how to hit a target.

1.4 Estimates as Probability Statements

If three-quarters of software projects overrun their estimates, the odds of any given software project completing on time and within budget are not 100%. Once we recognize that the odds of on-time completion are not 100%, an obvious question arises: "If the odds aren't 100%, what are they?" This is one of the central questions of software estimation.

Software estimates are routinely presented as single-point numbers, such as "This project will take 14 weeks." Such simplistic single-point estimates are meaningless because they don't include any indication of the probability associated with the single point. They imply a probability as shown in Figure 1-1—the only possible outcome is the single point given.

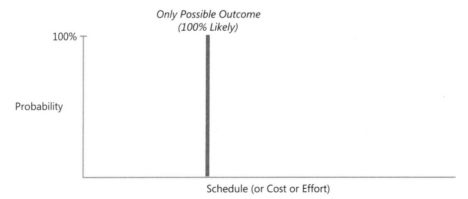

Figure 1-1   Single-point estimates assume 100% probability of the actual outcome equaling the planned outcome. This isn't realistic.

A single-point estimate is usually a target masquerading as an estimate. Occasionally, it is the sign of a more sophisticated estimate that has been stripped of meaningful probability information somewhere along the way.

Tip #3	When you see a single-point "estimate," ask whether the number is an estimate or whether it's really a target.

Accurate software estimates acknowledge that software projects are assailed by uncertainty from all quarters. Collectively, these various sources of uncertainty mean that project outcomes follow a probability distribution—some outcomes are more likely, some outcomes are less likely, and a cluster of outcomes in the middle of the distribution are most likely. You might expect that the distribution of project outcomes would look like a common bell curve, as shown in Figure 1-2.

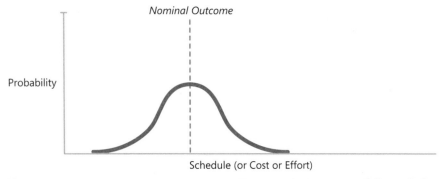

Figure 1-2   A common assumption is that software project outcomes follow a bell curve. This assumption is incorrect because there are limits to how efficiently a project team can complete any given amount of work.

Each point on the curve represents the chance of the project finishing exactly on that date (or costing exactly that much). The area under the curve adds up to 100%. This sort of probability distribution acknowledges the possibility of a broad range of outcomes. But the assumption that the outcomes are symmetrically distributed about the mean (average) is not valid. There is a limit to how well a project can be conducted, which means that the tail on the left side of the distribution is truncated rather than extending as far to the left as it does in the bell curve. And while there is a limit to how well a project can go, there is no limit to how poorly a project can go, and so the probability distribution does have a very long tail on the right.

Figure 1-3 provides an accurate representation of the probability distribution of a software project's outcomes.

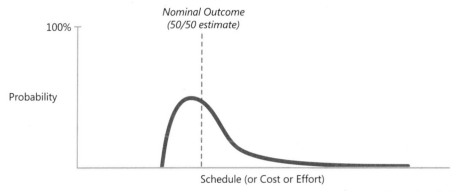

Figure 1-3   An accurate depiction of possible software project outcomes. There is a limit to how well a project can go but no limit to how many problems can occur.

The vertical dashed line shows the "nominal" outcome, which is also the "50/50" outcome—there's a 50% chance that the project will finish better and a 50% chance that it will finish worse. Statistically, this is known as the "median" outcome.

Figure 1-4 shows another way of expressing this probability distribution. While Figure 1-3 showed the probabilities of delivering on specific dates, Figure 1-5 shows the probabilities of delivering on each specific date *or earlier*.

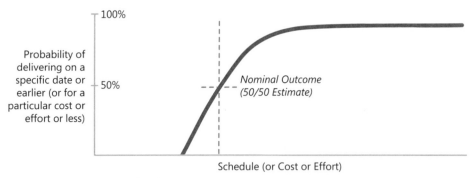

Figure 1-4   The probability of a software project delivering on or before a particular date (or less than or equal to a specific cost or level of effort).

Figure 1-5 presents the idea of probabilistic project outcomes in another way. As you can see from the figure, a naked estimate like "18 weeks" leaves out the interesting information that 18 weeks is only 10% likely. An estimate like "18 to 24 weeks" is more informative and conveys useful information about the likely range of project outcomes.

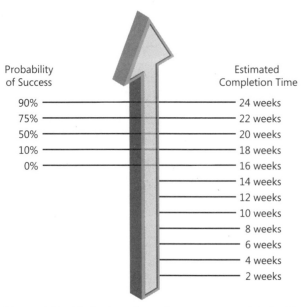

Probability of Success		Estimated Completion Time
90%		24 weeks
75%		22 weeks
50%		20 weeks
10%		18 weeks
0%		16 weeks
		14 weeks
		12 weeks
		10 weeks
		8 weeks
		6 weeks
		4 weeks
		2 weeks

Figure 1-5   All single-point estimates are associated with a probability, explicitly or implicitly.

Tip #4   When you see a single-point estimate, that number's probability is not 100%. Ask what the probability of that number is.

You can express probabilities associated with estimates in numerous ways. You could use a "percent confident" attached to a single-point number: "We're 90% confident in the 24-week schedule." You could describe estimates as best case and worst case, which implies a probability: "We estimate a best case of 18 weeks and a worst case of 24 weeks." Or you could simply state the estimated outcome as a range rather than a single-point number: "We're estimating 18 to 24 weeks." The key point is that all estimates include a probability, whether the probability is stated or implied. An explicitly stated probability is one sign of a good estimate.

You can make a commitment to the optimistic end or the pessimistic end of an estimation range—or anywhere in the middle. The important thing is for you to know where in the range your commitment falls so that you can plan accordingly.

1.5 Common Definitions of a "Good" Estimate

The answer to the question of what an "estimate" is still leaves us with the question of what a *good* estimate is. Estimation experts have proposed various definitions of a good estimate. Capers Jones has stated that accuracy with ±10% is possible, but only on well-controlled projects (Jones 1998). Chaotic projects have too much variability to achieve that level of accuracy.

In 1986, Professors S.D. Conte, H.E. Dunsmore, and V.Y. Shen proposed that a good estimation approach should provide estimates that are within 25% of the actual results 75% of the time (Conte, Dunsmore, and Shen 1986). This evaluation standard is the most common standard used to evaluate estimation accuracy (Stutzke 2005).

Numerous companies have reported estimation results that are close to the accuracy Conte, Dunsmore, and Shen and Jones have suggested. Figure 1-6 shows actual results compared to estimates from a set of U.S. Air Force projects.

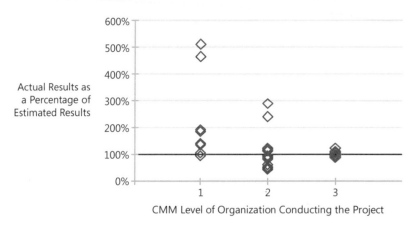

Source: "A Correlational Study of the CMM and Software Development Performance" (Lawlis, Flowe, and Thordahl 1995).

Figure 1-6   Improvement in estimation of a set of U.S. Air Force projects. The predictability of the projects improved dramatically as the organizations moved toward higher CMM levels.[1]

Figure 1-7 shows results of a similar improvement program at the Boeing Company.

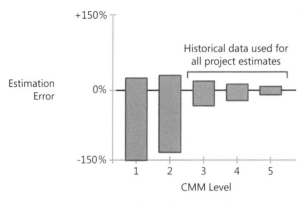

Figure 1-7   Improvement in estimation at the Boeing Company. As with the U.S. Air Force projects, the predictability of the projects improved dramatically at higher CMM levels.

---

[1]   The CMM (Capability Maturity Model) is a system defined by the Software Engineering Institute to assess the effectiveness of software organizations.

A final, similar example, shown in Figure 1-8, comes from improved estimation results at Schlumberger.

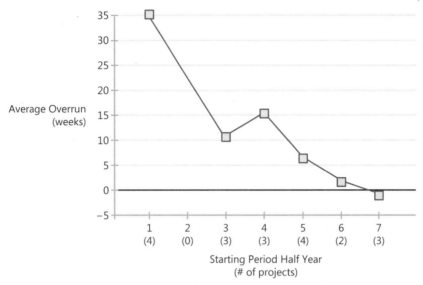

Figure 1-8   Schlumberger improved its estimation accuracy from an average overrun of 35 weeks to an average underrun of 1 week.

One of my client companies delivers 97% of its projects on time and within budget. Telcordia reported that it delivers 98% of its projects on time and within budget (Pitterman 2000). Numerous other companies have published similar results (Putnam and Myers 2003). Organizations are creating good estimates by both Jones's definition and Conte, Dunsmore, and Shen's definition. However, an important concept is missing from both of these definitions—namely, that accurate estimation results cannot be accomplished through estimation practices alone. They must also be supported by effective project control.

1.6 Estimates and Project Control

Sometimes when people discuss software estimation they treat estimation as a purely predictive activity. They act as though the estimate is made by an impartial estimator, sitting somewhere in outer space, disconnected from project planning and prioritization activities.

In reality, there is little that is pure about software estimation. If you ever wanted an example of Heisenberg's Uncertainty Principle applied to software, estimation would be it. (Heisenberg's Uncertainty Principle is the idea that the mere act of observing a thing changes it, so you can never be sure how that thing would behave if you weren't observing it.) Once we make an estimate and, on the basis of that estimate, make a commitment to deliver functionality and quality by a particular date, then we *control* the project to meet the target. Typical project control activities include removing non-critical requirements, redefining requirements, replacing less-experienced staff with more-experienced staff, and so on. Figure 1-9 illustrates these dynamics.

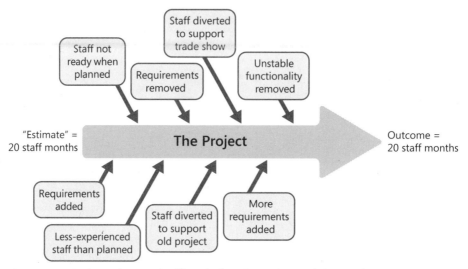

Figure 1-9   Projects change significantly from inception to delivery. Changes are usually significant enough that the project delivered is not the same as the project that was estimated. Nonetheless, if the outcome is similar to the estimate, we say the project met its estimate.

In addition to project control activities, projects are often affected by unforeseen external events. The project team might need to create an interim release to support a key customer. Staff might be diverted to support an old project, and so on.

Events that happen during the project nearly always invalidate the assumptions that were used to estimate the project in the first place. Functionality assumptions change, staffing assumptions change, and priorities change. It becomes impossible to make a clean analytical assessment of whether the project was estimated accurately—because the software project that was ultimately delivered is not the project that was originally estimated.

In practice, if we deliver a project with about the level of functionality intended, using about the level of resources planned, in about the time frame targeted, then we typically say that the project "met its estimates," despite all the analytical impurities implicit in that statement.

Thus, the criteria for a "good" estimate cannot be based on its predictive capability, which is impossible to assess, but on the estimate's ability to support project success, which brings us to the next topic: the Proper Role of Estimation.

1.7 Estimation's Real Purpose

Suppose you're preparing for a trip and deciding which suitcase to take. You have a small suitcase that you like because it's easy to carry and will fit into an airplane's overhead storage bin. You also have a large suitcase, which you don't like because you'll have to check it in and then wait for it at baggage claim, lengthening your trip. You lay your clothes beside the small suitcase, and it appears that they will almost fit. What do you do? You might try packing them very carefully, not wasting any space, and hoping they all fit. If that approach doesn't work, you might try stuffing them into the suitcase with brute force, sitting on the top and trying to squeeze the latches closed. If that still doesn't work, you're faced with a choice: leave a few clothes at home or take the larger suitcase.

Software projects face a similar dilemma. Project planners often find a gap between a project's business targets and its estimated schedule and cost. If the gap is small, the planner might be able to control the project to a successful conclusion by preparing extra carefully or by squeezing the project's schedule, budget, or feature set. If the gap is large, the project's targets must be reconsidered.

The primary purpose of software estimation is not to predict a project's outcome; it is to determine whether a project's targets are realistic enough to allow the project to be controlled to meet them. Will the clothes you want to take on your trip fit into the small suitcase or will you be forced to take the large suitcase? Can you take the small suitcase if you make minor adjustments? Executives want the same kinds of answers. They often don't want an accurate estimate that tells them that the desired clothes won't fit into the suitcase; they want a plan for making as many of the clothes fit as possible.

Problems arise when the gap between the business targets and the schedule and effort needed to achieve those targets becomes too large. I have found that if the initial target and initial estimate are within about 20% of each other, the project manager will have enough maneuvering room to control the feature set, schedule, team size, and other parameters to meet the project's business goals; other experts concur (Boehm 1981, Stutzke 2005). If the gap between the target and what is actually needed is too large, the manager will not be able to control the project to a successful conclusion by making minor adjustments to project parameters. No amount of careful packing or sitting on the suitcase will squeeze all your clothes into the smaller suitcase, and you'll have to take the larger one, even if it isn't your first choice, or you'll have to leave some clothes behind. The project targets will need to be brought into better alignment with reality before the manager can control the project to meet its targets.

Estimates don't need to be perfectly accurate as much as they need to be *useful*. When we have the combination of accurate estimates, good target setting, and good planning and control, we can end up with project results that are close to the "estimates." (As you've guessed, the word "estimate" is in quotation marks because the project that was estimated is not the same project that was ultimately delivered.)

These dynamics of changing project assumptions are a major reason that this book focuses more on the art of estimation than on the science. Accuracy of ±5% won't do you much good if the project's underlying assumptions change by 100%.

1.8 A Working Definition of a "Good Estimate"

With the background provided in the past few sections, we're now ready to answer the question of what qualifies as a good estimate.

> *A good estimate is an estimate that provides a clear enough view of the project reality to allow the project leadership to make good decisions about how to control the project to hit its targets..*

This definition is the foundation of the estimation discussion throughout the rest of this book.

Additional Resources

Conte, S. D., H. E. Dunsmore, and V. Y. Shen. *Software Engineering Metrics and Models.* Menlo Park, CA: Benjamin/Cummings, 1986. Conte, Dunsmore, and Shen's book contains the definitive discussion of evaluating estimation models. It discusses the "within 25% of actual 75% of the time" criteria, as well as many other evaluation criteria.

DeMarco, Tom. *Controlling Software Projects.* New York, NY: Yourdon Press, 1982. DeMarco discusses the probabilistic nature of software projects.

Stutzke, Richard D. *Estimating Software-Intensive Systems.* Upper Saddle River, NJ: Addison-Wesley, 2005. Appendix C of Stutzke's book contains a summary of measures of estimation accuracy.

Chapter 2

How Good an Estimator Are You?

> *The process is called estimation, not exactimation.*
>
> –Phillip Armour

Now that you know what a good estimate is, how good an estimator are you? The following section will help you find out.

2.1 A Simple Estimation Quiz

Table 2-1, appearing on the following page, contains a quiz designed to test your estimation skills. Please read and observe the following directions carefully:

For each question, fill in the upper and lower bounds that, in your opinion, give you a 90% chance of including the correct value. Be careful not to make your ranges either too wide or too narrow. Make them wide enough so that, in your best judgment, the ranges give you a 90% chance of including the correct answer. Please do not research any of the answers—this quiz is intended to assess your estimation skills, not your research skills. You must fill in an answer for each item; an omitted item will be scored as an incorrect item. Please limit your time on this exercise to 10 minutes.

(Also, you might want to photocopy the quiz before taking it so that the next person who reads this book can take it, too.)

The correct answers to this exercise (the latitude of Shanghai, for example) are listed in Appendix B in the back of the book. Give yourself one point for each of your ranges that includes the related correct answer.

Table 2-1   **How Good an Estimator Are You?**

[Low Estimate – High Estimate]	Description
[_____ – _____]	Surface temperature of the Sun
[_____ – _____]	Latitude of Shanghai
[_____ – _____]	Area of the Asian continent
[_____ – _____]	The year of Alexander the Great's birth
[_____ – _____]	Total value of U.S. currency in circulation in 2004
[_____ – _____]	Total volume of the Great Lakes
[_____ – _____]	Worldwide box office receipts for the movie *Titanic*
[_____ – _____]	Total length of the coastline of the Pacific Ocean
[_____ – _____]	Number of book titles published in the U.S. since 1776
[_____ – _____]	Heaviest blue whale ever recorded

Source: Inspired by a similar quiz in *Programming Pearls*, Second Edition (Bentley 2000).

This quiz is from *Software Estimation* by Steve McConnell (Microsoft Press, 2006) and is © 2006 Steve McConnell. All Rights Reserved. Permission to copy this quiz is granted provided that this copyright notice is included.

How did you do? (Don't feel bad. Most people do poorly on this quiz!) Please write your score here: _____

2.2 Discussion of Quiz Results

The purpose of this quiz is not to determine whether you know when Alexander the Great was born or the latitude of Shanghai. Its purpose is to determine how well you understand your own estimation capabilities.

How Confident Is "90% Confident"?

The directions above are specific that the goal of the exercise is to estimate at the 90% confidence level. Because there are 10 questions in the quiz, if you were truly estimating at the 90% confidence level, you should have gotten about 9 answers correct.[1]

If you were cautious, you made your ranges conservatively wide, in which case you scored 10 out of 10 correctly. If you were just a little hasty, you made your ranges narrower than they needed to be, in which case you scored 7 or 8 out of 10 correctly. I've given this quiz to hundreds of estimators. Figure 2-1 shows the results from the most recent 600 people who have taken the quiz.

---

[1]   The mathematics behind "90% confident" are a little complicated. If you were really estimating with 90% confidence, you would have a 34.9% chance of getting 10 answers correct, 38.7% chance of getting 9 answers correct, and a 19.4% chance of getting 8 answers correct. In other words, you'd have a 93% chance of getting 8 or more answers correct.

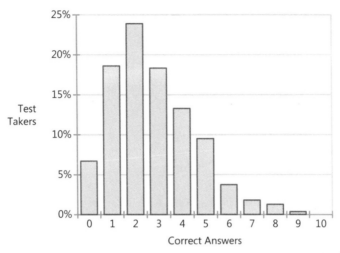

Figure 2-1   Results from administering the "How Good an Estimator Are You?" quiz. Most quiz-takers get 1–3 answers correct.

For the test takers whose results are shown in the figure, the average number of correct answers is 2.8. Only 2 percent of quiz takers score 8 or more answers correctly. No one has ever gotten 10 correct. I've concluded that most people's intuitive sense of "90% confident" is really comparable to something closer to "30% confident." Other studies have confirmed this basic finding (Zultner 1999, Jørgensen 2002).

Similarly, I've seen numerous project teams present "90% confident" schedules, and I've frequently seen those project teams overrun their "90% confident" schedules— more often than not. If those schedules represented a true 90% confidence, the project teams would overrun them only about 1 time out of 10.

I've concluded that specific percentages such as "90%" are not meaningful unless they are supported through some kind of statistical analysis. Otherwise those specific percentages are just wishful thinking. How to get to a *real* 90% confidence level will be discussed later in the book.

Tip #5	Don't provide "percentage confident" estimates (especially "90% confident") unless you have a quantitatively derived basis for doing so.

If you didn't take the quiz earlier in this chapter, this would be a good time to go back and take it. I think you'll be surprised at how few answers you get correct even after reading this explanation.

How Wide Should You Make Your Ranges?

When I find the rare person who gets 7 or 8 answers correct, I ask "How did you get that many correct?" The typical response? "I made my ranges too wide."

My response is, "No, you didn't! You didn't make your ranges wide enough!" If you got only 7 or 8 correct, your ranges were still too narrow to include the correct answer as often as you should have.

We are conditioned to believe that estimates expressed as narrow ranges are more accurate than estimates expressed as wider ranges. We believe that wide ranges make us appear ignorant or incompetent. The opposite is usually the case. (Of course, narrow ranges are desirable in the cases when the underlying data supports them.)

Tip #6	Avoid using artificially narrow ranges. Be sure the ranges you use in your estimates don't misrepresent your confidence in your estimates.

Where Does Pressure to Use Narrow Ranges Come From?

When you were taking the quiz, did you feel pressure to make your ranges wider? Or did you feel pressure to make your ranges narrower? Most people report that they feel pressure to make the ranges as narrow as possible. But if you go back and review the instructions, you'll find that they do not encourage you to use narrow ranges. Indeed, I was careful to state that you should make your ranges neither too wide nor too narrow—just wide enough to give you a 90% confidence in including the correct answer.

After discussing this issue with hundreds of developers and managers, I've concluded that much of the pressure to provide narrow ranges is self-induced. Some of the pressure comes from people's sense of professional pride. They believe that narrow ranges are a sign of a better estimate, even though that isn't the case. And some of the pressure comes from experiences with bosses or customers who insisted on the use of overly narrow ranges.

This same self-induced pressure has been found in interactions between customers and estimators. Jørgensen and Sjøberg reported that information about customers' expectations exerts strong influence on estimates and that estimators are typically not conscious of the degree to which their estimates are affected (Jørgensen and Sjøberg 2002).

Tip #7	If you are feeling pressure to make your ranges narrower, verify that the pressure actually is coming from an external source and not from yourself.

For those cases in which the pressure truly is coming from an external source, Chapter 22, "Estimate Presentation Styles," and Chapter 23, "Politics, Negotiation, and Problem Solving," discuss how to deal with that pressure.

How Representative Is This Quiz of Real Software Estimates?

In software, you aren't often asked to estimate the volume of the Great Lakes or the surface temperature of the Sun. Is it reasonable to expect you to be able to estimate the amount of U.S. currency in circulation or the number of books published in the U.S., especially if you're not in the U.S.?

Software developers are often asked to estimate projects in unfamiliar business areas, projects that will be implemented in new technologies, the impacts of new programming tools on productivity, the productivity of unidentified personnel, and so on. Estimating in the face of uncertainty is business as usual for software estimators. The rest of this book explains how to succeed in such circumstances.

Chapter 3
Value of Accurate Estimates

[The common definition of estimate is] "the most optimistic prediction that has a non-zero probability of coming true." ... Accepting this definition leads irrevocably toward a method called what's-the-earliest-date-by-which-you-can't-prove-you-won't-be-finished estimating.

—Tom DeMarco

The inaccuracy of software project estimates—as muddied by unrealistic targets and unachievable commitments—has been a problem for many years. In the 1970s, Fred Brooks pointed out that "more software projects have gone awry for lack of calendar time than all other causes combined" (Brooks 1975). A decade later, Scott Costello observed that "deadline pressure is the single greatest enemy of software engineering" (Costello 1984). In the 1990s, Capers Jones reported that "excessive or irrational schedules are probably the single most destructive influence in all of software" (Jones 1994, 1997).

Tom DeMarco wrote his common definition of an estimate in 1982. Despite the successes I mentioned in the first chapter, not much has changed in the years since he wrote that definition. You might already agree that accurate estimates are valuable. This chapter details the specific benefits of accurate estimates and provides supporting data for them.

3.1 Is It Better to Overestimate or Underestimate?

Intuitively, a perfectly accurate estimate forms the ideal planning foundation for a project. If the estimates are accurate, work among different developers can be coordinated efficiently. Deliveries from one development group to another can be planned to the day, hour, or minute. We know that accurate estimates are rare, so if we're going to err, is it better to err on the side of overestimation or underestimation?

Arguments Against Overestimation

Managers and other project stakeholders sometimes fear that, if a project is overestimated, Parkinson's Law will kick in—the idea that work will expand to fill available time. If you give a developer 5 days to deliver a task that could be completed in 4 days, the developer will find something to do with the extra day. If you give a project team 6 months to complete a project that could be completed in 4 months, the project team will find a way to use up the extra 2 months. As a result, some managers consciously squeeze the estimates to try to avoid Parkinson's Law.

Another concern is Goldratt's "Student Syndrome" (Goldratt 1997). If developers are given too much time, they'll procrastinate until late in the project, at which point they'll rush to complete their work, and they probably won't finish the project on time.

A related motivation for underestimation is the desire to instill a sense of urgency in the development team. The line of reason goes like this:

> *The developers say that this project will take 6 months. I think there's some padding in their estimates and some fat that can be squeezed out of them. In addition, I'd like to have some schedule urgency on this project to force prioritizations among features. So I'm going to insist on a 3-month schedule. I don't really believe the project can be completed in 3 months, but that's what I'm going to present to the developers. If I'm right, the developers might deliver in 4 or 5 months. Worst case, the developers will deliver in the 6 months they originally estimated.*

Are these arguments compelling? To determine that, we need to examine the arguments in favor of erring on the side of overestimation.

Arguments Against Underestimation

Underestimation creates numerous problems—some obvious, some not so obvious.

Reduced effectiveness of project plans   Low estimates undermine effective planning by feeding bad assumptions into plans for specific activities. They can cause planning errors in the team size, such as planning to use a team that's smaller than it should be. They can undermine the ability to coordinate among groups—if the groups aren't ready when they said they would be, other groups won't be able to integrate with their work.

If the estimation errors caused the plans to be off by only 5% or 10%, those errors wouldn't cause any significant problems. But numerous studies have found that software estimates are often inaccurate by 100% or more (Lawlis, Flowe, and Thordahl 1995; Jones 1998; Standish Group 2004; ISBSG 2005). When the planning assumptions are wrong by this magnitude, the average project's plans are based on assumptions that are so far off that the plans are virtually useless.

Statistically reduced chance of on-time completion   Developers typically estimate 20% to 30% lower than their actual effort (van Genuchten 1991). Merely using their normal estimates makes the project plans optimistic. Reducing their estimates even further simply reduces the chances of on-time completion even more.

Poor technical foundation leads to worse-than-nominal results   A low estimate can cause you to spend too little time on upstream activities such as requirements and design. If you don't put enough focus on requirements and design, you'll get to redo your requirements and redo your design later in the project—at greater cost than if you'd done those activities well in the first place (Boehm and Turner 2004, McConnell 2004a). This ultimately makes your project take longer than it would have taken with an accurate estimate.

Destructive late-project dynamics make the project worse than nominal   Once a project gets into "late" status, project teams engage in numerous activities that they don't need to engage in during an "on-time" project. Here are some examples:

- More status meetings with upper management to discuss how to get the project back on track.

- Frequent reestimation, late in the project, to determine just when the project will be completed.

- Apologizing to key customers for missing delivery dates (including attending meetings with those customers).

- Preparing interim releases to support customer demos, trade shows, and so on. If the software were ready on time, the software itself could be used, and no interim release would be necessary.

- More discussions about which requirements absolutely must be added because the project has been underway so long.

- Fixing problems arising from quick and dirty workarounds that were implemented earlier in response to the schedule pressure.

The important characteristic of each of these activities is that they don't need to occur *at all* when a project is meeting its goals. These extra activities drain time away from productive work on the project and make it take longer than it would if it were estimated and planned accurately.

Weighing the Arguments

Goldratt's Student Syndrome can be a factor on software projects, but I've found that the most effective way to address Student Syndrome is through active task tracking and buffer management (that is, project control), similar to what Goldratt suggests, not through biasing the estimates.

As Figure 3-1 shows, the best project results come from the most accurate estimates (Symons 1991). If the estimate is too low, planning inefficiencies will drive up the actual cost and schedule of the project. If the estimate is too high, Parkinson's Law kicks in.

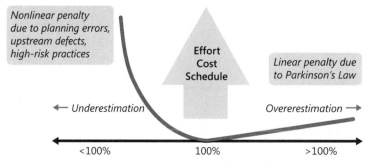

Target as a Percentage of Nominal Estimate

Figure 3-1   The penalties for underestimation are more severe than the penalties for overestimation, so, if you can't estimate with complete accuracy, try to err on the side of overestimation rather than underestimation.

I believe that Parkinson's Law does apply to software projects. Work does expand to fill available time. But deliberately underestimating a project because of Parkinson's Law makes sense only if the penalty for overestimation is worse than the penalty for underestimation. In software, the penalty for overestimation is *linear and bounded*—work will expand to fill available time, but it will not expand any further. But the penalty for underestimation is *nonlinear and unbounded*—planning errors, shortchanging upstream activities, and the creation of more defects cause more damage than overestimation does, and with little ability to predict the extent of the damage ahead of time.

Tip #8	Don't intentionally underestimate. The penalty for underestimation is more severe than the penalty for overestimation. Address concerns about overestimation through planning and control, not by biasing your estimates.

3.2 Details on the Software Industry's Estimation Track Record

The software industry's estimation track record provides some interesting clues to the nature of software's estimation problems. In recent years, The Standish Group has published a biennial survey called "The Chaos Report," which describes software project outcomes. In the 2004 report, 54% of projects were delivered late, 18% failed outright, and 28% were delivered on time and within budget. Figure 3-2 shows the results for the 10 years from 1994 to 2004.

What's notable about The Standish Group's data is that it doesn't even have a category for early delivery! The best possible performance is meeting expectations "On Time/On Budget"—and the other options are all downhill from there.

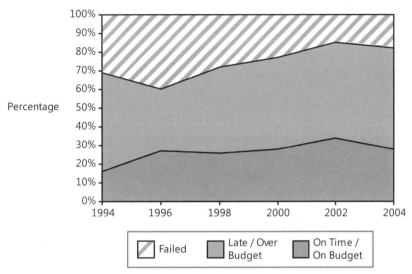

Figure 3-2   Project outcomes reported in The Standish Group's Chaos report have fluctuated year to year. About three quarters of all software projects are delivered late or fail outright.

Capers Jones presents another view of project outcomes. Jones has observed for many years that project success depends on project size. That is, larger projects struggle more than smaller projects do. Table 3-1 illustrates this point.

Table 3-1   **Project Outcomes by Project Size**

Size in Function Points (and Approximate Lines of Code)	**Early**	**On Time**	**Late**	**Failed (Canceled)**
10 FP (1,000 LOC)	11%	81%	6%	2%
100 FP (10,000 LOC)	6%	75%	12%	7%
1,000 FP (100,000 LOC)	1%	61%	18%	20%
10,000 FP (1,000,000 LOC)	<1%	28%	24%	48%
100,000 FP (10,000,000 LOC)	0%	14%	21%	65%

Source: *Estimating Software Costs* (Jones 1998).

As you can see from Jones's data, the larger a project, the less chance the project has of completing on time and the greater chance it has of failing outright.

Overall, a compelling number of studies have found results in line with the results reported by The Standish Group and Jones, that about one quarter of all projects are delivered on time; about one quarter are canceled; and about half are delivered late, over budget, or both (Lederer and Prasad 1992; Jones 1998; ISBSG 2001; Krasner 2003; Putnam and Myers 2003; Heemstra, Siskens and van der Stelt 2003; Standish Group 2004).

The reasons that projects miss their targets are manifold. Poor estimates are one reason but not the only reason. We'll discuss the reasons in depth in Chapter 4, "Where Does Estimation Error Come From?"

How Late Are the Late Projects?

The number of projects that run late or over budget is one consideration. The degree to which these projects miss their targets is another consideration. According to the first Standish Group survey, the average project schedule overrun was about 120% and the average cost overrun was about 100% (Standish Group 1994). But the estimation accuracy is probably worse than those numbers reflect. The Standish Group found that late projects routinely threw out significant amounts of functionality to achieve the schedules and budgets they eventually did meet. Of course, these projects' estimates weren't for the abbreviated versions they eventually delivered; they were for the originally specified, full-featured versions. If these late projects had delivered all of their originally specified functionality, they would have overrun their plans even more.

One Company's Experience

A more company-specific view of project outcomes is shown in the data reported by one of my clients in Figure 3-3.

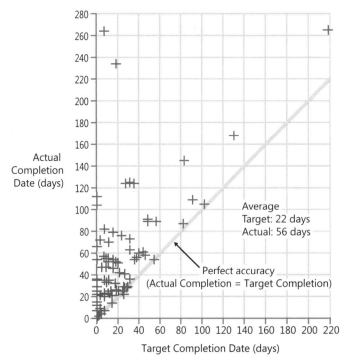

Figure 3-3   Estimation results from one organization. General industry data suggests that this company's estimates being about 100% low is typical. Data used by permission.

The points that are clustered on the "0" line on the left side of the graph represent projects for which the developers reported that they were done but which were found not to be complete when the software teams began integrating their work with other groups.

The diagonal line represents perfect scheduling accuracy. Ideally, the graph would show data points clustering tightly around the diagonal line. Instead, nearly all of the 80 data points shown are above the line and represent project overruns. One point is below the line, and a handful of points are on the line. The line illustrates DeMarco's common definition of an "estimate"—the earliest date by which you could possibly be finished.

The Software Industry's Systemic Problem

We often speak of the software industry's estimation problem as though it were a neutral estimation problem—that is, sometimes we overestimate, sometimes we underestimate, and we just can't get our estimates right.

But the software does not have a neutral estimation problem. The industry data shows clearly that *the software industry has an underestimation problem.* Before we can make our estimates more accurate, we need to start making the estimates *bigger*. That is the key challenge for many organizations.

3.3 Benefits of Accurate Estimates

Once your estimates become accurate enough that you get past worrying about large estimation errors on either the high or low side, truly accurate estimates produce additional benefits.

Improved status visibility   One of the best ways to track progress is to compare planned progress with actual progress. If the planned progress is realistic (that is, based on accurate estimates), it's possible to track progress according to plan. If the planned progress is fantasy, a project typically begins to run without paying much attention to its plan and it soon becomes meaningless to compare actual progress with planned progress. Good estimates thus provide important support for project tracking.

Higher quality   Accurate estimates help avoid schedule-stress-related quality problems. About 40% of all software errors have been found to be caused by stress; those errors could have been avoided by scheduling appropriately and by placing less stress on the developers (Glass 1994). When schedule pressure is extreme, about four times as many defects are reported in the released software as are reported for software developed under less extreme pressure (Jones 1994). One reason is that teams implement quick-and-dirty versions of features that absolutely must be completed in time to release the software. Excessive schedule pressure has also been found to be the most significant cause of extremely costly error-prone modules (Jones 1997).

Projects that aim from the beginning to have the lowest number of defects usually also have the shortest schedules (Jones 2000). Projects that apply pressure to create unrealistic estimates and subsequently shortchange quality are rudely awakened when they discover that they have also shortchanged cost and schedule.

Better coordination with nonsoftware functions   Software projects usually need to coordinate with other business functions, including testing, document writing, marketing campaigns, sales staff training, financial projections, software support training, and so on. If the software schedule is not reliable, that can cause related functions to slip, which can cause the *entire project schedule* to slip. Better software estimates allow for tighter coordination of the whole project, including both software and nonsoftware activities.

Better budgeting   Although it is almost too obvious to state, accurate estimates support accurate budgets. An organization that doesn't support accurate estimates undermines its ability to forecast the costs of its projects.

Increased credibility for the development team   One of the great ironies in software development is that after a project team creates an estimate, managers, marketers, and sales staff take the estimate and turn it into an optimistic business target—over the objections of the project team. The developers then overrun the optimistic business target, at which point, managers, marketers, and sales staff blame the developers for being poor estimators! A project team that holds its ground and insists on an accurate estimate will improve its credibility within its organization.

Early risk information   One of the most common wasted opportunities in software development is the failure to correctly interpret the meaning of an initial mismatch between project goals and project estimates. Consider what happens when the business sponsor says, "This project needs to be done in 4 months because we have a major trade show coming up," and the project team says, "Our best estimate is that this project will take 6 months." The most typical interaction is for the business sponsor and the project leadership to negotiate the *estimate*, and for the project team eventually to be pressured into committing to try to achieve the 4-month schedule.

Bzzzzzt! Wrong answer! The detection of a mismatch between the project goal and the project estimate should be interpreted as incredibly useful, incredibly rare, early-in-the-project risk information. The mismatch indicates a substantial chance that the project will fail to meet its business objective. Detected early, numerous corrective actions are available, and many of them are high leverage. You might redefine the scope of the project, you might increase staff, you might transfer your best staff onto the project, or you might stagger the delivery of different functionality. You might even decide the project is not worth doing after all.

But if this mismatch is allowed to persist, the options that will be available for corrective action will be far fewer and will be much lower leverage. The options will generally consist of "overrun the schedule and budget" or "cut painful amounts of functionality."

Tip #9	Recognize a mismatch between a project's business target and a project's estimate for what it is: valuable risk information that the project might not be successful. Take corrective action early, when it can do some good.

3.4 Value of Predictability Compared with Other Desirable Project Attributes

Software organizations and individual software projects try to achieve numerous objectives for their projects. Here are some of the goals they strive for:

- **Schedule**   Shortest possible schedule for the desired functionality at the desired quality level
- **Cost**   Minimum cost to deliver the desired functionality in the desired time
- **Functionality**   Maximum feature richness for the time and money available

Projects will prioritize these generic goals as well as more specific goals differently. Agile development tends to focus on the goals of flexibility, repeatability, robustness, sustainability, and visibility (Cockburn 2001, McConnell 2002). The SEI's CMM tends to focus on the goals of efficiency, improvability, predictability, repeatability, and visibility.

In my discussions with executives, I've frequently asked, "What is more important to you: the ability to change your mind about features, or the ability to know cost, schedule, and functionality in advance?" At least 8 times out of 10, executives respond "The ability to know cost, schedule, and functionality in advance"—in other words, *predictability*. Other software experts have made the same observation (Moseman 2002, Putnam and Myers 2003).

I often follow up by saying, "Suppose I could offer you project results similar to either Option #1 or Option #2 in Figure 3-4. Let's suppose Option #1 means that I can deliver a project with an expected duration of 4 months, but it might be 1 month early and it might be as many as 4 months late. Let's suppose Option #2 means that I can deliver a project with an expected duration of 5 months (rather than 4), and I can guarantee that it will be completed within a week of that date. Which would you prefer?"

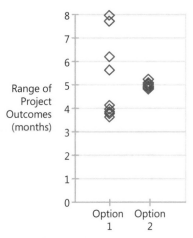

Figure 3-4   When given the option of a shorter average schedule with higher variability or a longer average schedule with lower variability, most businesses will choose the second option.

In my experience, nearly all executives will choose Option #2. The shorter schedule offered by Option #1 won't do the business any good because the business can't depend on it. Because the overrun could easily be as large as 4 months, the business has to plan on an 8-month schedule rather than a 4-month schedule. Or it delays making any plans at all until the software is actually ready. In comparison, the guaranteed 5-month schedule of Option #2 looks much better.

Over the years, the software industry has focused on time to market, cost, and flexibility. Each of these goals is desirable, but what top executives usually value most is predictability. Businesses need to make commitments to customers, investors, suppliers, the marketplace, and other stakeholders. These commitments are all supported by predictability.

None of this proves that predictability is the top priority for your business, but it suggests that you shouldn't make assumptions about your business's priorities.

Tip #10	Many businesses value predictability more than development time, cost, or flexibility. Be sure you understand what your business values the most.

3.5 Problems with Common Estimation Techniques

Considering the widespread poor results from software estimation, it shouldn't be a surprise that the techniques used to produce the estimates are not effective. These techniques should be carefully examined and thrown out!

Albert Lederer and Jayesh Prasad found that the most commonly used estimation technique was comparing a new project with a similar past project, based solely on personal memory. This technique was not found to be correlated with accurate estimates. The common techniques of "intuition" and "guessing" were found to be correlated with cost and schedule overruns (Lederer and Prasad 1992). Numerous other researchers have found that guessing, intuition, unstructured expert judgment, use of informal analogies, and similar techniques are the dominant strategies used for about 60 to 85% of all estimates (Hihn and Habib-Agahi 1991, Heemstra and Kusters 1991, Paynter 1996, Jørgensen 2002, Kitchenham et al. 2002).

Chapter 5, "Estimate Influences," presents a more detailed examination of sources of estimation error, and the rest of this book provides alternatives to these common techniques.

Additional Resources

Goldratt, Eliyahu M. *Critical Chain*. Great Barrington, MA: The North River Press, 1997. Goldratt describes an approach to dealing with Student Syndrome as well as an approach to buffer management that addresses Parkinson's Law.

Putnam, Lawrence H. and Ware Myers. *Five Core Metrics*. New York, NY: Dorset House, 2003. Chapter 4 contains an extended discussion of the importance of predictability compared to other project objectives.

Chapter 4
Where Does Estimation Error Come From?

> *There's no point in being exact about something if you don't even know what you're talking about.*
>
> *–John von Neumann*

A University of Washington Computer Science Department project was in serious estimation trouble. The project was months late and $20.5 million over budget. The causes ranged from design problems and miscommunications to last-minute changes and numerous errors. The university argued that the plans for the project weren't adequate. But this wasn't an ordinary software project. In fact, it wasn't a software project at all; it was the creation of the university's new Computer Science and Engineering Building (Sanchez 1998).

Software estimation presents challenges because estimation itself presents challenges. The Seattle Mariners' new baseball stadium was estimated in 1995 to cost $250 million. It was finally completed in 1999 at a cost of $517 million—an estimation error of more than 100% (Withers 1999). The most massive cost overrun in recent times was probably Boston's Big Dig highway construction project. Originally estimated to cost $2.6 billion, costs eventually totaled about $15 billion—an estimation error of more than 400% (Associated Press 2003).

Of course, the software world has its own dramatic estimation problems. The Irish Personnel, Payroll and Related Systems (PPARS) system was cancelled after it overran its €8.8 million system by €140 million (The Irish Times 2005). The FBI's Virtual Case File (VCF) project was shelved in March 2005 after costing $170 million and delivering only one-tenth of its planned capability (Arnone 2005). The software contractor for VCF complained that the FBI went through 5 different CIOs and 10 different project managers, not to mention 36 contract changes (Knorr 2005). Background chaos like that is not unusual in projects that have experienced estimation problems.

A chapter on sources of estimation error might just as well be titled "Classic Mistakes in Software Estimation." Merely avoiding the problems identified in this chapter will get you halfway to creating accurate estimates.

Estimation error creeps into estimates from four generic sources:

- Inaccurate information about the project being estimated

- Inaccurate information about the capabilities of the organization that will perform the project

- Too much chaos in the project to support accurate estimation (that is, trying to estimate a moving target)

- Inaccuracies arising from the estimation process itself

This chapter describes each source of estimation error in detail.

4.1 Sources of Estimation Uncertainty

How much does a new house cost? It depends on the house. How much does a Web site cost? It depends on the Web site. Until each specific feature is understood in detail, it's impossible to estimate the cost of a software project accurately. It isn't possible to estimate the amount of work required to build something when that "something" has not been defined.

Software development is a process of gradual refinement. You start with a general product concept (the vision of the software you intend to build), and you refine that concept based on the product and project goals. Sometimes your goal is to estimate the budget and schedule needed to deliver a specific amount of functionality. Other times your goal is to estimate how much functionality can be built in a predetermined amount of time under a fixed budget. Many projects navigate under a happy medium of some flexibility in budget, schedule, and features. In any of these cases the different ways the software could ultimately take shape will produce widely different combinations of cost, schedule, and feature set.

Suppose you're developing an order-entry system and you haven't yet pinned down the requirements for entering telephone numbers. Some of the uncertainties that could affect a software estimate from the requirements activity through release include the following:

- When telephone numbers are entered, will the customer want a Telephone Number Checker to check whether the numbers are valid?

- If the customer wants the Telephone Number Checker, will the customer want the cheap or expensive version of the Telephone Number Checker? (There are typically 2-hour, 2-day, and 2-week versions of any particular feature—for example, U.S.-only versus international phone numbers.)

- If you implement the cheap version of the Telephone Number Checker, will the customer later want the expensive version after all?

- Can you use an off-the-shelf Telephone Number Checker, or are there design constraints that require you to develop your own?

- How will the Telephone Number Checker be designed? (Typically there is at least a factor of 10 difference in design complexity among different designs for the same feature.)

- How long will it take to code the Telephone Number Checker? (There can be a factor of 10 difference—or more—in the time that different developers need to code the same feature.)

- Do the Telephone Number Checker and the Address Checker interact? How long will it take to integrate the Telephone Number Checker and the Address Checker?

- What will the quality level of the Telephone Number Checker be? (Depending on the care taken during implementation, there can be a factor of 10 difference in the number of defects contained in the original implementation.)

- How long will it take to debug and correct mistakes made in the implementation of the Telephone Number Checker? (Individual performance among different programmers with the same level of experience varies by at least a factor of 10 in debugging and correcting the same problems.)

As you can see just from this short list of uncertainties, potential differences in how a single feature is specified, designed, and implemented can introduce cumulative differences of a hundredfold or more in implementation time for any given feature. When you combine these uncertainties across hundreds or thousands of features in a large feature set, you end up with significant uncertainty in the project itself.

4.2 The Cone of Uncertainty

Software development consists of making literally thousands of decisions about all the feature-related issues described in the previous section. Uncertainty in a software estimate results from uncertainty in how the decisions will be resolved. As you make a greater percentage of those decisions, you reduce the estimation uncertainty.

As a result of this process of resolving decisions, researchers have found that project estimates are subject to predictable amounts of uncertainty at various stages. The Cone of Uncertainty in Figure 4-1 shows how estimates become more accurate as a project progresses. (The following discussion initially describes a sequential development approach for ease of explanation. The end of this section will explain how to apply the concepts to iterative projects.)

The horizontal axis contains common project milestones, such as Initial Concept, Approved Product Definition, Requirements Complete, and so on. Because of its origins, this terminology sounds somewhat product-oriented. "Product Definition" just refers to the agreed-upon vision for the software, or the *software concept*, and applies equally to Web services, internal business systems, and most other kinds of software projects.

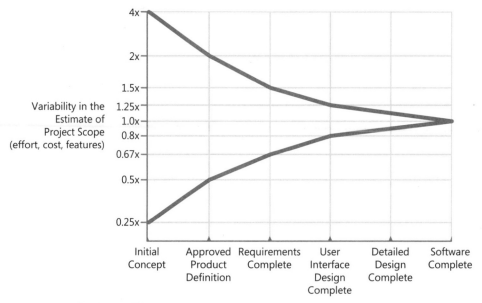

Figure 4-1   The Cone of Uncertainty based on common project milestones.

The vertical axis contains the degree of error that has been found in estimates created by skilled estimators at various points in the project. The estimates could be for how much a particular feature set will cost and how much effort will be required to deliver that feature set, or it could be for how many features can be delivered for a particular amount of effort or schedule. This book uses the generic term *scope* to refer to project size in effort, cost, features, or some combination thereof.

As you can see from the graph, estimates created very early in the project are subject to a high degree of error. Estimates created at Initial Concept time can be inaccurate by a factor of 4x on the high side or 4x on the low side (also expressed as 0.25x, which is just 1 divided by 4). The total range from high estimate to low estimate is 4x divided by 0.25x, or 16x!

One question that managers and customers ask is, "If I give you another week to work on your estimate, can you refine it so that it contains less uncertainty?" That's a reasonable request, but unfortunately it's not possible to deliver on that request. Research by Luiz Laranjeira suggests that the accuracy of the software estimate depends on the level of refinement of the software's definition (Laranjeira 1990). The more refined the definition, the more accurate the estimate. The reason the estimate contains variability is that the software project itself contains variability. The only way to reduce the variability in the estimate is to reduce the variability in the project.

One misleading implication of this common depiction of the Cone of Uncertainty is that it looks like the Cone takes forever to narrow—as if you can't have very good estimation accuracy until you're nearly done with the project. Fortunately, that impression is created because the milestones on the horizontal axis are equally spaced, and we naturally assume that the horizontal axis is calendar time.

In reality, the milestones listed tend to be front-loaded in the project's schedule. When the Cone is redrawn on a calendar-time basis, it looks like Figure 4-2.

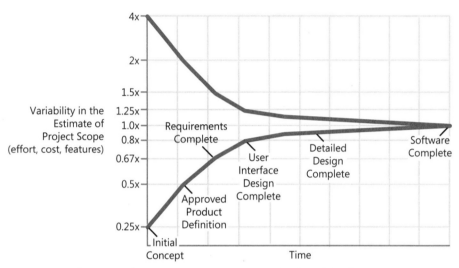

Figure 4-2 The Cone of Uncertainty based on calendar time. The Cone narrows much more quickly than would appear from the previous depiction in Figure 4-1.

As you can see from this version of the Cone, estimation accuracy improves rapidly for the first 30% of the project, improving from ±4x to ±1.25x.

Can You Beat the Cone?

An important—and difficult—concept is that the Cone of Uncertainty represents the *best-case accuracy* that is possible to have in software estimates at different points in a project. The Cone represents the error in estimates created by skilled estimators. It's easily possible to do worse. It isn't possible to be more accurate; it's only possible to be more lucky.

Tip #11	Consider the effect of the Cone of Uncertainty on the accuracy of your estimate. Your estimate cannot have more accuracy than is possible at your project's current position within the Cone.

The Cone Doesn't Narrow Itself

Another way in which the Cone of Uncertainty represents a best-case estimate is that if the project is not well controlled, or if the estimators aren't very skilled, estimates can fail to improve. Figure 4-3 shows what happens when the project doesn't focus on reducing variability—the uncertainty isn't a Cone, but rather a Cloud that persists to the end of the project. The issue isn't really that the estimates don't converge; the issue is that the project itself doesn't converge—that is, it doesn't drive out enough variability to support more accurate estimates.

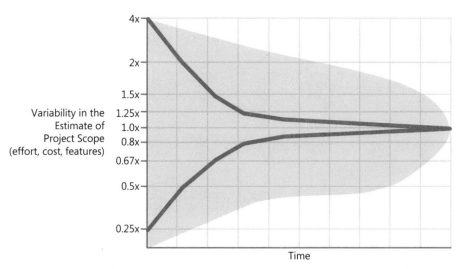

Figure 4-3   If a project is not well controlled or well estimated, you can end up with a Cloud of Uncertainty that contains even more estimation error than that represented by the Cone.

The Cone narrows only as you make decisions that eliminate variability. As Figure 4-4 illustrates, defining the product vision (including committing to what you will *not* do) reduces variability. Defining requirements—again, including what you are *not* going to do—eliminates variability further. Designing the user interface helps to reduce the risk of variability arising from misunderstood requirements. Of course, if the product isn't really defined, or if the product definition gets redefined later, the Cone will widen, and estimation accuracy will be poorer.

Tip #12	Don't assume that the Cone of Uncertainty will narrow itself. You must force the Cone to narrow by removing sources of variability from your project.

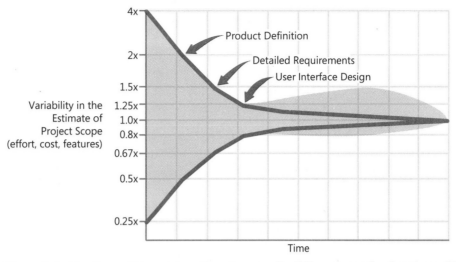

Figure 4-4   The Cone of Uncertainty doesn't narrow itself. You narrow the Cone by making decisions that remove sources of variability from the project. Some of these decisions are about what the project will deliver; some are about what the project will *not* deliver. If these decisions change later, the Cone will widen.

Accounting for the Cone of Uncertainty in Software Estimates

Studies of software estimates have found that estimators who start with single-point estimates and create ranges based on their original single-point numbers do not usually adjust their minimum and maximum values sufficiently to account for the uncertainty in the estimate, especially in circumstances that contain high uncertainty (Jørgensen 2002). This tendency to use ranges that are too narrow can be addressed two ways. The first is to start with a "most likely" estimate and then compute the ranges using predefined multipliers, as shown in Table 4-1.

Table 4-1   **Estimation Error by Software-Development Activity**

| Phase | Scoping Error | | |
	Possible Error on Low Side	**Possible Error on High Side**	**Range of High to Low Estimates**
Initial Concept	0.25x (–75%)	4.0x (+300%)	16x
Approved Product Definition	0.50x (–50%)	2.0x (+100%)	4x
Requirements Complete	0.67x (–33%)	1.5x (+50%)	2.25x
User Interface Design Complete	0.80x (–20%)	1.25x (+25%)	1.6x
Detailed Design Complete (for sequential projects)	0.90x (–10%)	1.10x (+10%)	1.2x

Source: Adapted from *Software Estimation with Cocomo II* (Boehm et al. 2000).

If you use the entries from this table, recognize that at the point when you create the estimate you won't know whether the actual project outcome will fall toward the high end or the low end of your range.

Tip #13	Account for the Cone of Uncertainty by using predefined uncertainty ranges in your estimates.

A second approach is based on the finding that estimation "know-how-much" and estimation "know-how-uncertain" are two different skills. You can have one person estimate the best-case and worst-case ends of the range and a second person estimate the likelihood that the actual result will fall within that range (Jørgensen 2002).

Tip #14	Account for the Cone of Uncertainty by having one person create the "how much" part of the estimate and a different person create the "how uncertain" part of the estimate.

Relationship Between the Cone of Uncertainty and Commitment

Software organizations routinely sabotage their own projects by making commitments too early in the Cone of Uncertainty. If you commit at Initial Concept or Product Definition time, you will have a factor of 2x to 4x error in your estimates. As discussed in Chapter 1, "What Is an 'Estimate'?", a skilled project manager can navigate a project to completion if the estimate is within about 20% of the project reality. But no manager can navigate a project to a successful conclusion when the estimates are off by several hundred percent.

Meaningful commitments are not possible in the early, wide part of the Cone. Effective organizations delay their commitments until they have done the work to force the Cone to narrow. Meaningful commitments in the early-middle part of the project (about 30% of the way in) are possible and appropriate.

The Cone of Uncertainty and Iterative Development

Applying the Cone of Uncertainty to iterative projects is somewhat more involved than applying it to sequential projects is.

If you're working on a project that does a full development cycle each iteration—that is, from requirements definition through release—you'll go through a miniature Cone on each iteration. Before you do the requirements work for the iteration, you'll be at the Approved Product Definition point in the Cone, subject to 4x variability from high to low estimates. With short iterations (less than a month), you can move from Approved Product Definition to Requirements Complete and User Interface Design

Complete in a few days, reducing your variability from 4x to 1.6x. If your schedule is immovable, the 1.6x variability will apply to the specific features you can deliver in the time available, rather than to the effort or schedule. There are estimation advantages that flow from short iterations, which are discussed in Section 8.4, "Using Data from Your Current Project."

What you give up with approaches that leave requirements undefined until the beginning of each iteration is long-range predictability about the combination of cost, schedule, and features you'll deliver several iterations down the road. As Chapter 3, "Value of Accurate Estimates," discussed, your business might prioritize that flexibility highly, or it might prefer that your projects provide more predictability.

The alternative to *total* iteration is not *no* iteration. That option has been found to be almost universally ineffective. The alternatives are *less* iteration or *different* iteration.

Many development teams settle on a middle ground in which a majority of requirements are defined at the front end of the project, but design, construction, test, and release are performed in short iterations. In other words, the project moves sequentially through the User Interface Design Complete milestone (about 30% of the calendar time into the project) and then shifts to a more iterative approach from that point forward. This drives down the variability arising from the Cone to about ±25%, which allows for project control that is good enough to hit a target while still tapping into major benefits of iterative development. Project teams can leave some amount of planned time for as-yet-to-be-determined requirements at the end of the project. That introduces a little bit of variability related to the feature set, which in this case is positive variability because you'll exercise it only if you identify desirable features to implement. This middle ground supports long-range predictability of cost and schedule as well as a moderate amount of requirements flexibility.

4.3 Chaotic Development Processes

The Cone of Uncertainty represents uncertainty that is inherent even in well-run projects. Additional variability can arise from poorly run projects—that is, from avoidable project chaos.

Common examples of project chaos include the following:

- Requirements that weren't investigated very well in the first place
- Lack of end-user involvement in requirements validation
- Poor designs that lead to numerous errors in the code
- Poor coding practices that give rise to extensive bug fixing

- Inexperienced personnel

- Incomplete or unskilled project planning

- Prima donna team members

- Abandoning planning under pressure

- Developer gold-plating

- Lack of automated source code control

This is just a partial list of possible sources of chaos. For a more complete discussion, see Chapter 3, "Classic Mistakes," of my book *Rapid Development* (McConnell 1996) and on the Web at *www.stevemcconnell.com/rdenum.htm*.

These sources of chaos share two commonalities. The first is that each introduces variability that makes accurate estimation difficult. The second is that the best way to address each of these issues is not through estimation, but through better project control.

Tip #15	Don't expect better estimation practices alone to provide more accurate estimates for chaotic projects. You can't accurately estimate an out-of-control process. As a first step, fixing the chaos is more important than improving the estimates.

4.4 Unstable Requirements

Requirements changes have often been reported as a common source of estimation problems (Lederer and Prasad 1992, Jones 1994, Stutzke 2005). In addition to all the general challenges that unstable requirements create, they present two specific estimation challenges.

The first challenge is that unstable requirements represent one specific flavor of project chaos. If requirements cannot be stabilized, the Cone of Uncertainty can't be narrowed, and estimation variability will remain high through the end of the project.

The second challenge is that requirements changes are often not tracked and the project is often not reestimated when it should be. In a well-run project, an initial set of requirements will be baselined, and cost and schedule will be estimated from that baselined set of requirements. As new requirements are added or old requirements are revised, cost and schedule estimates will be modified to reflect those changes. In practice, project managers often neglect to update their cost and schedule assumptions as their requirements change. The irony in these cases is that the estimate for the original functionality might have been accurate, but after dozens of new requirements have been piled onto the project—requirements that have been agreed to but not accounted for—the project won't have any chance of meeting its original estimates, and the project will be perceived as being late, even though everyone agreed that the feature additions were good ideas.

The estimation techniques described in this book will certainly help you estimate *better* when you have high requirements volatility, but better estimation alone cannot address problems arising from requirements instability. The more powerful responses are project control responses rather than estimation responses. If your environment doesn't allow you to stabilize requirements, consider alternative development approaches that are designed to work in high-volatility environments, such as short iterations, Scrum, Extreme Programming, DSDM (Dynamic Systems Development Method), time box development, and so on.

| Tip #16 | To deal with unstable requirements, consider project control strategies instead of or in addition to estimation strategies. |

Estimating Requirements Growth

If you do want to estimate the effect of unstable requirements, you might consider simply incorporating an allowance for requirements growth, requirements changes, or both into your estimates. Figure 4-5 shows a revised Cone of Uncertainty that accounts for approximately 50% growth in requirements over the course of a project. (This particular Cone is for purposes of illustration only. The specific data points are not supported by the same research as the original Cone.)

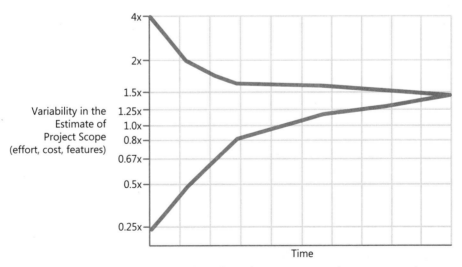

Figure 4-5   A Cone of Uncertainty that allows for requirements increases over the course of the project.

This approach has been used by leading organizations, including NASA's Software Engineering Laboratory, which plans on a 40% increase in requirements (NASA SEL 1990). A similar concept is incorporated into the Cocomo II estimation model, which includes the notion of requirements "breakage" (Boehm et al. 2000).

4.5 Omitted Activities

The previous sections described sources of error arising from the project itself. The remaining sections in this chapter turn to a discussion of errors that arise from the estimation practices.

One of the most common sources of estimation error is forgetting to include necessary tasks in the project estimates (Lederer and Prasad 1992, Coombs 2003). Researchers have found that this phenomenon applies both at the project planning level and at the individual developer level. One study found that developers tended to estimate pretty accurately the work they remembered to estimate, but they tended to overlook 20% to 30% of the necessary tasks, which led to a 20 to 30% estimation error (van Genuchten 1991).

Omitted work falls into three general categories: missing requirements, missing software-development activities, and missing non-software-development activities.

Table 4-2 lists requirements that are commonly missing from estimates.

Table 4-2 **Functional and Nonfunctional Requirements Commonly Missing from Software Estimates**

Functional Requirements Areas	Nonfunctional Requirements
Setup/installation program	Accuracy
Data conversion utility	Interoperability
Glue code needed to use third-party or open-source software	Modifiability
	Performance
Help system	Portability
Deployment modes	Reliability
Interfaces with external systems	Responsiveness
	Reusability
	Scalability
	Security
	Survivability
	Usability

Tip #17	Include time in your estimates for stated requirements, implied requirements, and nonfunctional requirements—that is, *all* requirements. Nothing can be built for free, and your estimates shouldn't imply that it can.

Table 4-3 lists software activities that estimators often overlook.

Table 4-3   Software-Development Activities Commonly Missing from Software Estimates

Ramp-up time for new team members	Technical support of existing systems during the project
Mentoring of new team members	Maintenance work on previous systems during the project
Management coordination/manager meetings	Defect-correction work
Cutover/deployment	Performance tuning
Data conversion	Learning new development tools
Installation	Administrative work related to defect tracking
Customization	Coordination with test (for developers)
Requirements clarifications	Coordination with developers (for test)
Maintaining the revision control system	Answering questions from quality assurance
Supporting the build	Input to user documentation and review of user documentation
Maintaining the scripts required to run the daily build	Review of technical documentation
Maintaining the automated smoke test used in conjunction with the daily build	Demonstrating software to customers or users
Installation of test builds at user location(s)	Demonstrating software at trade shows
Creation of test data	Demonstrating the software or prototypes of the software to upper management, clients, and end users
Management of beta test program	Interacting with clients or end users; supporting beta installations at client locations
Participation in technical reviews	
Integration work	Reviewing plans, estimates, architecture, detailed designs, stage plans, code, test cases, and so on
Processing change requests	
Attendance at change-control/triage meetings	
Coordinating with subcontractors	

Tip #18	Include all necessary software-development activities in your estimates, not just coding and testing.

Table 4-4 lists the non-software-development activities that are often missing from estimates.

Table 4-4   Non-Software-Development Activities Commonly Missing from Software Estimates

Vacations	Company meetings
Holidays	Department meetings
Sick days	Setting up new workstations
Training	Installing new versions of tools on workstations
Weekends	Troubleshooting hardware and software problems

Some projects deliberately plan to exclude many of the activities in Table 4-4 for a small project. That can work for a short time, but these activities tend to creep back into any project that lasts longer than a few weeks.

Tip #19	On projects that last longer than a few weeks, include allowances for overhead activities such as vacations, sick days, training days, and company meetings.

In addition to using the entries in these tables to avoid omitting parts of the software or kinds of activities from your estimates, you might also consider looking at a Work Breakdown Structure (WBS) for the standard kinds of activities to be considered. Section 10.3, "Hazards of Adding Up Best Case and Worst Case Estimates," discusses estimating with a WBS and provides a generic WBS.

4.6 Unfounded Optimism

Optimism assails software estimates from all sources. On the developer side of the project, Microsoft Vice President Chris Peters observed that "You never have to fear that estimates created by developers will be too pessimistic, because developers will always generate a too-optimistic schedule" (Cusumano and Selby 1995). In a study of 300 software projects, Michiel van Genuchten reported that developer estimates tended to contain an optimism factor of 20% to 30% (van Genuchten 1991). Although managers sometimes complain otherwise, developers don't tend to sandbag their estimates—their estimates tend to be too low!

Tip #20	Don't reduce developer estimates—they're probably too optimistic already.

Optimism applies within the management ranks as well. A study of about 100 schedule estimates within the U.S. Department of Defense found a consistent "fantasy factor" of about 1.33 (Boehm 1981). Project managers and executives might not *assume* that projects can be done 30% faster or cheaper than they can be done, but they certainly *want* the projects to be done faster and cheaper, and that is a kind of optimism in itself.

Common variations on this optimism theme include the following:

■ We'll be more productive on this project than we were on the last project.

■ A lot of things went wrong on the last project. Not so many things will go wrong on this project.

■ We started the project slowly and were climbing a steep learning curve. We learned a lot of lessons the hard way, but all the lessons we learned will allow us to finish the project much faster than we started it.

Considering that optimism is a near-universal fact of human nature, software estimates are sometimes undermined by what I think of as a Collusion of Optimists. Developers present estimates that are optimistic. Executives like the optimistic estimates because they imply that desirable business targets are achievable. Managers like the estimates because they imply that they can support upper management's objectives. And so the software project is off and running with no one ever taking a critical look at whether the estimates were well founded in the first place.

4.7 Subjectivity and Bias

Subjectivity creeps into estimates in the form of optimism, in the form of conscious bias, and in the form of unconscious bias. I differentiate between estimation *bias*, which suggests an intent to fudge an estimate in one direction or another, and estimation *subjectivity*, which simply recognizes that human judgment is influenced by human experience, both consciously and unconsciously.

As far as bias is concerned, the response of customers and managers when they discover that the estimate does not align with the business target is sometimes to apply more pressure to the estimate, to the project, and to the project team. Excessive schedule pressure occurs in 75% to 100% of large projects (Jones 1994).

As far as subjectivity is concerned, when considering different estimation techniques our natural tendency is to believe that the more "control knobs" we have on an estimate—that is, the more places there are to tweak the estimate to match our specific project—the more accurate the estimate will be.

The reality is the opposite. The more control knobs an estimate has, the more chances there are for subjectivity to creep in. The issue is not so much that estimators deliberately bias their estimates. The issue is more that the estimate gets shaded slightly higher or slightly lower with each of the subjective inputs. If the estimation technique has a large number of subjective inputs, the cumulative effect can be significant.

I've seen one example of this while teaching several hundred estimators to use the Cocomo II estimation model. Cocomo II includes 17 Effort Multipliers and 5 Scaling Factors. To create a Cocomo II estimate, the estimator must decide what adjustment is needed for each of these 22 factors. The factors adjust for whether your team is above average or below average, whether your software is more or less complex than average, and so on. In theory, these 22 control knobs should allow virtually any estimate to be fine-tuned. In practice, the control knobs seem to introduce 22 chances for error to creep into the estimate.

Figure 4-6 shows the ranges of results of about 100 groups of estimators applying Cocomo II's 17 Effort Multipliers to the same estimation problem. For each bar, the bottom of the bar represents the lowest group estimate in a session and the top of the bar represents the highest group estimate in a session. The total height of the bar represents the variation in the estimates.

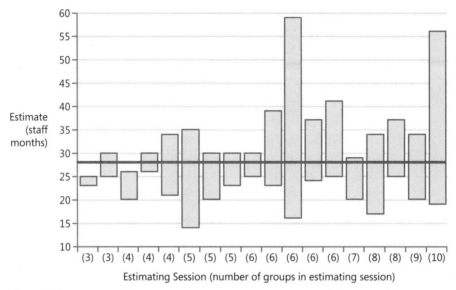

Figure 4-6 Example of variations in estimates when numerous adjustment factors are present. The more adjustment factors an estimation method provides, the more opportunity there is for subjectivity to creep into the estimate.

If the estimation technique produced consistent results, we would see a tight clustering of results along the horizontal blue bar (the average of all the estimates). But, as you can see, the variation among the estimates is enormous. The total variation from highest to lowest is a factor of 4. The average variation from the low group to the high group within any one session is a factor of 1.7.

An important aspect of this data is that *this particular estimation exercise is free of external bias.* It occurs in an estimation class in which the emphasis is on accuracy. The only bias that is affecting these estimates are the biases inherent in the estimators' experiences. In a real estimation situation, the range of results would probably be even greater because of the increased amount of external bias that would affect the estimates.

In contrast, Figure 4-7 illustrates the range of estimation outcomes with an estimation technique that includes only one place to insert a subjective judgment into the estimate—that is, one control knob. (The control knob in this case is unrelated to the Cocomo II factors.)

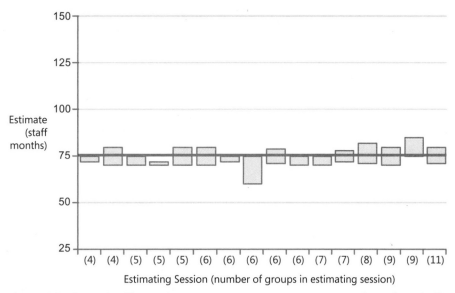

Figure 4-7   Example of low variation in estimates resulting from a small number of adjustment factors. (The scales of the two graphs are different, but they are directly comparable when you account for the difference in the average values on the two graphs.)

As you can see, the variation in these results is dramatically smaller than the variation when there are 17 control knobs present. The average variation from the low group to the high group within any one session is a factor of only 1.1.

The finding that "more control knobs isn't better" extends beyond software estimation. As forecasting guru J. Scott Armstrong states, "One of the most enduring and useful conclusions from research on forecasting is that simple methods are generally as accurate as complex methods" (Armstrong 2001).

Tip #21	Avoid having "control knobs" on your estimates. While control knobs might give you a feeling of better accuracy, they usually introduce subjectivity and degrade actual accuracy.

4.8 Off-the-Cuff Estimates

Project teams are sometimes trapped by off-the-cuff estimates. Your boss asks, for example, "How long would it take to implement print preview on the Gigacorp Web site?" You say, "I don't know. I think it might take about a week. I'll check into it." You go off to your desk, look at the design and code for the program you were asked about, notice a few things you'd forgotten when you talked to your manager, add up the changes, and decide that it would take about five weeks. You hurry over to your manager's office to update your first estimate, but the manager is in a meeting. Later that day, you catch up with your manager, and before you can open your mouth, your manager says, "Since it seemed like a small project, I went ahead and asked for approval for the print-preview function at the budget meeting this afternoon. The rest of the budget committee was excited about the new feature and can't wait to see it next week. Can you start working on it today?"

I've found that the safest policy is not to give off-the-cuff estimates. Lederer and Prasad found that intuition and guessing in software project estimates were both correlated with cost and schedule overruns (Lederer and Prasad 1992). I've collected data on off-the-cuff estimates from 24 groups of estimators. Figure 4-8 shows the average error of estimates in these 24 groups of estimators for off-the-cuff estimates versus estimates that go through a group review process.

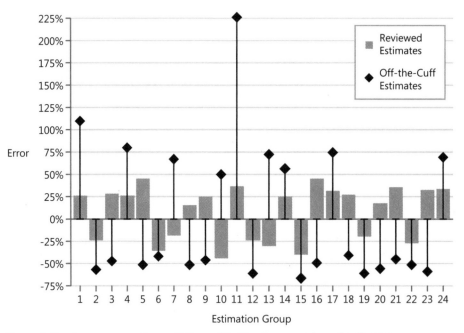

Figure 4-8   Average error from off-the-cuff estimates vs. reviewed estimates.

The average off-the-cuff estimate has a mean magnitude of relative error (MMRE[1]) of 67%, whereas the average reviewed estimate has an error of only 30%—less than half. (These are not software estimates, so the percentage errors shouldn't be applied literally to software project estimates.)

---

[1]   MMRE is equal to AbsoluteValue [(ActualResult – EstimatedResult) / ActualResult].

One of the errors people commit when estimating solely from personal memory is that they compare the new project to their memory of how long a past project took, or how much effort it required. Unfortunately, people sometimes remember their *estimate* for the past project rather than the *actual outcome* of the past project. If they use their past estimate as the basis for a new estimate, and the past project's actual outcome was that it overran its estimate, guess what? The estimator has just calibrated a project overrun into the estimate for the new project.

While Lederer and Prasad found that guessing and intuition were positively correlated with project overruns, they also found that the use of "documented facts" was *negatively* correlated with project overruns. In other words, there is a world of difference between giving your boss an off-the-cuff answer versus saying, "I can't give you an answer off the top of my head, but let me go back to my desk, check a few notes, and get back to you in 15 minutes. Would that be OK?"

While this is a simple point, off-the-cuff estimation is one of the most common errors that project teams make (Lederer and Prasad 1992, Jørgensen 1997, Kitchenham et al. 2002). Avoiding off-the-cuff estimates is one of the most important points in this book.

Tip #22	Don't give off-the-cuff estimates. Even a 15-minute estimate will be more accurate.

What if your boss calls on a cell phone and insists on getting an estimate *right now?* Consider your performance on the estimation quiz in Chapter 2, "How Good an Estimator Are You?" Did you get 8 to 10 answers correct? If not, what are the odds that the off-the-cuff answer you give your boss on the cell phone—even an estimate padded for uncertainty—will give you a 90% chance of including the correct answer?

4.9 Unwarranted Precision

In casual conversation, people tend to treat "accuracy" and "precision" as synonyms. But for estimation purposes, the distinctions between these two terms are critical.

Accuracy refers to how close to the real value a number is. *Precision* refers merely to how exact a number is. In software estimation, this amounts to how many significant digits an estimate has. A measurement can be precise without being accurate, and it can be accurate without being precise. The single digit 3 is an accurate representation of pi to one significant digit, but it is not precise. 3.37882 is a more precise representation of pi than 3 is, but it is not any more accurate.

Airline schedules are precise to the minute, but they are not very accurate. Measuring people's heights in whole meters might be accurate, but it would not be at all precise.

Table 4-5 provides examples of numbers that are accurate, precise, or both.

Table 4-5   **Examples of Accuracy and Precision**

Example	Comment
pi = 3	Accurate to 1 significant digit, but not precise
pi = 3.37882	Precise to 6 significant digits, but accurate only to 1 significant digit
pi = 3.14159	Both accurate and precise, to 6 significant digits
My height = 2 meters	Accurate to 1 significant digit, but not very precise
Airline flight times	Precise to the minute, but not very accurate
"This project will take 395.7 days, ± 2 months"	Highly precise, but not accurate to the precision stated
"This project will take 1 year"	Not very precise, but could be accurate
"This project will require 7,214 staff hours"	Highly precise, but probably not accurate to the precision stated
"This project will require 4 staff years"	Not very precise, but could be accurate

For software estimation purposes, the distinction between accuracy and precision is critical. Project stakeholders make assumptions about project accuracy based on the precision with which an estimate is presented. When you present an estimate of 395.7 days, stakeholders assume the estimate is accurate to 4 significant digits! The accuracy of the estimate might be better reflected by estimating 1 year, 4 quarters, or 13 months, rather than 395.7 days. Using an estimate of 395.7 days instead of 1 year is like representing pi as 3.37882–the number is more precise, but it's really less accurate.

Tip #23	Match the number of significant digits in your estimate (its precision) to to your estimate's accuracy.

4.10 Other Sources of Error

The sources of error described in the first nine sections of this chapter are the most common and the most significant, but they are not exhaustive. Here are some of the other ways that error can creep into an estimate:

- Unfamiliar business area

- Unfamiliar technology area

- Incorrect conversion from estimated time to project time (for example, assuming the project team will focus on the project eight hours per day, five days per week)

- Misunderstanding of statistical concepts (especially adding together a set of "best case" estimates or a set of "worst case" estimates)

- Budgeting processes that undermine effective estimation (especially those that require final budget approval in the wide part of the Cone of Uncertainty)

- Having an accurate size estimate, but introducing errors when converting the size estimate to an effort estimate

- Having accurate size and effort estimates, but introducing errors when converting those to a schedule estimate

- Overstated savings from new development tools or methods

- Simplification of the estimate as it's reported up layers of management, fed into the budgeting process, and so on

These topics are all discussed in more detail in later chapters.

Additional Resources

Armstrong, J. Scott, ed. *Principles of forecasting: A handbook for researchers and practitioners.* Boston, MA: Kluwer Academic Publishers, 2001. Armstrong is one of the leading researchers in forecasting in a marketing context. Many of the observations in this book are relevant to software estimation. Armstrong has been a leading critic of overly complex estimation models.

Boehm, Barry, et al. *Software Cost Estimation with Cocomo II.* Reading, MA: Addison-Wesley, 2000. Boehm was the first to popularize the Cone of Uncertainty (he calls it a funnel curve). This book contains his most current description of the phenomenon.

Cockburn, Alistair. *Agile Software Development.* Boston, MA: Addison-Wesley, 2001. Cockburn's book introduces Agile development approaches, which are especially useful in environments characterized by highly volatile requirements.

Laranjeira, Luiz. "Software Size Estimation of Object-Oriented Systems," *IEEE Transactions on Software Engineering,* May 1990. This paper provided a theoretical-research foundation for the empirical observation of the Cone of Uncertainty.

Tockey, Steve. *Return on Software.* Boston, MA: Addison-Wesley, 2005. Chapters 21 through 23 discuss basic estimation concepts, general estimation techniques, and allowing for inaccuracy in estimates. Tockey includes a detailed discussion of how to build your own Cone of Uncertainty.

Wiegers, Karl. *More About Software Requirements: Thorny Issues and Practical Advice.* Redmond, WA: Microsoft Press, 2006.

Wiegers, Karl. *Software Requirements, Second Edition.* Redmond, WA: Microsoft Press, 2003. In these two books, Wiegers describes numerous practices that help elicit good requirements in the first place, which substantially reduces requirements volatility later in a project.

Chapter 5
Estimate Influences

How much is 68 + 73?

ENGINEER: *"It's 141." Short and sweet.*

MATHEMATICIAN: *"68 + 73 = 73 + 68 by the commutative law of addition."*
True, but not very helpful.

ACCOUNTANT: *"Normally it's 141, but what are you going to use it for?"*

–Barry W. Boehm and Richard E. Fairley

Influences on a software project can be sliced and diced in several ways. Understanding these influences helps improve estimation accuracy and helps improve understanding of software project dynamics overall.

Project size is easily the most significant determinant of effort, cost, and schedule. The kind of software you're developing comes in second, and personnel factors are a close third. The programming language and environment you use are not first-tier influences on the project outcome, but they are a first-tier influence on the estimate. This chapter presents these first-tier influences in decreasing order of significance and concludes with a discussion of second-tier influences.

5.1 Project Size

The largest driver in a software estimate is the size of the software being built, because there is more variation in the size than in any other factor. Figure 5-1 shows the way that effort grows in an average business-systems project as project size increases from 25,000 lines of code to 1,000,000 lines of code. The figure expresses size in lines of code (LOC), but the dynamic would be the same whether you measured size in function points, number of requirements, number of Web pages, or any other measure that expressed the same range of sizes.

As the diagram shows, a system consisting of 1,000,000 LOC requires dramatically more effort than a system consisting of only 100,000 LOC.

These comments about software size being the largest cost driver might seem obvious, yet organizations routinely violate this fundamental fact in two ways:

- Costs, effort, and schedule are estimated without knowing how big the software will be.

- Costs, effort, and schedule are not adjusted when the size of the software is consciously increased (that is, in response to change requests).

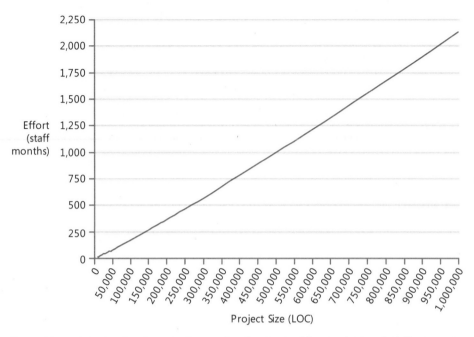

Source: Computed using data from the Cocomo II estimation model, assuming nominal diseconomy
of scale (Boehm, et al 2000).

Figure 5-1   Growth in effort for a typical business-systems project. The specific numbers are
meaningful only for the average business-systems project. The general dynamic applies to
software projects of all kinds.

Tip #24	Invest an appropriate amount of effort assessing the size of the software that will be built. The size of the software is the single most significant contributor to project effort and schedule.

Why Is This Book Discussing Size in Lines of Code?

People new to estimation sometimes have questions about whether lines of code are really a meaningful way to measure software size. One issue is that many modern programming environments are not as lines-of-code-oriented as older environments were. Another issue is that a lot of software development work—such as requirements, design, and testing—doesn't produce lines of code. If you're interested in seeing how these issues affect the usefulness of measuring size in lines of code, see Section 18.1, "Challenges with Estimating Size."

Diseconomies of Scale

People naturally assume that a system that is 10 times as large as another system will require something like 10 times as much effort to build. But the effort for a

1,000,000-LOC system is more than 10 times as large as the effort for a 100,000-LOC system, as is the effort for a 100,000-LOC system compared to the effort for a 10,000-LOC system.

The basic issue is that, in software, larger projects require coordination among larger groups of people, which requires more communication (Brooks 1995). As project size increases, the number of communication paths among different people increases as a *squared* function of the number of people on the project.[1] Figure 5-2 illustrates this dynamic.

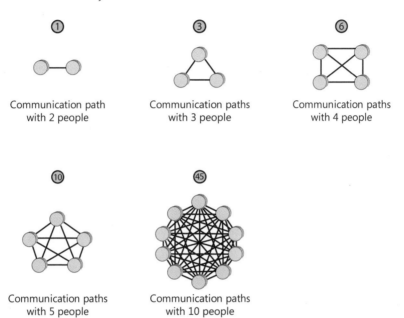

Figure 5-2   The number of communication paths on a project increases proportionally to the square of the number of people on the team.

The consequence of this exponential increase in communication paths (along with some other factors) is that projects also have an exponential increase in effort as a project size increases. This is known as a *diseconomy of scale*.

Outside software, we usually discuss *economies* of scale rather than *diseconomies* of scale. An economy of scale is something like, "If we build a larger manufacturing plant, we'll be able to reduce the cost per unit we produce." An economy of scale implies that the bigger you get, the smaller the unit cost becomes.

A diseconomy of scale is the opposite. In software, the larger the system becomes, the greater the cost of each unit. If software exhibited economies of scale, a 100,000-LOC

---

[1]   The actual number of paths is n x (n − 1) / 2, which is an n^2 function.

system would be less than 10 times as costly as a 10,000-LOC system. But the opposite is almost always the case.

Figure 5-3 illustrates a typical diseconomy of scale in software compared with the increase of effort that would be associated with linear growth.

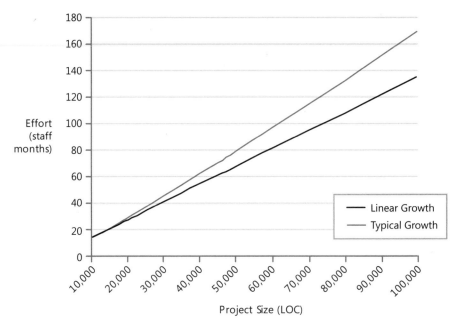

Source: Computed using data from the Cocomo II estimation model, assuming nominal diseconomy of scale (Boehm, et al 2000).

Figure 5-3   Diseconomy of scale for a typical business-systems project ranging from 10,000 to 100,000 lines of code.

As you can see from the graph, in this example, the 10,000-LOC system would require 13.5 staff months. If effort increased linearly, a 100,000-LOC system would require 135 staff months, but it actually requires 170 staff months.

As Figure 5-3 is drawn, the effect of the diseconomy of scale doesn't look very dramatic. Indeed, within the 10,000 LOC to 100,000 LOC range, the effect is usually not all that dramatic. But two factors make the effect more dramatic. One factor is greater difference in project size, and the other factor is project conditions that degrade productivity more quickly than average as project size increases. Figure 5-4 shows the range of outcomes for projects ranging from 10,000 LOC to 1,000,000 LOC. In addition to the nominal diseconomy, the graph also shows the worst-case diseconomy.

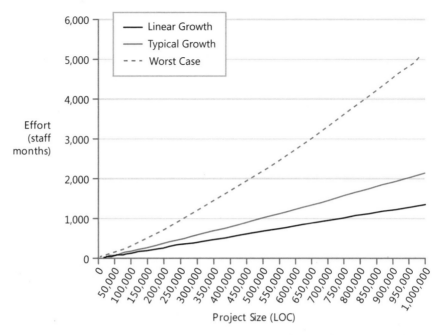

Source: Computed using data from the Cocomo II estimation model, assuming nominal and worst-case diseconomies of scale (Boehm, et al 2000).

Figure 5-4   Diseconomy of scale for projects with greater size differences and the worst-case diseconomy of scale.

In this graph, you can see that the worst-case effort growth increases much faster than the nominal effort growth, and that the effect becomes much more pronounced at larger project sizes. Along the nominal effort growth curve, effort at 100,000 lines of code is 13 times what it is at 10,000 lines of code, rather than 10 times. At 1,000,000 LOC, effort is 160 times the 10,000-LOC effort, rather than 100 times.

The worst-case growth is much worse. Effort on the worst-case curve at 100,000 LOC is 17 times what it is at 10,000 LOC, and at 1,000,000 LOC it isn't 100 times as large— it's 300 times as large!

Table 5-1 illustrates the general relationship between project size and productivity.

Table 5-1   Relationship Between Project Size and Productivity

Project Size (in Lines of Code)	Lines of Code per Staff Year (Cocomo II Nominal in Parentheses)
10K	2,000–25,000 (3,200)
100K	1,000–20,000 (2,600)
1M	700–10,000 (2,000)
10M	300–5,000 (1,600)

Source: Derived from data in *Measures for Excellence* (Putnam and Meyers 1992), *Industrial Strength Software* (Putnam and Meyers 1997), *Software Cost Estimation with Cocomo II* (Boehm et al. 2000), and "Software Development Worldwide: The State of the Practice" (Cusumano et al. 2003).

The numbers in this table are valid only for purposes of comparison between size ranges. But the general trend the numbers show is significant. Productivity on small projects can be 2 to 3 times as high as productivity on large projects, and productivity can vary by a factor of 5 to 10 from the smallest projects to the largest.

Tip #25	Don't assume that effort scales up linearly as project size does. Effort scales up exponentially.

For software estimation, the implications of diseconomies of scale are a case of good news, bad news. The bad news is that if you have large variations in the sizes of projects you estimate, you can't just estimate a new project by applying a simple effort ratio based on the effort from previous projects. If your effort for a previous 100,000-LOC project was 170 staff months, you might figure that your productivity rate is 100,000/170, which equals 588 LOC per staff month. That might be a reasonable assumption for another project of about the same size as the old project, but if the new project is 10 times bigger, the estimate you create that way could be off by 30% to 200%.

There's more bad news: There isn't a simple technique in the art of estimation that will account for a significant difference in the size of two projects. If you're estimating a project of a significantly different size than your organization has done before, you'll need to use estimation software that applies the science of estimation to compute the estimate for the new project based on the results of past projects. My company provides a free software tool called Construx® Estimate™ that will do this kind of estimate. You can download a copy at *www.construx.com/estimate*.

Tip #26	Use software estimation tools to compute the impact of diseconomies of scale.

When You Can Safely Ignore Diseconomies of Scale

After all that bad news, there is actually some good news. The majority of projects in an organization are often similar in size. If the new project you're estimating will be similar in size to your past projects, it is usually safe to use a simple effort ratio, such as lines of code per staff month, to estimate a new project. Figure 5-5 illustrates the relatively minor difference in linear versus exponential estimates that occurs within a specific size range.

If you use a ratio-based estimation approach within a restricted range of sizes, your estimates will not be subject to much error. If you used an average ratio from projects in the middle of the size range, the estimation error introduced by economies of scale would be no more than about 10%. If you work in an environment that experiences higher-than-average diseconomies of scale, the differences could be higher.

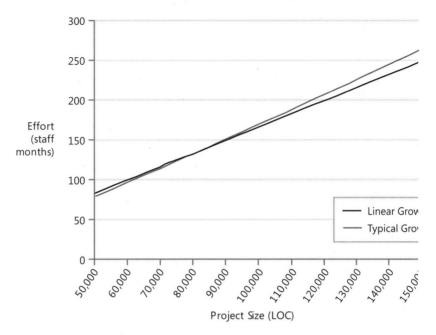

Source: Computed using data from the Cocomo II estimation model, assuming nominal diseco of scale (Boehm, et al 2000).

Figure 5-5   Differences between ratio-based estimates and estimates based on diseconomy of scale will be minimal for projects within a similar size range.

Tip #27	If you've completed previous projects that are about the same size as the project you're estimating—defined as being within a factor of 3 from largest to smallest—you can safely use a ratio-based estimating approach, such as lines of code per staff month, to estimate your new project.

Importance of Diseconomy of Scale in Software Estimation

Much of the software-estimating world's focus has been on determining the exact significance of diseconomies of scale. Although that is a significant factor, remember that the raw size is the largest contributor to the estimate. The effect of diseconomy of scale on the estimate is a second-order consideration, so put the majority of your effort into developing a good size estimate. We'll discuss how to create software size estimates more specifically in Chapter 18, "Special Issues in Estimating Size."

5.2 Kind of Software Being Developed

After project size, the kind of software you're developing is the next biggest influence on the estimate. If you're working on life-critical software, you can expect your project to require far more effort than a similarly sized business-systems project. Table 5-2 shows examples of lines of code per staff month for projects of different kinds.

Table 5-2   **Productivity Rates for Common Project Types**

Kind of Software	LOC/Staff Month Low-High (Nominal)		
	10,000-LOC Project	**100,000-LOC Project**	**250,000-LOC Project**
Avionics	100–1,000 **(200)**	20–300 **(50)**	20–200 **(40)**
Business Systems	800–18,000 **(3,000)**	200–7,000 **(600)**	100–5,000 **(500)**
Command and Control	200–3,000 **(500)**	50–600 **(100)**	40–500 **(80)**
Embedded Systems	100–2,000 **(300)**	30–500 **(70)**	20–400 **(60)**
Internet Systems (public)	600–10,000 **(1,500)**	100–2,000 **(300)**	100–1,500 **(200)**
Intranet Systems (internal)	1,500–18,000 **(4,000)**	300–7,000 **(800)**	200–5,000 **(600)**
Microcode	100–800 **(200)**	20–200 **(40)**	20–100 **(30)**
Process Control	500–5,000 **(1,000)**	100–1,000 **(300)**	80–900 **(200)**
Real-Time	100–1,500 **(200)**	20–300 **(50)**	20–300 **(40)**
Scientific Systems/ Engineering Research	500–7,500 **(1,000)**	100–1,500 **(300)**	80–1,000 **(200)**
Shrink wrap/Packaged Software	400–5,000 **(1,000)**	100–1,000 **(200)**	70–800 **(200)**
Systems Software/Drivers	200–5,000 **(600)**	50–1,000 **(100)**	40–800 **(90)**
Telecommunications	200–3,000 **(600)**	50–600 **(100)**	40–500 **(90)**

Source: Adapted and extended from *Measures for Excellence* (Putnam and Meyers 1992), *Industrial Strength Software* (Putnam and Meyers 1997), and *Five Core Metrics* (Putnam and Meyers 2003).

As you can see from the table, a team developing an intranet system for internal use might generate code 10 to 20 times faster than a team working on an avionics project, real-time project, or embedded systems project. The table also again illustrates the diseconomy of scale: projects of 100,000 LOC generate code far less efficiently than 10,000-LOC projects. Projects of 250,000 LOC generate code even less efficiently.

You can account for the industry in which you're working in one of three ways:

■ Use the results from Table 5-2 as a starting point. If you do that, notice that the ranges in the table are large—typically a factor of 10 difference between the high and the low ends of the ranges.

- Use an estimating model such as Cocomo II, and adjust the estimating parameters to match the kind of software you develop. If you do that, remember the cautions from Chapter 4, "Where Does Estimation Error Come From?" about using too many control knobs on your estimates.

- Use historical data from your own organization, which will automatically incorporate the development factors specific to the industry you work in. This is by far the best approach, and we'll discuss the use of historical data in more detail in Chapter 8, "Calibration and Historical Data."

Tip #28	Factor the kind of software you develop into your estimate. The kind of software you're developing is the second-most significant contributor to project effort and schedule.

5.3 Personnel Factors

Personnel factors also exert significant influence on project outcomes. According to Cocomo II, on a 100,000-LOC project the combined effect of personnel factors can swing a project estimate by as much as a factor of 22! In other words, if your project ranked worst in each category shown in Figure 5-6 (shown by the gray bars), it would require 22 times as much total effort as a project that ranked best in each category (shown by the blue bars).

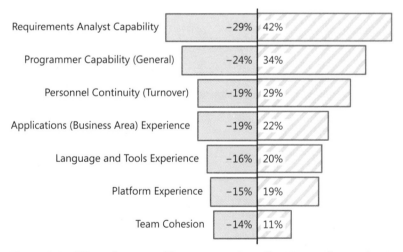

Figure 5-6   Effect of personnel factors on project effort. Depending on the strength or weakness in each factor, the project results can vary by the amount indicated—that is, a project with the worst requirements analysts would require 42% more effort than nominal, whereas a project with the best analysts would require 29% less effort than nominal.

The magnitude of these factors from the Cocomo II model is confirmed by numerous studies since the 1960s that show 10:1 to 20:1 differences in individual and team performance (Sackman, Erikson, and Grant 1968; Weinberg and Schulman 1974; Curtis 1981; Mills 1983; Boehm, Gray, and Seewaldt 1984; DeMarco and Lister 1985; Curtis et al. 1986; Card 1987; Boehm 1987b; Boehm and Papaccio 1988; Valett and McGarry 1989; Boehm et al. 2000).

One implication of these variations among individuals is that you can't accurately estimate a project if you don't have some idea of who will be doing the work—because individual performance varies by a factor of 10 or more. Within any particular organization, however, your estimates probably won't need to account for that much variation because both top-tier and bottom-tier developers tend to migrate toward organizations that employ other people with similar skill levels (Mills 1983, DeMarco and Lister 1999).

Another implication is that the most accurate estimation approach will depend on whether you know who specifically will be doing the work that's being estimated. That issue is discussed in Chapter 16, "Flow of Software Estimates on a Well-Estimated Project."

5.4 Programming Language

The specific programming language a project uses will affect your estimates in at least four ways.

First, as Figure 5-6 suggested, the project team's experience with the specific language and tools that will be used on the project has about a 40% impact on the overall productivity rate of the project.

Second, some languages generate more functionality per line of code than others. Table 5-3 shows the amount of functionality that several languages produce relative to the C programming language.

Table 5-3   **Ratio of High-Level-Language Statements to Equivalent C Code**

Language	Level Relative to C
C	1 to 1
C#	1 to 2.5
C++	1 to 2.5
Cobol	1 to 1.5
Fortran 95	1 to 2
Java	1 to 2.5
Macro Assembly	2 to 1

Table 5-3   **Ratio of High-Level-Language Statements to Equivalent C Code**

Language	Level Relative to C
Perl	1 to 6
Smalltalk	1 to 6
SQL	1 to 10
Visual Basic	1 to 4.5

Source: Adapted from *Estimating Software Costs* (Jones 1998) and *Software Cost Estimation with Cocomo II* (Boehm 2000).

If you don't have any choice about the programming language you're using, this point is not relevant to your estimate. But if you have some leeway in choosing a programming language, you can see that using a language such as Java, C#, or Microsoft Visual Basic would tend to be more productive than using C, Cobol, or Macro Assembly.

A third factor related to languages is the richness of the tool support and environment associated with the language. According to Cocomo II, the weakest tool set and environment will increase total project effort by about 50% compared to the strongest tool set and environment (Boehm et al. 2000). Realize that the choice of programming language might determine the choice of tool set and environment.

A final factor related to programming language is that developers working in interpreted languages tend to be more productive than those working in compiled languages, perhaps as much as a factor of 2 (Jones 1986a, Prechelt 2000).

The concept of amount of functionality produced per line of code will be discussed further in Section 18.2, "Function-Point Estimation."

5.5 Other Project Influences

I've mentioned the Cocomo II estimating model several times in this chapter. As discussed in Chapter 4, I have reservations about subjectivity creeping into the use of Cocomo II's adjustment factors. However, my reservations stem from concerns about "usage failure" more than concerns about "method failure." The Cocomo II project has done a much better job than other studies of rigorously isolating the impacts of specific factors on project outcomes. Most studies combine multiple factors intentionally or unintentionally. A study might examine the impact of software process improvement, but it might not isolate the impact of switching from one programming language to another, or of consolidating staff from two locations to one location. The Cocomo II project has conducted the most statistically rigorous analysis of specific factors that I've seen. So, although I prefer other methods for estimation, I do recommend studying Cocomo II's adjustment factors to gain an understanding of the significance of different software project influences.

Table 5-4 lists the Cocomo II ratings factors for Cocomo's 17 Effort Multipliers (EMs). The Very Low column represents the amount you would adjust an effort estimate for the best (or worst) influence of that factor. For example, if a team had very low "Applications (Business Area) Experience," you would multiply your nominal Cocomo II effort estimate by 1.22. If the team had very high experience, you would multiply the estimate by 0.81 instead.

Table 5-4 **Cocomo II Adjustment Factors**

| | Ratings | | | | | | |
Factor	Very Low	Low	Nominal	High	Very High	Extra High	Influence
Applications (Business Area) Experience	1.22	1.10	1.00	0.88	0.81		1.51
Database Size		0.90	1.00	1.14	1.28		1.42
Developed for Reuse		0.95	1.00	1.07	1.15	1.24	1.31
Extent of Documentation Required	0.81	0.91	1.00	1.11	1.23		1.52
Language and Tools Experience	1.20	1.09	1.00	0.91	0.84		1.43
Multisite Development	1.22	1.09	1.00	0.93	0.86	0.78	1.56
Personnel Continuity (turnover)	1.29	1.12	1.00	0.90	0.81		1.59
Platform Experience	1.19	1.09	1.00	0.91	0.85		1.40
Platform Volatility		0.87	1.00	1.15	1.30		1.49
Product Complexity	0.73	0.87	1.00	1.17	1.34	1.74	2.38
Programmer Capability (general)	1.34	1.15	1.00	0.88	0.76		1.76
Required Software Reliability	0.82	0.92	1.00	1.10	1.26		1.54
Requirements Analyst Capability	1.42	1.19	1.00	0.85	0.71		2.00
Storage Constraint			1.00	1.05	1.17	1.46	1.46
Time Constraint			1.00	1.11	1.29	1.63	1.63
Use of Software Tools	1.17	1.09	1.00	0.90	0.78		1.50

The Influence column on the far right of the table shows the degree of influence that each factor, in isolation, has on the overall effort estimate. The Applications (Business Area) Experience factor has an influence of 1.51, which means that a project performed by a team with very low skills in that area will require 1.51 times as much total effort as a project performed by a team with very high skills in that area. (Influence is computed by dividing the largest value by the smallest value. For example, 1.51 is 1.22/0.8.)

Figure 5-7 presents another view of the impact of the Cocomo II factors, in which the factors are arranged from most significant influence to least significant influence.

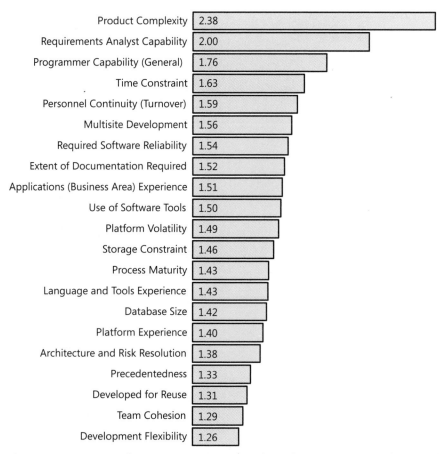

Figure 5-7   Cocomo II factors arranged in order of significance. The relative lengths of the bars represent the sensitivity of the estimate to the different factors.

Figure 5-8 shows the same factors represented in terms of their potential to increase total effort (the gray bars) versus decrease effort (the blue bars).

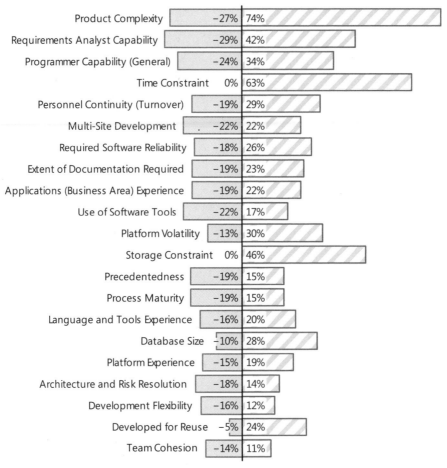

Figure 5-8   Cocomo II factors arranged by potential to increase total effort (gray bars) and potential to decrease total effort (blue bars).

I've listed some observations about these factors in Table 5-5 in alphabetical order.

Table 5-5   Cocomo II Adjustment Factors

Cocomo II Factor	Influence	Observation
Applications (Business Area) Experience	1.51	Teams that aren't familiar with the project's business area need significantly more time. This shouldn't be a surprise.
Architecture and Risk Resolution	1.38*	The more actively the project attacks risks, the lower the effort and cost will be. This is one of the few Cocomo II factors that is controllable by the project manager.
Database Size	1.42	Large, complex databases require more effort project-wide. Total influence is moderate.

Table 5-5   **Cocomo II Adjustment Factors**

Cocomo II Factor	Influence	Observation
Developed for Reuse	1.31	Software that is developed with the goal of later reuse can increase costs as much as 31%. This doesn't say whether the initiative actually succeeds. Industry experience has been that forward-looking reuse programs often fail.
Extent of Documentation Required	1.52	Too much documentation can negatively affect the whole project. Impact is moderately high.
Language and Tools Experience	1.43	Teams that have experience with the programming language and/or tool set work moderately more productively than teams that are climbing a learning curve. This is not a surprise.
Multi-Site Development	1.56	Projects conducted by a team spread across multiple sites around the globe will take 56% more effort than projects that are conducted by a team co-located at one facility. Projects that are conducted at multiple sites, including outsourced or offshore projects, need to take this effect seriously.
Personnel Continuity (turnover)	1.59	Project turnover is expensive—in the top one-third of influential factors.
Platform Experience	1.40	Experience with the underlying technology platform affects overall project performance moderately.
Platform Volatility	1.49	If the platform is unstable, development can take moderately longer. Projects should weigh this factor in their decision about when to adopt a new technology. This is one reason that systems projects tend to take longer than applications projects.
Precedentedness	1.33*	Refers to how "precedented" (we usually say "unprecedented") the application is. Familiar systems are easier to create than unfamiliar systems.
Process Maturity	1.43*	Projects that use more sophisticated development processes take less effort than projects that use unsophisticated processes. Cocomo II uses an adaptation of the CMM process maturity model to apply this criterion to a specific project.
Product Complexity	2.38	Product complexity (software complexity) is the single most significant adjustment factor in the Cocomo II model. Product complexity is largely determined by the type of software you're building.
Programmer Capability (general)	1.76	The skill of the programmers has an impact of a factor of almost 2 on overall project results.

Table 5-5 **Cocomo II Adjustment Factors**

Cocomo II Factor	Influence	Observation
Required Reliability	1.54	More reliable systems take longer. This is one reason (though not the only reason) that embedded systems and life-critical systems tend to take more effort than other projects of similar sizes. In most cases, your marketplace determines how reliable your software must be. You don't usually have much latitude to change this.
Requirements Analyst Capability	2.00	The single largest personnel factor—good requirements capability—makes a factor of 2 difference in the effort for the entire project. Competency in this area has the potential to reduce a project's overall effort from nominal more than any other factor.
Requirements Flexibility	1.26*	Projects that allow the development team latitude in how they interpret requirements take less effort than projects that insist on rigid, literal interpretations of all requirements.
Storage Constraint	1.46	Working on a platform on which you're butting up against storage limitations moderately increases project effort.
Team Cohesion	129*	Teams with highly cooperative interactions develop software more efficiently than teams with more contentious interactions.
Time Constraint	1.63	Minimizing response time increases effort across the board. This is one reason that systems projects and real-time projects tend to consume more effort than other projects of similar sizes.
Use of Software Tools	1.50	Advanced tool sets can reduce effort significantly.

* Exact effect depends on project size. Effect listed is for a project size of 100,000 LOC. These factors are discussed in the next section.

As I hinted earlier, studying the Cocomo II adjustment factors to gain insight into your project's strengths and weaknesses is a high-leverage activity. For the estimate itself, using historical data from your past or current projects tends to be easier and more accurate than tweaking Cocomo's 22 adjustment factors.

Chapter 8 will discuss the ins and outs of collecting and using historical data.

5.6 Diseconomies of Scale Revisited

The Cocomo II adjustment factors provide an interesting viewpoint into how diseconomies of scale operate. In Figure 5-9, 5 of the factors in the figure are called *scaling factors*. These are the factors that contribute to software's diseconomies of scale. They affect projects to different degrees at different sizes. Figure 5-9 shows the same graph with these factors highlighted in blue.

Figure 5-9   Cocomo II factors with diseconomy of scale factors highlighted in blue. Project size is 100,000 LOC.

None of the factors that contribute to software's diseconomy of scale is in the top half of factors in terms of significance. In fact, 4 of the 5 least-influential factors are scaling factors. However, because the scaling factors contribute different amounts at different project sizes, this diagram must be drawn from the point of view of a project of a specific size. The factors in Figure 5-9 are shown for a project of 100,000 lines of code. Figure 5-10 shows what happens when the factors are recalculated for a much larger project of 5,000,000 lines of code.

The scaling factors all become significant as project size increases. Although none of them was in the top half at 100,000 LOC, all the scaling factors are in the top half at 5,000,000 LOC.

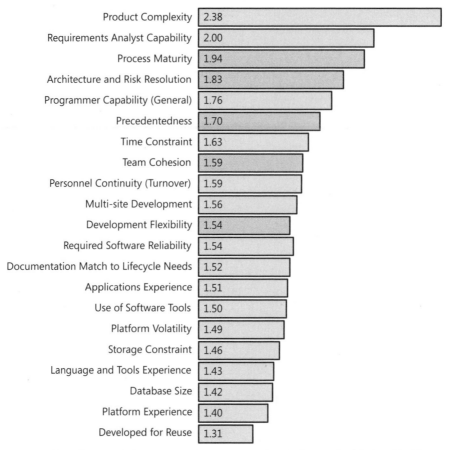

Figure 5-10   Cocomo II factors with diseconomy of scale factors highlighted in blue. Project size is 5,000,000 LOC.

What this means from an estimating point of view is that different factors need to be weighted differently at different project sizes. What this means from a project planning and control point of view is that small and medium-sized projects can succeed largely on the basis of strong individuals. Large projects still need strong individuals, but how well the project is managed (especially in terms of risk management), how mature the organization is, and how well the individuals coalesce into a team become as significant.

Additional Resources

Boehm, Barry, et al. *Software Cost Estimation with Cocomo II*. Reading, MA: Addison-Wesley, 2000. This book is the definitive description of Cocomo II. The book's size is daunting, but it describes the basic Cocomo model within the first 80 pages, including detailed definitions of the effort multipliers and scaling factors discussed in this chapter and how Cocomo II accounts for diseconomies of scale. The rest of the book describes extensions of the model.

Putnam, Lawrence H. and Ware Myers. *Measures for Excellence: Reliable Software On Time, Within Budget.* Englewood Cliffs, NJ: Yourdon Press, 1992. This book describes Putnam's estimation method including how it addresses diseconomies of scale. I like Putnam's model because it contains few control knobs and works best when it is calibrated with historical data. The book is mathematically oriented, so it can be slow going.

Part II
Fundamental Estimation Techniques

Chapter 6
Introduction to Estimation Techniques

Chapters 1 through 5 described the critical concepts that underlie all software estimates. This book now turns to a discussion of detailed estimation techniques that can be applied to specific estimation problems.

One important consideration in the use of these techniques is that different techniques will apply in different circumstances. This chapter introduces the major considerations in choosing which techniques to choose.

6.1 Considerations in Choosing Estimation Techniques

The most useful techniques in any given situation are determined by both a desire to account for the estimation influences described in Chapter 5, "Estimate Influences," and a desire to avoid the sources of estimation error described in Chapter 4, "Where Does Estimation Error Come From?" The following sections describe the major issues you should consider.

What's Being Estimated

Some projects determine their features and then focus on estimating the schedule and effort needed to deliver those features. Other projects determine their budgets and development time frames and then focus on estimating how many features they can deliver.

Many estimation techniques are applicable regardless of what is being estimated; a few techniques are better suited to estimating how much effort a project will require, how long a project will take, or how many features can be delivered.

In this book, estimating *size* refers to estimating the scope of technical work of a given feature set—in units such as lines of code, function points, stories, or some other measure. Estimating *features* refers to estimating how many features can be delivered within schedule and budget constraints. These terms are not industry standards; I'm defining them here for the sake of clarity.

Project Size

Project size is another factor to consider in choosing the best estimation technique.

Small   I characterize a small project as a project with five or fewer total technical staff, but that is a loose characterization. Small projects typically can't use the statistically oriented techniques that larger projects can use because variations in individual productivity drown out other factors.

Small projects are more likely to use a flat staffing model (using the same number of people on the team for the entire project), which invalidates some of the more algorithmically oriented large-project estimation approaches.

The best estimation techniques for small projects tend to be "bottom-up" techniques based on estimates created by the individuals who will actually do the work.

Large   A large project is a project with a team of approximately 25 people or more that lasts 6 to 12 months or more.

The best techniques for large projects change significantly from the beginning of the project to the end. In the early stages, the best estimation approaches tend to be "top-down" techniques based on algorithms and statistics. These are valid at the point in the project when specific team members are not yet known—when plans are based on a team that consists of, for example, "11 senior engineers, 25 staff developers, and 8 testers," rather than specific individuals.

In the middle stages, a combination of top-down and bottom-up techniques based on the project's own historical data will produce the most accurate estimates. In the later stages of large projects, bottom-up techniques will provide the most accurate estimates.

Medium   Medium-size projects consist of approximately 5 to 25 people and last 3 to 12 months. They have the advantage of being able to use virtually all the estimation techniques that large projects can use and several of the small-project techniques, too.

Software Development Style

For purposes of estimation, the two major development styles are *sequential* and *iterative*. Industry terminology surrounding iterative, Agile, and sequential projects can be confusing. For this book's purposes, the primary difference between these kinds of projects is the percentage of requirements they define early in the project compared to the percentage they define after construction is underway.

Here is how several common development approaches stack up according to these criteria.

Evolutionary prototyping   Evolutionary prototyping is used when requirements are unknown, and one of the primary reasons to use evolutionary prototyping is to help define requirements (McConnell 1996). For estimation purposes, this is an iterative development style.

Extreme Programming   Extreme Programming deliberately defines only the requirements that will be developed in the next iteration, which typically lasts less than a month (Beck 2004). For estimation purposes, Extreme Programming is a highly iterative approach.

Evolutionary delivery   An evolutionary delivery project can define anywhere from "hardly any" to "most" of its requirements up front (Gilb 1988, McConnell 1996). Depending on which end of the scale the project falls on, an evolutionary delivery project can be either sequential or iterative. Most evolutionary delivery projects leave enough requirements undefined at the beginning of construction that the approach as normally practiced is iterative.

Staged delivery   Staged delivery attempts to define the majority of its requirements prior to beginning the majority of construction (McConnell 1996). It uses iterations within design, construction, and test, so in some sense it is iterative. For estimation purposes, however, it is a sequential development style.

Rational Unified Process   The Rational Unified Process (RUP) describes its stages as "iterations." However, a nominal RUP project seeks to define about 80% of its requirements before construction begins (Jacobson, Booch, and Rumbaugh 1999). For estimation purposes, RUP is a sequential development style.

Scrum   Scrum is a development style in which a project team takes on a set of features that it can implement within a 30-day "sprint" (Schwaber and Beedle 2002). Once a sprint begins, the customer is not allowed to change requirements. From the point of view of an individual sprint, for estimation purposes, Scrum is sequential. Because features are not allocated for more than one sprint at a time, from a multiple-sprint (multiple iteration) point of view, Scrum is iterative.

Effect of Development Style on Choice of Estimation Techniques

Both iterative and sequential projects tend to start with top-down or statistically based estimation techniques and both eventually migrate toward bottom-up techniques. Iterative projects transition to refining their estimates more quickly using project-specific data.

Development Stage

As a team works its way through a project, it develops information that supports more accurate estimates. Requirements become better understood, designs become more detailed, plans become firmer, and the project itself generates productivity data that can be used to estimate the remainder of the project.

This book defines development stages as follows:

Early   On sequential projects, the early stage will be the period from the beginning of the project concept until requirements have been mostly defined. On iterative projects, *early* refers to the initial planning period.

Middle   The middle stage is the time between initial planning and early construction. On a sequential project, this time will extend from requirements and architecture time until enough construction has been completed to generate project productivity data that can be used for estimation. On iterative projects, *middle* refers to the first two to four iterations—the iterations that occur before the project can confidently base its estimates on its own productivity data.

Late   *Late* refers to the time from mid-construction through release.

Some techniques work best in the wide part of the Cone of Uncertainty. Others work better after the project has begun to generate data that can be used to estimate the remainder of the project.

Accuracy Possible

The accuracy of a technique is a function partly of the technique, partly of whether the technique is being applied to a suitable estimation problem, and partly of when in the project the technique is applied.

Some estimation techniques produce high accuracy but at high cost. Others produce lower accuracy, but at lower cost. Normally you'll want to use the most accurate techniques available, but depending on the stage of the project and how much accuracy is possible at that point in the Cone of Uncertainty, a low-cost, low-accuracy approach can be appropriate.

6.2 Technique Applicability Tables

Most of the remaining chapters in this book begin with tables that describe the applicability of techniques in the chapter. Here's an example:

Applicability of Techniques in this Chapter—SAMPLE

	Group Reviews	**Calibration with Project-Specific Data**
What's Estimated	Size, Effort, Schedule, Features	Size, Effort, Schedule, Features
Size of project	- M L	S M L
Development Stage	Early–Middle	Middle—Late
Iterative or Sequential	Both	Both
Accuracy Possible	Medium–High	High

The entries in the table are based on the considerations described in the previous section. Table 6-1 describes how to interpret the entries in these tables.

Table 6-1   **Possible Entries in the "Applicability of Techniques in This Chapter" Tables**

Table Entry	**Possible Entries**
What's estimated	Size, Effort, Schedule, Features
Size of project	S M L (Small, Medium, Large)
Development stage	Early, Middle, Late
Iterative or sequential	Iterative, Sequential, or Both
Accuracy possible	Low, Medium, High

Tip #29	When choosing estimation techniques, consider what you want to estimate, the size of the project, the development stage, the project's development style, and what accuracy you need.

Chapter 7
Count, Compute, Judge

Applicability of Techniques in This Chapter

	Count	Compute
What's estimated	Size, Features	Size, Effort, Schedule, Features
Size of project	S M L	S M L
Development stage	Early–Late	Early–Middle
Iterative or sequential	Both	Both
Accuracy possible	High	High

Suppose you're at a reception for the world's best software estimators. The room is packed, and you're seated in the middle of the room at a table with three other estimators. All you can see as you scan the room are wall-to-wall estimators. Suddenly, the emcee steps up to the microphone and says, "We need to know exactly how many people are in this room so that we can order dessert. Who can give me the most accurate estimate for the number of people in the room?"

The estimators at your table immediately break out into a vigorous discussion about the best way to estimate the answer. Bill, the estimator to your right, says, "I make a hobby of estimating crowds. Based on my experience, it looks to me like we've got about 335 people in the room."

The estimator sitting across the table from you, Karl, says, "This room has 11 tables across and 7 tables deep. One of my friends is a banquet planner, and she told me that they plan for 5 people per table. It looks to me like most of the tables do actually have about 5 people at them. If we multiple 11 times 7 times 5, we get 385 people. I think we should use that as our estimate."

The estimator to your left, Lucy, says, "I noticed on the way into the room that there was an occupancy limit sign that says this room can hold 485 people. This room is pretty full. I'd say 70 to 80 percent full. If we multiply those percentages by the room limit, we get 340 to 388 people. How about if we use the average of 364 people, or maybe just simplify it to 365?"

Bill says, "We have estimates of 335, 365, and 385. It seems like the right answer must be in there somewhere. I'm comfortable with 365."

"Me too," Karl says.

Everyone looks at you. You say, "I need to check something. Would you excuse me for a minute?" Lucy, Karl, and Bill give you curious looks and say, "OK."

You return a few minutes later. "Remember how we had to have our tickets scanned before we entered the room? I noticed on my way into the room that the handheld ticket scanner had a counter. So I went back and talked to the ticket taker at the front door. She said that, according to her scanner, she has scanned 407 tickets. She also said no one has left the room so far. I think we should use 407 as our estimate. What do you say?"

7.1 Count First

What do you think the right answer is? Is it the answer of 335, created by Bill, whose specialty is estimating crowd sizes? Is it the answer of 385, derived by Karl from a few reasonable assumptions? Is it Lucy's 365, also derived from a few reasonable assumptions? Or is the right number the 407 that was counted by the ticket scanner? *Is there any doubt in your mind that 407 is the most accurate answer?* For the record, the story ended by your table proposing the answer of 407, which turned out to be the correct number, and your table was served dessert first.

One of the secrets of this book is that you should avoid doing what we traditionally think of as estimating! If you can *count* the answer directly, you should do that first. That approach produced the most accurate answer in the story.

If you can't count the answer directly, you should count something else and then *compute* the answer by using some sort of calibration data. In the story, Karl had the historical data of knowing that the banquet was planned to have 5 people per table. He *counted* the number of tables and then computed the answer from that.

Similarly, Lucy based her estimate on the documented fact of the room's occupancy limit. She used her *judgment* to estimate the room was 70 to 80 percent full.

The least accurate estimate came from, Bill, the person who used only *judgment* to create the answer.

Tip #30	*Count* if at all possible. *Compute* when you can't count. Use *judgment* alone only as a last resort.

7.2 What to Count

Software projects produce numerous things that you can count. Early in the development life cycle, you can count marketing requirements, features, use cases, and stories, among other things.

In the middle of the project, you can count at a finer level of granularity—engineering requirements, Function Points, change requests, Web pages, reports, dialog boxes, screens, and database tables, just to name a few.

Late in the project, you can count at an even finer level of detail—code already written, defects reported, classes, and tasks, as well as all the detailed items you were counting earlier in the project.

You can decide what to count based on a few goals.

Find something to count that's highly correlated with the size of the software you're estimating   If your features are fixed and you're estimating cost and schedule, the biggest influence on a project estimate is the size of the software. When you look for something to count, look for something that will be a strong indicator of the software's size. Number of marketing requirements, number of engineering requirements, and Function Points are all examples of countable quantities that are strongly associated with final system size.

In different environments, different quantities are the most accurate indicators of project size. In one environment, the best indicator might be the number of Web pages. In another environment, the best indicator might be the number of marketing requirements, test cases, stories, or configuration settings. The trick is to find something that's a relevant indicator of size in your environment.

Tip #31	Look for something you can count that is a meaningful measure of the scope of work in your environment.

Find something to count that's available sooner rather than later in the development cycle   The sooner you can find something meaningful to count, the sooner you'll be able to provide long-range predictability. The count of lines of code for a project is often a great indicator of project effort, but the code won't be available to count until the very end of the project. Function Points are strongly associated with ultimate project size, but they aren't available until you have detailed requirements. If you can find something you can count earlier, you can use that to create an estimate earlier. For example, you might create a rough estimate based on a count of marketing requirements and then tighten up the estimate later based on a Function Point count.

Find something to count that will produce a statistically meaningful average   Find something that will produce a count of 20 or more. Statistically, you need a sample of at least 20 items for the average to be meaningful. Twenty is not a magic number, but it's a good guideline for statistical validity.

Understand what you're counting   For your count to serve as an accurate basis for estimation, you need to be sure the same assumptions apply to the count that your historical data is based on and to the count that you're using for your estimate. If you're counting marketing requirements, be sure that what you counted as a "marketing requirement" for your historical data is similar to what you count as a "marketing requirement" for your estimate. If your historical data indicates that a past project team in your company delivered 7 user stories per week, be sure your assumptions about team size, programmer experience, development technology, and other factors are similar in the project you're estimating.

Find something you can count with minimal effort   All other things being equal, you'd rather count something that requires the least effort. In the story at the beginning of the chapter, the count of people in the room was readily available from the ticket scanner. If you had to go around to each table and count people manually, you might decide it wasn't worth the effort.

One of the insights from the Cocomo II project is that a size estimation measure called Object Points is about as strongly correlated with effort as the Function Points measure is but requires only about half as much effort to count. Thus, Object Points are seen as an effective alternative to Function Points for estimation in the wide part of the Cone of Uncertainty (Boehm et al 2000).

7.3 Use Computation to Convert Counts to Estimates

If you collect historical data related to counts, you can convert the counts to something useful, such as estimated effort. Table 7-1 lists examples of quantities you might count and the data you would need to compute an estimate from the count.

Table 7-1   **Examples of Quantities That Can Be Counted for Estimation Purposes**

Quantity to Count	Historical Data Needed to Convert the Count to an Estimate
Marketing requirements	■ Average effort hours per requirement for development
	■ Average effort hours per requirement for independent testing
	■ Average effort hours per requirement for documentation
	■ Average effort hours per requirement to create engineering requirements from marketing requirements

Table 7-1   **Examples of Quantities That Can Be Counted for Estimation Purposes**

Quantity to Count	Historical Data Needed to Convert the Count to an Estimate
Features	■ Average effort hours per feature for development and/or testing
Use cases	■ Average total effort hours per use case ■ Average number of use cases that can be delivered in a particular amount of calendar time
Stories	■ Average total effort hours per story ■ Average number of stories that can be delivered in a particular amount of calendar time
Engineering requirements	■ Average number of engineering requirements that can be formally inspected per hour ■ Average effort hours per requirement for development/ test/documentation
Function Points	■ Average development/test/documentation effort per Function Point ■ Average lines of code in the target language per Function Point
Change requests	■ Average development/test/documentation effort per change request (depending on variability of the change requests, the data might be decomposed into average effort per small, medium, and large change request)
Web pages	■ Average effort per Web page for user interface work ■ Average whole-project effort per Web page (less reliable, but can be an interesting data point)
Reports	■ Average effort per report for report work
Dialog boxes	■ Average effort per dialog for user interface work
Database tables	■ Average effort per table for database work ■ Average whole-project effort per table (less reliable, but can be an interesting data point)
Classes	■ Average effort hours per class for development ■ Average effort hours to formally inspect a class ■ Average effort hours per class for testing
Defects found	■ Average effort hours per defect to fix ■ Average effort hours per defect to regression test ■ Average number of defects that can be corrected in a particular amount of calendar time
Configuration settings	■ Average effort per configuration setting

Table 7-1   **Examples of Quantities That Can Be Counted for Estimation Purposes**

Quantity to Count	Historical Data Needed to Convert the Count to an Estimate
Lines of code already written	■ Average number of defects per line of code ■ Average lines of code that can be formally inspected per hour ■ Average new lines of code from one release to the next
Test cases already written	■ Average amount of release-stage effort per test case

Tip #32	Collect historical data that allows you to compute an estimate from a count.

Example of counting defects late in a project   Once you have the kind of data described in the table, you can use that data as a more solid basis for creating estimates than expert judgment. If you know that you have 400 open defects, and you know that the 250 defects you've fixed so far have averaged 2 hours per defect, you know that you have about 400 x 2 equals 800 hours of work to fix the open defects.

Example of estimation by counting Web pages   If your data says that so far your project has taken an average of 40 hours to design, code, and test each Web page with dynamic content, and you have 12 Web pages left, you know that you have something like 12 x 40 equals 480 hours of work left on the remaining Web pages.

The important point in these examples is that *there is no judgment in these estimates.* You count, and then you compute. This process helps keep the estimates free from bias that would otherwise degrade their accuracy. For counts that you already have available—such as number of defects—such estimates also require very low effort.

Tip #33	Don't discount the power of simple, coarse estimation models such as average effort per defect, average effort per Web page, average effort per story, and average effort per use case.

7.4 Use Judgment Only as a Last Resort

So-called expert judgment is the least accurate means of estimation. Estimates seem to be the most accurate if they can be tied to something concrete. In the story told at the beginning of this chapter, the worst estimate was the one created by the expert who used judgment alone. Tying the estimate to the room occupancy limit was a little better, although it was subject to more error because that approach required a judgment about how full the room was as a percentage of maximum occupancy, which is an opportunity for subjectivity or bias to contaminate the estimate.

Historical data combined with computation is remarkably free from the biases that can undermine more judgment-based estimates. Avoid the temptation to tweak computed estimates to conform to your expert judgment. When I wrote the second edition of *Code Complete* (McConnell 2004a), I had a team that formally inspected the entire first edition—all 900 pages of it. During our first inspection meeting, our inspection rate averaged 3 minutes per page. Realizing that 3 minutes per page implied 45 hours of inspection meetings, I commented after the first meeting that I thought we were just beginning to gel as a team, and, in my judgment, we would speed up in future meetings. I suggested using a working number of 2 or 2.5 minutes per page instead of 3 minutes to plan future meetings. The project manager responded that, because we had only one meeting's worth of data, we should use that meeting's number of 3 minutes per page as a guide for planning the next few meetings. We could adjust our plans later based on different data from later meetings, if we needed to.

Nine hundred pages later, how many minutes per page do you think we averaged for the entire book? If you guessed 3 minutes per page, you're right!

Tip #34	Avoid using expert judgment to tweak an estimate that has been derived through computation. Such "expert judgment" usually degrades the estimate's accuracy.

Additional Resources

Boehm, Barry, et al. *Software Cost Estimation with Cocomo II*. Reading, MA: Addison-Wesley, 2000. Boehm provides a brief description of Object Points.

Lorenz, Mark and Jeff Kidd. *Object-Oriented Software Metrics*. Upper Saddle River, NJ: PTR Prentice Hall, 1994. Lorenz and Kidd present numerous suggestions of quantities that can be counted in object-oriented programs.

Chapter 8
Calibration and Historical Data

Applicability of Techniques in This Chapter

	Calibration with Industry-Average Data	Calibration with Organizational Data	Calibration with Project-Specific Data
What's estimated	Size, Effort, Schedule, Features	Size, Effort, Schedule, Features	Size, Effort, Schedule, Features
Size of project	S M L	S M L	S M L
Development stage	Early–Middle	Early–Middle	Middle–Late
Iterative or sequential	Both	Both	Both
Accuracy possible	Low–Medium	Medium–High	High

Calibration is used to convert counts to estimates—lines of code to effort, user stories to calendar time, requirements to number of test cases, and so on. Estimates always involve some sort of calibration, whether explicit or implicit. Calibration using various kinds of data makes up the second piece of the "count, then compute" approach described in Chapter 7, "Count, Compute, Judge."

Your estimates can be calibrated using any of three kinds of data:

- *Industry data*, which refers to data from other organizations that develop the same basic kind of software as the software that's being estimated

- *Historical data*, which in this book refers to data from the organization that will conduct the project being estimated

- *Project data*, which refers to data generated earlier in the same project that's being estimated

Historical data and project data are both tremendously useful and can support creation of highly accurate estimates. Industry data is a temporary backup that can be useful when you don't have historical data or project data.

8.1 Improved Accuracy and Other Benefits of Historical Data

The most important reason to use historical data from your own organization is that it improves estimation accuracy. The use of historical data, or "documented facts," is negatively correlated with cost and schedule overruns—that is, projects that have been estimated using historical data tend not to have overruns (Lederer and Prasad 1992).

The following sections discuss some of the reasons that historical data improves accuracy.

Accounts for Organizational Influences

First and foremost, use of historical data accounts for a raft of organizational influences that affect project outcomes. For very small projects, individual capabilities dictate the project outcome. As project size increases, talented individuals still matter, but their efforts are either supported or undermined by organizational influences. For medium and large projects, organizational characteristics start to matter as much as or more than individual capabilities.

Here are some of the organizational influences that affect project outcomes:

- How complex is the software, what is the execution time constraint, what reliability is required, how much documentation is required, how precedented is the application—that is, how does the project stack up against the Cocomo II factors related to the kind of software being developed (as discussed in Chapter 5, "Estimate Influences")?

- Can the organization commit to stable requirements, or must the project team deal with volatile requirements throughout the project?

- Is the project manager free to remove a problem team member from the project, or do the organization's Human Resources policies make it difficult or impossible to remove a problem employee?

- Is the team free to concentrate on the current project, or are team members frequently interrupted with calls to support production releases of previous projects?

- Can the organization add team members to the new project as planned, or does it refuse to pull people off other projects before those projects have been completed?

- Does the organization support the use of effective design, construction, quality assurance, and testing practices?

- Does the organization operate in a regulated environment (for example, under FAA or FDA regulations) in which certain practices are dictated?

- Can the project manager depend on team members staying until the project is complete, or does the organization have high turnover?

Accounting for each of these influences in an estimate one by one is difficult and error-prone. But historical data adjusts for all these factors, whether you're aware of the specifics or not.

Avoids Subjectivity and Unfounded Optimism

One way that subjectivity creeps into estimates is that project managers or estimators look at a new project, compare it with an old project, observe numerous differences between the two projects, and then conclude that the new project will go better than the old one did. They say, "We had a lot of turnover on the last project. That won't happen this time, so we'll be more productive. Also, people kept getting called back to support the previous version, and we'll make sure that that doesn't happen this time either. We also had a lot of late-breaking requirements from marketing. We'll do a better job on that, too. Plus we're working with better technology this time and newer, more effective development methods. With all those improvements, we should be able to be *way* more productive."

It's easy to identify with the optimism in these lines of reasoning. But the factors listed are controlled more by the organization than by the specific project manager, so most of these factors tend to be difficult to control for one specific project. The other factors tend to be interpreted optimistically, which introduces bias into the estimate.

With historical data, you use a simplifying assumption that the next project will go about the same as the last project did. This is a reasonable assumption. As estimation guru Lawrence Putnam says, productivity is an organizational attribute that cannot easily be varied from project to project (Putnam and Myers 1992, Putnam and Myers 2003). The same concept shows up in Extreme Programming as "Yesterday's Weather": the weather today won't always be the same as it was yesterday, but it's more likely to be like yesterday's weather than like anything else (Beck and Fowler 2001).

Tip #35	Use historical data as the basis for your productivity assumptions. Unlike mutual fund disclosures, your organization's past performance really is your best indicator of future performance.

Reduces Estimation Politics

One of the traps in estimation models that include a lot of control knobs is that many of the higher-leverage knobs are related to personnel. Cocomo II, for example, requires you to make assessments of your requirements analysts' and programmers' capabilities, along with several less subjective personnel factors related to experience. Cocomo requires the estimator to rate the programmers as 90th percentile, 75th percentile, 55th percentile, 35th percentile, or 15th percentile. (All these percentiles are industrywide.)

Suppose a manager takes a Cocomo II estimate into a meeting with an executive and the meeting agenda is to look for fat in the manager's estimate. It's easy to imagine the conversation going like this:

> MANAGER: *I know we had a goal of finishing this release in 12 weeks, but my estimates indicate that it will take 16 weeks. Let's walk through the estimate using this software estimation tool. Here are the assumptions I made. First, I had to calibrate the estimation model. For the "programmer capability" factor, I assumed our programmers are 35th percentile–*

> EXECUTIVE: *What?! No one on our staff is below average! You need to have more confidence in your staff! What kind of manager are you? Well, maybe we've got a few people who aren't quite as good as the rest, but the overall team can't be that bad. Let's assume they're at least average, right? Can you enter that into the software?*

> MANAGER: *Well, OK. Now, the next factor is the capability of the requirements engineers. We've never focused on recruiting good requirements engineers or developing those skills in our engineers, so I assumed they were 15th percentile–*

> EXECUTIVE: *Hold on! 15th percentile? These people are very talented, even if they haven't had formal training in requirements engineering. They've got to be at least average. Can we change that factor to average?*

> MANAGER: *I can't justify making them average. We really don't even have any staff we can call requirements specialists.*

> EXECUTIVE: *Fine. Let's compromise and change the factor to 35th percentile then.*

> MANAGER: *OK (sigh).*

In this interaction, if the manager was using the Cocomo II adjustment factors, his estimate of effort required was just reduced by 23%. If the executive had succeeded in talking the manager into rating the requirements engineers as average rather than 35th percentile, the estimate would be reduced by 39%. In either case, a single conversation would result in a significant difference.

A manager who calibrates the estimate with historical data sidesteps the whole issue of whether the programmers are above average or below average. Productivity is whatever the data says it is. It's difficult for a non-technical stakeholder to argue with a statement like this one: "We've averaged 300 to 450 delivered lines of code per staff month, so we've calibrated the model with an assumption of 400 lines of code per staff month, which we believe is a little on the optimistic side but within a prudent planning range."

Clearly, half the programmers in the industry are below average, but I rarely meet project managers or executives who believe *their* programmers are the people who are below average.

Tip #36	Use historical data to help avoid politically charged estimation discussions arising from assumptions like "My team is below average."

8.2 Data to Collect

If you're not already collecting historical data, you can start with a very small set of data:

- Size (lines of code or something else you can count after the software has been released)
- Effort (staff months)
- Time (calendar months)
- Defects (classified by severity)

This small amount of data, even if you collect it only at the completion of two or three projects, will give you enough data to calibrate any of several commercial software estimation tools. It will also allow you to compute simple ratios such as lines of code per staff month.

In addition to the fact that these four kinds of data are sufficient to calibrate estimation models, most experts recommend starting small so that you understand what you're collecting (Pietrasanta 1990, NASA SEL 1995). If you don't start small, you can end up with data that's defined inconsistently across projects, which makes the data meaningless. Depending on how you define these four kinds of data, the numbers you come up with for each can vary by a factor of 2 or more.

Issues Related to Size Measures

You can measure the size of completed projects in Function Points, stories, Web pages, database tables, and numerous other ways, but most organizations eventually settle on capturing size-related historical data in terms of lines of code. (More details on the strengths and weaknesses of using LOC measurements are discussed in Section 18.1, "Challenges with Estimating Size.")

For size in lines of code, you'll need to define several issues, including the following:

- Do you count all code or only code that's included in the released software? (For example, do you count scaffolding code, mock object code, unit test code, and system test code?)

- How do you count code that's reused from previous versions?

- How do you count open source code or third-party library code?

- Do you count blank lines and comments, or only non-blank, non-comment source lines?

- Do you count class interfaces?

- Do you count data declarations?

- How do you count lines that make up one logical line of code but that are broken across multiple lines for the sake of readability?

There isn't any industry standard on this topic, and it doesn't particularly matter how you answer these questions.[1] What does matter is that you answer these questions consistently across projects so that whatever assumptions are baked into the data you collected is *consciously* projected forward in your estimates.

Issues Related to Effort Measures

Similar cautions apply to collecting effort data:

- Do you count time in hours, days, or some other unit?

- How many hours per day do you count? Standard 8 hours or actual hours applied to the specific project?

- Do you count unpaid overtime?

- Do you count holidays, vacation, and training?

- Do you make allowances for all-company meetings?

- What kinds of effort do you count? Testing? First-level management? Documentation? Requirements? Design? Research?

- How do you count time that's divided across multiple projects?

- How do you count time spent supporting previous releases of the same software?

- How do you count time spent supporting sales calls, trade shows, and so on?

- How do you count travel time?

- How do you count fuzzy front-end time—the time spent firming up the software concept before the project is fully defined?

---

[1] The closest the software industry has to a standard definition is a non-blank, non-comment, deliverable source statement that includes interfaces and data declarations. That definition still leaves a few of the questions unanswered, such as how to count code reused from previous projects.

Again, the main goal here is to define the data you're collecting well enough so that you know what you're estimating. If your data from past projects includes a high percentage of unpaid overtime and you use that historical data to estimate a future project, guess what? You've just calibrated a high percentage of overtime into your future project.

Issues Related to Calendar Time Measures

It's surprisingly difficult in many organizations to determine how long a particular project lasted.

- When does the project start? Does it start when it gets formal budget approval? Does it start when initial discussions about the project begin? Does it start when it's fully staffed? Capers Jones reports that fewer than 1% of projects have a clearly defined starting point (Jones 1997).

- When does the project end? Does it end when the software is released to the customer? When the final release candidate is delivered to testing? What if most programmers have rolled off the project a month before the official release? Jones reports that 15% of projects have ambiguous end times (Jones 1997).

In this area, it's very helpful if the organization has well-defined project launch and project completion milestones. The main goal, again, is simply to understand the data you're collecting.

Issues Related to Defect Measures

Finally, defect measures also vary by a factor of 2 or 3 depending on what's counted as a defect:

- Do you count all change requests as defects, or only those that are ultimately classified as defects rather than feature requests?

- Do you count multiple reports of the same defect as a single defect or as multiple defects?

- Do you count defects that are detected by developers, or only those detected by testers?

- Do you count requirements and design defects that are found prior to the beginning of system testing?

- Do you count coding defects that are found prior to the beginning of alpha or beta testing?

- Do you count defects reported by users after the software has been released?

> **Tip #37**   In collecting historical data to use for estimation, start small, be sure you understand what you're collecting, and collect the data consistently.

Other Data Collection Issues

Historical data tends to be easiest to collect if it's collected while the project is underway. It's difficult to go back six months after a project has been completed and reconstruct the "fuzzy front end" of the project to determine when the project began. It's also easy to forget how much overtime people worked at the end of the project.

> **Tip #38**   Collect a project's historical data *as soon as possible* after the end of the project.

While it's useful to collect data at the end of a project, it's even more useful to collect snapshots of a project as it's underway. Collecting data on size, effort, and defects every 1 to 2 weeks can provide valuable insight into your project's dynamics.

For example, collecting a snapshot of reported defects can help you predict the rate at which defects will be discovered and will need to be fixed on future projects. Collecting data on effort over time can help you understand your organization's ability to mobilize staff to support a project. If one project staffs up more slowly than desired, it might be a fluke. If your historical data says that the last three projects have each staffed up at about the same rate, that suggests that you're facing an organizational influence that can't easily be changed on the next project.

> **Tip #39**   As a project is underway, collect historical data on a periodic basis so that you can build a data-based profile of how your projects run.

8.3 How to Calibrate

The ultimate goal of collecting data is to convert the data to a model that you can use for estimation. Here are some examples of models you could create:

- Our developers average X lines of code per staff month.
- A 3-person team can deliver X stories per calendar month.
- Our team is averaging X staff hours per use case to create the use case, and Y hours per use case to construct and deliver the use case.
- Our testers create test cases at a rate of X hours per test case.
- In our environment, we average X lines of code per function point in C# and Y lines of code per function point in Python.
- On this project so far, defect correction work has averaged X hours per defect.

These are just examples to illustrate the kinds of models you can build using historical data. Table 7-1 in the previous chapter listed many more examples.

One characteristic these models have in common is that they are all linear. The math works the same whether you're building a 10,000-LOC system or a 1,000,000-LOC system. But because of software's diseconomies of scale, some models will need to be adjusted for different size ranges. You could try to handle the size differentiation informally. Table 8-1 shows one example of how you might do that.

Table 8-1   Example of Accounting for Diseconomies of Scale Informally—For Purposes of Illustration Only

Team Size	Average Stories Delivered per Calendar Month
1	5
2–3	12
4–5	22
6–7	31
8	No data for projects of this size

This approach is valid when you have small variations in project size. To account for larger variations in project size, see Section 5.1, "Project Size," and Section 5.6, "Diseconomies of Scale Revisited."

8.4 Using Project Data to Refine Your Estimates

Earlier in this chapter, I pointed out that historical data is useful because it accounts for organizational influences—both recognized and unrecognized. The same idea applies to the use of historical data within a specific project (Gilb 1988, Cohn 2006). Individual projects have dynamics that will vary somewhat from the dynamics of their surrounding organizations. Using data from the project itself will account for the influences that are unique to that specific project. The sooner on a project you can begin basing your estimates on data from the project itself, the sooner your estimates will become truly accurate.

Tip #40	Use data from your current project (project data) to create highly accurate estimates for the remainder of the project.

Even if you don't have historical data from past projects, you can collect data from your current project and use that as a basis for estimating the remainder of your project. Your goal should be to switch from using organizational data or industry-average data to project data as soon as you can. The more iterative your project is, the sooner you'll be able to do this.

Collecting and using data from your own project will be discussed in more detail in Section 16.4, "Estimate Refinement." Section 12.3, "Story Points," presents a specific example of using project data to refine your estimates.

8.5 Calibration with Industry Average Data

If you don't have your own historical data, you have little choice but to use industry-average data, which is adequate but no better. As Table 5-2 illustrated, the productivity rates for different organizations within the same industries typically vary by a factor of 10. If you use the average productivity for your industry, you won't be accounting for the possibility that your organization might be at the top end of the productivity range or at the bottom.

Figure 8-1 shows an example of an estimate created using industry-average data. Each point in the graph represents a possible project outcome created using a statistical technique known as a Monte Carlo simulation. The solid black lines represent the median effort and schedule found during the simulation. The dashed black lines represent the 25th and 75th percentiles for effort and schedule.

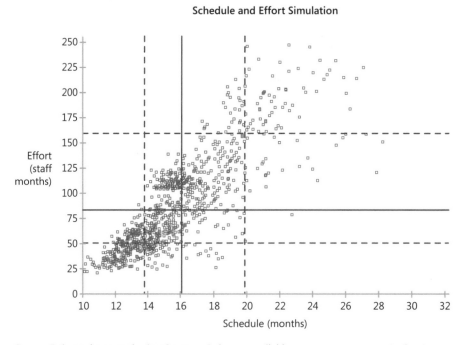

Source: Estimated prepared using Construx Estimate, available at www.construx.com/estimate.

Figure 8-1   An example of estimated outcomes for an estimate calibrated using industry-average data. Total variation in the effort estimates is about a factor of 10 (from about 25 staff months to about 250 staff months).

Figure 8-2 shows an example of a comparable estimate calibrated using historical data from one of my clients.

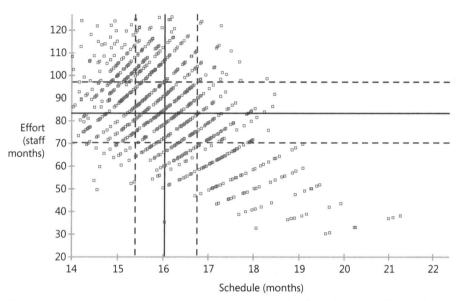

Schedule and Effort Simulation

Figure 8-2   An estimate calibrated using historical productivity data. The effort estimates vary by only about a factor of 4 (from about 30 staff months to about 120 staff months).

The sizes and nominal productivity rates of the two projects are identical, but the amount of variability in the two estimates is dramatically different. Because the industry-average estimate must account for factor-of-10 differences in productivity, the standard deviation on the effort estimate created using industry-average data is about 100%! If you wanted to give your boss an estimate that ranged from 25% confident to 75% confident using industry-average data, in this case you'd need to quote a range of 50 to 160 staff months—a factor of 3 difference!

If you could use historical data instead of industry-average data, you could quote a range of 70 to 95 staff months—a factor of only 1.4 from the top end of the range to the bottom. The standard deviation in the estimate created using historical data is only about 25%.

A review of studies on estimation accuracy found that in studies in which estimation models were not calibrated to the estimation environment, expert estimates were more accurate than the models. But the studies that used models calibrated with historical data found that the models were as good as or better than expert estimates (Jørgensen 2002).

Tip #41	Use project data or historical data rather than industry-average data to calibrate your estimates whenever possible. In addition to making your estimates more accurate, historical data will reduce variability in your estimate arising from uncertainty in the productivity assumptions.

8.6 Summary

If you haven't previously been exposed to the power of historical data, you can be excused for not currently having any data to use for your estimates. But now that you know how valuable historical data is, you don't have any excuse not to collect it. Be sure that when you reread this chapter next year you're not still saying, "I wish I had some historical data!"

Tip #42	If you don't currently have historical data, begin collecting it as soon as possible.

Additional Resources

Boehm, Barry, et al. *Software Cost Estimation with Cocomo II*. Reading, MA: Addison-Wesley, 2000. Appendix E of Boehm's book contains a checklist that's useful for precisely defining what constitutes a "line of code."

Gilb, Tom. *Principles of Software Engineering Management*. Wokingham, England: Addison-Wesley, 1988. Section 7.14 of Gilb's book describes using project-specific data to refine estimates. The description of evolutionary delivery throughout the book is based on the expectation that projects will build feedback loops allowing them to be estimated, planned, and managed in a way that allows the projects to be self-correcting.

Grady, Robert B. and Deborah L. Caswell. *Software Metrics: Establishing a Company-Wide Program*. Englewood Cliffs, NJ: Prentice Hall, 1987. This book and the following one describe Grady's experiences setting up a measurement program at Hewlett-Packard. The books contain many hard-won insights into the pitfalls of setting up a measurement program plus some interesting examples of the useful data you can ultimately obtain.

Grady, Robert B. *Practical Software Metrics for Project Management and Process Improvement*. Englewood Cliffs, NJ: PTR Prentice Hall, 1992.

Jones, Capers. *Applied Software Measurement: Assuring Productivity and Quality, 2d Ed.* New York, NY: McGraw-Hill, 1997. Chapter 3 of this book presents an excellent discussion of the sources of errors in size, effort, and quality measurements.

Putnam, Lawrence H. and Ware Myers. *Five Core Metrics*. New York, NY: Dorset House, 2003. This book presents a compelling argument for collecting data on the five core metrics of size, productivity, time, effort, and reliability.

Software Engineering Institute's *Software Engineering Measurement and Analysis (SEMA)* Web site: *www.sei.cmu.edu/sema/*. This comprehensive Web site helps organizations create data collection (measurement) practices and use the data they collect.

Chapter 9
Individual Expert Judgment

Applicability of Techniques in This Chapter

	Use of Structured Process	Use of Estimation Checklist	Estimating Task Effort in Ranges	Comparing Task Estimates to Actuals
What's estimated	Effort, Schedule, Features	Effort, Schedule, Features	Size, Effort, Schedule, Features	Size, Effort, Schedule, Features
Size of project	S M L	S M L	S M L	S M L
Development stage	Early–Late	Early–Late	Early–Late	Middle–Late
Iterative or sequential	Both	Both	Both	Both
Accuracy possible	High	High	High	N/A

Individual expert judgment is by far the most common estimation approach used in practice (Jørgensen 2002). Hihn and Habib-agahi found that 83% of estimators used "informal analogy" as their primary estimation technique (Hihn and Habib-agahi 1991). A New Zealand survey found that 86% of software organizations used "expert estimation" (Paynter 1996). Barbara Kitchenham and her colleagues found that 72% of project estimates were based on "expert opinion" (Kitchenham et al. 2002).

Expert-judgment estimates of individual tasks form the foundation for bottom-up estimation, but not all expert judgments are equal. Indeed, as Chapter 7, "Count, Compute, Judge," indicated, judgment is the most hazardous kind of estimation.

When discussing "expert judgment," we need first to ask "expert in what?" Being expert in the technology or development practices that will be employed does not make someone an expert in estimation. Magne Jørgensen reports that increased experience in the activity being estimated does not lead to increased accuracy in the estimates for the activity (Jørgensen 2002). Other studies have found that "experts" tend to use simple estimation strategies, even when their level of expertise in the subject being estimated is high (Josephs and Hahn 1995, Todd and Benbasat 2000).

This chapter describes how to ensure that, when you use expert judgment, the judgment is effective. The discussion in this chapter is closely related to the discussion in

Chapter 10, "Decomposition and Recomposition," which explains how to combine the individual estimates accurately.

9.1 Structured Expert Judgment

Individual expert judgment does not have to be informal or intuitive. Researchers have found significant accuracy differences between "intuitive expert judgment," which tends to be inaccurate (Lederer and Prasad 1992) and "structured expert judgment," which can produce estimates that are about as accurate as model-based estimates (Jørgensen 2002).

Who Creates the Estimates?

For the estimation of specific tasks—such as the time needed to code and debug a particular feature or to create a specific set of test cases—the people who will actually do the work will create the most accurate estimates. Estimates prepared by people who aren't doing the work are less accurate (Lederer and Prasad 1992). In addition, separate estimators are more likely to underestimate than estimator-developers are (Lederer and Prasad 1992).

Tip #43	To create the task-level estimates, have the people who will actually do the work create the estimates.

This guideline is for task-level estimates. If your project is still in the wide part of the Cone of Uncertainty (that is, specific tasks haven't yet been identified or assigned to individuals), the estimate should be created by an expert estimator or by the most expert development, quality assurance, and documentation staff available.

Granularity

One of the best ways to improve the accuracy of task-level estimates is to separate large tasks into smaller tasks. When creating estimates, developers, testers, and managers tend to concentrate on the tasks that they understand and deemphasize tasks that are unfamiliar to them. The common result is that a 1-line entry on the schedule, such as "data conversion," which was supposed to take 2 weeks, instead takes 2 months because no one investigated what was actually involved.

When estimating at the task level, decompose estimates into tasks that will require no more than about 2 days of effort. Tasks larger than that will contain too many places that unexpected work can hide. Ending up with estimates that are at the 1/4 day, 1/2 day, or full day of granularity is appropriate.

Use of Ranges

If you ask a developer to estimate a set of features, the developer will often come back with an estimate that looks like Table 9-1.

Table 9-1   **Example of Developer Single-Point Estimates**

Feature	Estimated Days to Complete
Feature 1	1.5
Feature 2	1.5
Feature 3	2.0
Feature 4	0.5
Feature 5	0.5
Feature 6	0.25
Feature 7	2.0
Feature 8	1.0
Feature 9	0.75
Feature 10	1.25
TOTAL	**11.25**

If you then ask the same developer to reestimate each feature's best case and worst case, the developer will often return with estimates similar to those in Table 9-2.

Table 9-2   **Example of Individual Estimation Using Best Case and Worst Case**

Feature	Estimated Days to Complete	
	Best Case	**Worst Case**
Feature 1	1.25	2.0
Feature 2	1.5	2.5
Feature 3	2.0	3.0
Feature 4	0.75	2.0
Feature 5	0.5	1.25
Feature 6	0.25	0.5
Feature 7	1.5	2.5
Feature 8	1.0	1.5
Feature 9	0.5	1.0
Feature 10	1.25	2.0
TOTAL	**10.5**[1]	**18.25**

[1]   Some statistical anomalies arise when you simply total the Best Case estimates and the Worst Case estimates. Chapter 10 discusses these in detail.

When you compare the original single-point estimates to the Best Case and Worst Case estimates, you see that the 11.25 total of the single-point estimates is much closer to the Best Case estimate of 10.5 days than to the Worst Case total of 18.25 days.

If you examine the estimate for Feature 4, you'll also notice that both the Best Case and the Worst Case estimates are higher than the original single-point estimate. Thinking through the worst case result sometimes exposes additional work that must be done even in the best case, which can raise the nominal estimate. In thinking through the worst case, I like to ask developers how long the task would take if *everything* went wrong. People's worst cases are often optimistic worst cases rather than *true* worst cases.

If you're a manager or a lead, have your developers create a set of single-point estimates. Hide those estimates from them. Then have the developers create a set of Best Case and Worst Case estimates. Have them compare their Best Case and Worst Case estimates to their original single-point estimates. This is often an eye-opening experience.

This exercise yields two benefits. First, it raises awareness that single-point estimates tend to be akin to Best Case estimates. Second, going through the process of writing down Best Case and Worst Case estimates a few times begins to engrain the habit of thinking through the worst case outcome when estimating. Once you get into the habit of considering both best case and worst case outcomes, you'll get better at factoring the full range of possible outcomes into your single-point task estimates, regardless of whether you actually write down the best and worst cases.

Tip #44	Create both Best Case and Worst Case estimates to stimulate thinking about the full range of possible outcomes.

Formulas

Creating the Best Case and the Worst Case estimates is just the first step. You're still left with the question of which estimate to use. Or maybe you should use the mathematical midpoint instead? The answer is none of the above. In many cases, the Worst Case is much worse than what's called the Expected Case. Taking the midpoints of the ranges could result in an unnecessarily high estimate.

A technique called the Program Evaluation and Review Technique (PERT) allows you to compute an Expected Case that might not be exactly in the middle of the range from best case to worst case (Putnam and Myers 1992, Stutzke 2005). To use PERT, you add an additional Most Likely Case to your set of cases. You can estimate the

Most Likely Case using expert judgment. You then calculate the Expected Case using this formula:

Equation #1	Expected Case = [BestCase + (4 × MostLikelyCase) + WorstCase] / 6

This formula accounts for the full width of the range as well as the position of the Most Likely Case within the range. Table 9-3 shows the estimates from Table 9-2 with the addition of Most Likely Case and Expected Case. As you can see from the table, the overall estimate of 13.62 is closer to the lower end of the range than the midpoint of 14.4 would have been.

Table 9-3   **Example of Individual Estimation Using Best Case, Worst Case, and Most Likely Case**

Feature	Estimated Days to Complete			
	Best Case	**Most Likely Case**	**Worst Case**	**Expected Case**
Feature 1	1.25	1.5	2.0	**1.54**
Feature 2	1.5	1.75	2.5	**1.83**
Feature 3	2.0	2.25	3.0	**2.33**
Feature 4	0.75	1	2.0	**1.13**
Feature 5	0.5	0.75	1.25	**0.79**
Feature 6	0.25	0.5	0.5	**0.46**
Feature 7	1.5	2	2.5	**2.00**
Feature 8	1.0	1.25	1.5	**1.25**
Feature 9	0.5	0.75	1.0	**0.75**
Feature 10	1.25	1.5	2.0	**1.54**
TOTAL	**10.5**	**13.25**	**18.25**	**13.62**

As discussed in Chapter 4, "Where Does Estimation Error Come From?" people's "most likely" estimates tend to be optimistic, which can yield optimistic overall estimates when using this approach. Some estimation experts suggest altering the basic PERT formula to account for a downward bias in the estimates (Stutzke 2005). Here's the altered formula:

Equation #2	Expected Case = [BestCase + (3 × MostLikelyCase) + (2 × WorstCase)] / 6

This is a reasonable short-term solution to the problem. The long-term solution to this problem is to work with people to make their Most Likely Case estimates more accurate.

Checklists

Even experts occasionally forget to consider everything they should. Studies of fore-casting in a variety of disciplines have found that simple checklists help improve accuracy by reminding people of considerations they might otherwise forget (Park 1996, Harvey 2001, Jørgensen 2002). Table 9-4 presents a checklist you might use to improve the accuracy of your estimates.

Table 9-4 **Checklist for Individual Estimates**

1. Is what's being estimated clearly defined?
2. Does the estimate include all the *kinds of work* needed to complete the task?
3. Does the estimate include all the *functionality areas* needed to complete the task?
4. Is the estimate broken down into enough detail to expose hidden work?
5. Did you look at documented facts (written notes) from past work rather than estimating purely from memory?
6. Is the estimate approved by the person who will actually do the work?
7. Is the productivity assumed in the estimate similar to what has been achieved on similar assignments?
8. Does the estimate include a Best Case, Worst Case, and Most Likely Case?
9. Is the Worst Case really the worst case? Does it need to be made even worse?
10. Is the Expected Case computed appropriately from the other cases?
11. Have the assumptions in the estimate been documented?
12. Has the situation changed since the estimate was prepared?

To avoid omitting work from your estimates, you might also review the lists of over-looked activities in Section 4.5, "Omitted Activities."

Tip #45	Use an estimation checklist to improve your individual estimates. Develop and maintain your own personal checklist to improve your estimation accuracy.

9.2 Compare Estimates to Actuals

Prying yourself loose from single-point/Best Case estimates is half the battle. The other half is comparing your actual results to your estimated results so that you can refine your personal estimating abilities.

Keep a list of your estimates, and fill in your actual results when you complete them. Then compute the Magnitude of Relative Error (MRE) of your estimates (Conte, Dunsmore, and Shen 1986). MRE is computed using this formula:

Equation #3	MRE = AbsoluteValue × [(ActualResult − EstimatedResult) / ActualResult]

Table 9-5 shows how the MRE calculations would work out for the Best Case and Worst Case estimates presented earlier.

Table 9-5   **Table 9-5 Example of Spreadsheet for Tracking Accuracy of Individual Estimates**

| | **Estimated Days to Complete** | | | | | |
Feature	**Best Case**	**Worst Case**	**Expected Case**	**Actual Outcome**	**MRE**	**In Range from Best Case to Worst Case?**
Feature 1	1.25	2	1.54	2	23%	Yes
Feature 2	1.5	2.5	1.83	2.5	27%	Yes
Feature 3	2	3	2.33	1.25	87%	No
Feature 4	0.75	2	1.13	1.5	25%	Yes
Feature 5	0.5	1.25	0.79	1	21%	Yes
Feature 6	0.25	0.5	0.46	0.5	8%	Yes
Feature 7	1.5	2.5	2.00	3	33%	No
Feature 8	1	1.5	1.25	1.5	17%	Yes
Feature 9	0.5	1	0.75	1	25%	Yes
Feature 10	1.25	2	1.54	2	23%	Yes
TOTAL	**10.50**	**18.25**	**13.625**	**16.25**		**80% Yes**
Average					**29%**	

In this spreadsheet, the MRE is calculated for each estimate. The average MRE, shown in the bottom row, is 29% for the set of estimates. You can use this average MRE to measure the accuracy of your estimates. As your estimates improve, you should see the MRE decline. The right-most column shows how many estimates are within the best case/worst case range. You should also see the percentage of estimates that fall within the range increase over time.

Tip #46	Compare actual performance to estimated performance so that you can improve your individual estimates over time.

When you compare your actual performance to your estimates, you should try to understand what went right, what went wrong, what you overlooked, and how to avoid making those mistakes in the future.

Another practice that sets up a feedback loop and encourages accurate estimates is a public estimation review. I've worked with companies that have their developers report on their actual results versus their estimates at a Monday morning standup meeting. This reinforces the idea that accurate estimates are an organizational priority.

Regardless of how you do it, the key principle is to set up a feedback loop based on actual results so that your estimates improve over time. To be effective, the feedback should be as timely as possible; delay reduces effectiveness of the feedback loop (Jørgensen 2002).

Additional Resources

Jørgensen, M. "A Review of Studies on Expert Estimation of Software Development Effort." 2002. This paper presents a comprehensive review of the research on expert estimation approaches. The author draws numerous conclusions from the common research threads and presents 12 tips for achieving accurate expert estimates.

Humphrey, Watts S. *A Discipline for Software Engineering*. Reading, MA: Addison-Wesley, 1995. Humphrey lays out a detailed methodology by which developers can collect personal productivity data, compare their planned results to their actual results, and improve over time.

Stutzke, Richard D. *Estimating Software-Intensive Systems*. Upper Saddle River, NJ: Addison-Wesley, 2005. Chapter 5 of Stutzke's book discusses judgment-based estimation techniques and provides background on some of the math described in this chapter.

Decomposition and Recomposition

Applicability of Techniques in This Chapter

	Decomposition by Feature or Task	Decomposition by Work Breakdown Structure (WBS)	Computing Best and Worst Cases from Standard Deviation
What's estimated	Size, Effort, Features	Effort	Effort, Schedule
Size of project	S M L	- M L	S M L
Development stage	Early–Late (small projects); Middle–Late (medium and large projects)	Early–Middle	Early–Late (small projects); Middle–Late (medium and large projects)
Iterative or sequential	Both	Both	Both
Accuracy possible	Medium–High	Medium	Medium

Decomposition is the practice of separating an estimate into multiple pieces, estimating each piece individually, and then recombining the individual estimates into an aggregate estimate. This estimation approach is also known as "bottom up," "micro estimation," "module build up," "by engineering procedure," and by many other names (Tockey 2005).

Decomposition is a cornerstone estimation practice—as long as you watch out for a few pitfalls. This chapter discusses the basic practice in more detail and explains how to avoid such pitfalls.

10.1 Calculating an Accurate Overall Expected Case

Scene: The weekly team meeting...

> YOU: *We need to create an estimate for a new project. I want to emphasize how important accurate estimation is to this group, and so I'm betting a pizza lunch that I can create a more accurate estimate for this project than you can. If you win, I'll buy the pizza. If I win, you'll buy. Any takers?*
>
> TEAM: *You're on!*
>
> YOU: *OK, let's get started.*

You look up information about a similar past project, and you find that that project took 18 staff weeks. You estimate that this project is about 20 percent larger than the past project, so you create a total estimate of 22 staff weeks.

Meanwhile, your team has created a more detailed, feature-by-feature estimate. They come back with the estimate shown in Table 10-1.

Table 10-1   **Example of Estimation by Decomposition**

Feature	Estimated Staff Weeks to Complete
Feature 1	1.5
Feature 2	4
Feature 3	3
Feature 4	1
Feature 5	4
Feature 6	6
Feature 7	2
Feature 8	1
Feature 9	3
Feature 10	1.5
TOTAL	**27**

YOU: *27 weeks? Wow, I think your estimate is high, but I guess we'll find out.*

A few weeks later...

YOU: *Now that the project is done, we know that it took a total of 29 staff weeks. It looks like your estimate of 27 staff weeks was optimistic by 2 weeks, which is an error of 7%. My estimate of 22 staff weeks was off by 7 staff weeks, about 24%. It looks like you win, so I'm buying the pizza.*

By the way, I want to see which of you good estimators cost me the pizza. Let's take a look at which detailed estimates were the most accurate.

You take a few minutes to compute the magnitude of relative error of each individual estimate and write the results on the whiteboard. Table 10-2 shows the results.

Table 10-2   **Example Results of Estimation by Decomposition**

Feature	Estimated Staff Weeks to Complete	Actual Effort	Raw Error	Magnitude of Relative Error
Feature 1	1.5	3.0	–1.5	50%
Feature 2	4.5	2.5	2.0	80%
Feature 3	3	1.5	1.5	100%
Feature 4	1	2.5	–1.5	60%

Table 10-2   **Example Results of Estimation by Decomposition**

Feature	Estimated Staff Weeks to Complete	Actual Effort	Raw Error	Magnitude of Relative Error
Feature 5	4	4.5	–0.5	11%
Feature 6	6	4.5	1.5	33%
Feature 7	2	3.0	–1.0	33%
Feature 8	1	1.5	–0.5	33%
Feature 9	3	2.5	0.5	20%
Feature 10	1.5	3.5	–2.0	57%
TOTAL	**27**	**29**	**–2**	-
Average	-	-	**–7%**	**46%**

TEAM: Wow, that's interesting. Most of our individual estimates weren't any more accurate than yours. Our estimates were nearly all wrong by 30% to 50% or more. Our average error was 46%–which is way higher than your error. But our overall error was still only 7% and yours was 24%.

But the joke is on you. Even though our estimates were worse than yours, you're still buying the pizza!

Somehow the team's estimate was more accurate than your estimate even though their individual feature estimates were worse. How is that possible?

The Law of Large Numbers

The team's estimate benefited from a statistical property called the Law of Large Numbers. The gist of this law is that if you create one big estimate, the estimate's error tendency will be completely on the high side or completely on the low side. But if you create several smaller estimates, some of the estimation errors will be on the high side, and some will be on the low side. The errors will tend to cancel each other out to some degree. Your team underestimated in some cases, but it also overestimated in some cases, so the error in the aggregate estimate is only 7%. In your estimate, all 24% of the error was on the same side.

This approach should work in theory, and research says that it also works in practice. Lederer and Prasad found that summing task durations was negatively correlated with cost and schedule overruns (Lederer and Prasad 1992).

Tip #47	Decompose large estimates into small pieces so that you can take advantage of the Law of Large Numbers: the errors on the high side and the errors on the low side cancel each other out to some degree.

How Small Should the Estimated Pieces Be?

Seen from the perspective shown in Figure 10-1, software development is a process of making larger numbers of steadily smaller decisions. At the beginning of the project, you make such decisions as "What major *areas* should this software contain?" A simple decision to include or exclude an area can significantly swing total project effort and schedule in one direction or another. As you approach top-level requirements, you make a larger number of decisions about which features should be in or out, but each of those decisions on average exerts a smaller impact on the overall project outcome. As you approach detailed requirements, you typically make hundreds of decisions, some with larger implications and some with smaller implications, but on average the impact of these decisions is far smaller than the impact of the decisions made earlier in the project.

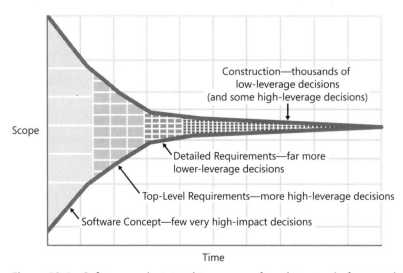

Figure 10-1   Software projects tend to progress from large-grain focus at the beginning to fine-grain focus at the end. This progression supports increasing the use of estimation by decomposition as a project progresses.

By the time you focus on software construction, the granularity of the decisions you make is tiny: "How should I design this class interface? How should I name this variable? How should I structure this loop?" And so on. These decisions are still important, but the effect of any single decision tends to be localized compared with the big decisions that were made at the initial, software-concept level.

The implication of software development being a process of steady refinement is that the further into the project you are, the finer-grained your decomposed estimates can be. Early in the project, you might base a bottom-up estimate on feature areas. Later, you might base the estimate on marketing requirements. Still later, you might use detailed requirements or engineering requirements. In the project's endgame, you might use developer and tester task-based estimates.

The limits on the number of items to estimate are more practical than theoretical. Very early in a project, it can be a struggle to get enough detailed information to create a decomposed estimate. Later in the project, you might have too much detail. You need 5 to 10 individual items before you get much benefit from the Law of Large Numbers, but even 5 items are better than 1.

10.2 Decomposition via an Activity-Based Work Breakdown Structure

Sometimes unseen work hides in the form of forgotten features. Sometimes it hides in the form of forgotten tasks. Decomposing a project via an activity-based work breakdown structure (WBS) helps you avoid forgetting tasks. It also helps fine-tune thinking about whether the project you're estimating is bigger or smaller than similar past projects. Comparing the new project to the old project in each WBS category can sharpen your assessment of which parts are bigger and which are smaller.

Table 10-3 shows a generic, activity-based WBS for a small-to-medium-sized software project. The left column lists the category of activities such as Planning, Requirements, Coding, and so on. The other columns list the kinds of work within each categories, such as Creating, Planning, Reviewing, and so on.

Table 10-3   **Generic Work Breakdown Structure for a Small-to-Medium-Sized Software Project**

Category	Create/ Do	Plan	Manage	Review	Rework	Report Defects
General management	●	●	●	●		
Planning	●		●	●	●	
Corporate activities (meetings, vacation, holidays, and so on)	●					
Hardware setup/Software setup/Maintenance	●	●	●	●	●	●
Staff preparation	●	●	●	●		
Technical Processes/Practices	●	●	●	●	●	●
Requirements work	●	●	●	●	●	●
Coordinate with other projects	●	●	●	●		
Change management	●	●	●	●	●	●
User-interface prototyping	●	●	●	●	●	●
Architecture work	●	●	●	●	●	●
Detailed designing	●	●	●	●	●	●
Coding	●	●	●	●	●	●
Component acquisition	●	●	●	●	●	●
Automated build	●	●	●	●	●	●

Table 10-3   **Generic Work Breakdown Structure for a Small-to-Medium-Sized Software Project**

Category	Create/ Do	Plan	Manage	Review	Rework	Report Defects
Integration	●	●	●	●	●	●
Manual system tests	●	●	●	●	●	●
Automated system tests	●	●	●	●	●	●
Software release (interim, alpha, beta, and final releases)	●	●	●	●	●	●
Documents (user docs, technical docs)	●	●	●	●	●	●

To use the generic WBS, you combine the column descriptions with the categories—for example, Create/Do Planning, Manage Planning, Review Planning, Create/Do Requirements Work, Manage Requirements Work, Review Requirements Work, Create/Do Coding, Manage Coding, Review Coding, and so on. The dots in the table represent the most common combinations.

This WBS presents an extensive list of the kinds of activities that you might consider when creating an estimate. You will probably need to extend the list to include at least a few additional entries related to specifics of your organization's software-development approach. You might also decide to exclude some of this WBS's categories, which will be fine as long as that's a conscious decision.

Tip #48	Use a generic software-project work breakdown structure (WBS) to avoid omitting common activities.

10.3 Hazards of Adding Up Best Case and Worst Case Estimates

Have you ever had the following experience? You put together a detailed task list. You carefully estimate each of the tasks on the list, thinking, "We can pull this off if we try hard enough." After you go through meticulous planning, you work hard on the first task and deliver it on time. The second task turns up some unexpected problems, but you work late and get it done on schedule. The third task turns up a few more problems, and you leave it unfinished at the end of the day, thinking you'll polish it off the next morning. By the end of the next day, you've barely finished that task, and haven't yet started the task you were supposed to do that day. By the end of the week, you're more than a full task behind schedule.

How did that happen? Were your estimates wrong, or did you just not perform very well?

Warning: Math Ahead!

The answer lies in some of the statistical subtleties involved in combining individual estimates. *Statistical subtleties?* Yes, for better or worse, this is an area in which we must dig into the mathematics a little to understand how to avoid common problems associated with building up an estimate from decomposed task or feature estimates.

What Went Wrong?

To see what happened in the preceding scenario, let's take another look at the case study from the beginning of the chapter. The team in the case study produced an accurate estimate. But the accuracy of their single-point estimates was unusual. A more common attempt to produce an estimate by decomposition would not produce the estimates listed in Table 10-1; it would be much more likely to produce estimates such as those shown in Table 10-4.

Table 10-4 Example of More Typical, Error-Prone Attempt to Estimate by Decomposition

Feature	Estimated Staff Weeks to Complete	Actual Effort
Feature 1	1.6	3.0
Feature 2	1.8	2.5
Feature 3	2.0	1.5
Feature 4	0.8	2.5
Feature 5	3.8	4.5
Feature 6	3.8	4.5
Feature 7	2.2	3.0
Feature 8	0.8	1.5
Feature 9	1.6	2.5
Feature 10	1.6	3.5
TOTAL	**20.0**	**29.0**

In this example, the accuracy of the 20-staff-week estimate obtained through a simple summation of decomposed, single-point estimates is actually worse than the aggregate estimate of 22 staff weeks that you provided earlier in the case study. How can this be?

The root cause is a combination of the "90% confident" problem that that was discussed in Chapter 1 ("What Is an 'Estimate'?") and the optimism problem discussed in Chapter 4 ("Where Does Estimation Error Come From?"). When developers are asked to provide single-point estimates, they often unconsciously present Best Case estimates. Let's say that each of the individual Best Case estimates is 25% likely, meaning that you have only a 25% chance of doing as well or better than the estimate. The odds of delivering any individual task according to a Best Case estimate are not great: only 1 in 4 (25%). But the odds of delivering *all* the tasks are vanishingly small. To deliver both the first task and the second task on time, you have to beat 1 in 4 odds for the first task and 1 in 4 odds for the second task. Statistically, those odds are multiplied together, so the odds of completing both tasks on time is only 1 in 16. To complete all 10 tasks on time you have to multiply the 1/4s 10 times, which gives you odds of only about 1 in 1,000,000, or 0.000095%. The odds of 1 in 4 might not seem so bad at the individual task level, but the combined odds kill software schedules. The statistics of combining a set of Worst Case estimates work similarly.

These statistical anomalies are another reason to create Best Case, Worst Case, Most Likely Case, and Expected Case estimates, as described in Chapter 9, "Individual Expert Judgment." Table 10-5 shows how that might work out if the developers who produced the estimates in Table 10-4 were asked to produce Best Case, Worst Case, and Most Likely Case estimates, and if the Expected Case estimates were computed from those.

Table 10-5   **Example of Estimation by Decomposition Using Best Case, Expected Case, and Worst Case Estimates**

	Weeks to Complete			
Feature	**Best Case (25% Likely)**	**Most Likely Case**	**Worst Case (75% Likely)**	**Expected Case (50% Likely)**
Feature 1	1.6	2.0	3.0	2.10
Feature 2	1.8	2.5	4.0	2.63
Feature 3	2.0	3.0	4.2	3.03
Feature 4	0.8	1.2	1.6	1.20
Feature 5	3.8	4.5	5.2	4.50
Feature 6	3.8	5.0	6.0	4.97
Feature 7	2.2	2.4	3.4	2.53
Feature 8	0.8	1.2	2.2	1.30
Feature 9	1.6	2.5	3.0	2.43
Feature 10	1.6	4.0	6.0	3.93
TOTAL	**20.0**	**28.3**	**38.6**	**28.62**

As usual, it turns out that the developers' single-point estimates in Table 10-4 were actually their Best Case estimates.

10.4 Creating Meaningful Overall Best Case and Worst Case Estimates

If you can't use the sum of the best cases and worst cases to produce overall Best Case and Worst Case estimates, what do you do? A common approximation in statistics is to assume that 1/6 of the range between a minimum and a maximum approximately equals one standard deviation. This is based on the assumption that the minimum is only 0.135% likely and the assumption that the maximum includes 99.86% of all possible values.

Computing Aggregate Best and Worst Cases for Small Numbers of Tasks (Simple Standard Deviation Formula)

For a small number of tasks (about 10 or fewer), you can base the best and worst cases on a simple standard deviation calculation. First, you add the best cases together and add the worst cases together. Then you compute the standard deviation using this formula:

Equation #4	StandardDeviation = (SumOfWorstCaseEstimates − SumOfBestCaseEstimates) / 6

If you take 1/6 of the range between 20.0 and 38.6 in Table 10-5, that will be 1 standard deviation of the distribution of project outcomes for that project. One-sixth of that difference is 3.1. You can then use a table of standard deviations to compute a percentage likelihood. In a business context, this is often referred to as *percentage confident*. Table 10-6 provides the standard deviation numbers.

Table 10-6   **Percentage Confident Based on Use of Standard Deviation**

Percentage Confident	Calculation
2%	Expected case − (2 x StandardDeviation)
10%	Expected case − (1.28 x StandardDeviation)
16%	Expected case − (1 x StandardDeviation)
20%	Expected case − (0.84 x StandardDeviation)
25%	Expected case − (0.67 x StandardDeviation)
30%	Expected case − (0.52 x StandardDeviation)
40%	Expected case − (0.25 x StandardDeviation)
50%	Expected case
60%	Expected case + (0.25 x StandardDeviation)
70%	Expected case + (0.52 x StandardDeviation)
75%	Expected case + (0.67 x StandardDeviation)
80%	Expected case + (0.84 x StandardDeviation)
84%	Expected case + (1 x StandardDeviation)
90%	Expected case + (1.28 x StandardDeviation)
98%	Expected case + (2 x StandardDeviation)

Using this approach, a statistically valid 75%-likely estimate would be the *Expected case* (29 weeks) plus 0.67 x *StandardDeviation*, which is 29 + (0.67 x 3.1), which equals 31 weeks.

Why do I say the answer is 31 weeks instead of 31.1? Because the garbage in, garbage out principle applies. The underlying task estimates are not accurate to more than 2 significant digits, much less 3, so be humble about the results. In this example, presenting an estimate of 31 weeks probably overstates the accuracy of the result, and 30 might be a more meaningful number.

Tip #49	Use the simple standard deviation formula to compute meaningful aggregate Best Case and Worst Case estimates for estimates containing 10 tasks or fewer.

Computing Aggregate Best and Worst Cases for Large Numbers of Tasks (Complex Standard Deviation Formula)

If you have more than about 10 tasks, the formula for standard deviation in the previous section isn't valid, and you have to use a more complicated approach. A science-of-estimation approach begins by applying the standard deviation formula to each of the individual estimates (Stutzke 2005):

Equation #5	IndividualStandardDeviation = (IndividualWorstCaseEstimate − IndividualBestCaseEstimate) / 6

You use this formula to compute the Standard Deviation column in Table 10-7. You then go through some fairly complicated math to compute the standard deviation of the aggregate estimate.

1. Compute the standard deviation of each task or feature using the preceding formula.

2. Compute the square of each task's standard deviation, which is known as the *variance*. This is shown in the right-most column of Table 10-7.

3. Total the variances.

4. Take the square root of the total.

In the table, the sum of the variances is 1.22, and the square root of that is 1.1, so that's the standard deviation of the aggregate estimate.

Table 10-7   **Example of Complex Standard Deviation Calculations**

	Weeks to Complete			
Feature	**Best Case**	**Worst Case**	**Standard Deviation**	**Variance (Standard Deviation Squared)**
Feature 1	1.6	3.0	0.233	0.054
Feature 2	1.8	4.0	0.367	0.134
Feature 3	2.0	4.2	0.367	0.134

Table 10-7   **Example of Complex Standard Deviation Calculations**

	Weeks to Complete			
Feature	**Best Case**	**Worst Case**	**Standard Deviation**	**Variance (Standard Deviation Squared)**
Feature 4	0.8	1.6	0.133	0.018
Feature 5	3.8	5.2	0.233	0.054
Feature 6	3.8	6.0	0.367	0.134
Feature 7	2.2	3.4	0.200	0.040
Feature 8	0.8	2.2	0.233	0.054
Feature 9	1.6	3.0	0.233	0.054
Feature 10	1.6	6.0	0.733	0.538
TOTAL	**20.0**	**38.6**	-	**1.22**
Standard Deviation	-	-	-	**1.1**

Tip #50	Use the complex standard deviation formula to compute meaningful aggregate Best Case and Worst Case estimates when you have about 10 tasks or more.

If you recall that the standard deviation produced by the preceding approach was 3.1, you'll realize that this approach produces an answer of 1.10 from the same data, which is quite a discrepancy! How can that be?

This turns out to be a case of the difference between precision and accuracy. The problem with using the formula *(WorstCaseEstimate − BestCaseEstimate) / 6*, is that, statistically speaking, you're assuming that the person who created the Best Case and Worst Case estimates included a 6 standard deviation range from best case to worst case. For that to be true, the estimation range would have to account for 99.7% of all possible outcomes. In other words, out of 1000 estimates, only 3 actual outcomes could fall outside their estimated ranges!

Of course, this is a ridiculous assumption. In the example, 2 outcomes out of 10 fell outside the estimation range. As Chapter 1 illustrated, most people's sense of 90% confident is really closer to 30% confident. With practice, people might be able to estimate an all-inclusive range 70% of the time, but estimators don't have a ghost of a chance of estimating a 99.7% confidence interval.

A realistic approach to computing standard deviation from best and worst cases is to divide each individual range by a number that's closer to 2 than 6. Statistically, dividing by 2 implies that the estimator's ranges will include the actual outcome 68% of the time, which is a goal that can be achieved with practice.

Table 10-8 lists the number you should divide by based on the percentage of your actual outcomes that are falling within your estimated ranges.

Table 10-8   **Divisor to Use for the Complex Standard Deviation Calculation**

If this percentage of your actual outcomes fall within your estimation range...	...use this number as the divisor in the standard deviation calculation for individual estimates
10%	0.25
20%	0.51
30%	0.77
40%	1.0
50%	1.4
60%	1.7
70%	2.1
80%	2.6
90%	3.3
99.7%	6.0

You would then plug the appropriate number from this table into the complex standard deviation formula:

Equation #6	IndividualStandardDeviation = (IndividualWorstCaseEstimate − Individual BestCaseEstimate) / DivisorFromTable10-8

Tip #51	Don't divide the range from best case to worst case by 6 to obtain standard deviations for individual task estimates. Choose a divisor based on the accuracy of your estimation ranges.

Creating the Aggregate Best and Worst Case Estimates

In the case study, the team's actual results fell within its best case–worst case ranges 8 out of 10 times. Table 10-8 indicates that teams hitting the actual result 80% of the time should use a divisor of 2.6. Table 10-9 shows the results of recomputing the standard deviations, variances, and aggregate standard deviation based on dividing the ranges by 2.6 instead of 6.

Table 10-9   **Example of Computing Standard Deviation Using a Divisor Other Than 6**

Feature	Weeks to Complete			
	Best Case	Worst Case	Standard Deviation	Variance (Standard Deviation Squared)
Feature 1	1.6	3.0	0.538	0.290
Feature 2	1.8	4.0	0.846	0.716
Feature 3	2.0	4.2	0.846	0.716

Table 10-9   **Example of Computing Standard Deviation Using a Divisor Other Than 6**

	Weeks to Complete			
Feature	**Best Case**	**Worst Case**	**Standard Deviation**	**Variance (Standard Deviation Squared)**
Feature 4	0.8	1.6	0.308	0.095
Feature 5	3.8	5.2	0.538	0.290
Feature 6	3.8	6.0	0.846	0.716
Feature 7	2.2	3.4	0.462	0.213
Feature 8	0.8	2.2	0.538	0.290
Feature 9	1.6	3.0	0.538	0.290
Feature 10	1.6	6.0	1.692	2.864
TOTAL	**20.0**	**38.6**	-	**6.48**
Standard Deviation	-	-	-	**2.55**

This approach produces a standard deviation for the aggregate estimate of 2.55 weeks. To compute percentage-confident estimates, you would then use the Expected Case estimate of 28.6 weeks from Table 10-5 and the multipliers from Table 10-6. This would produce a set of percentage-confident estimates such as the ones shown in Table 10-10.

Table 10-10   **Example of Percentage-Confident Estimates Computed From Standard Deviation**

Percentage Confident	**Effort Estimate**
2%	23.5
10%	25.4
16%	26.1
20%	26.5
25%	26.9
30%	27.3
40%	28.0
50%	28.6
60%	29.3
70%	30.0
75%	30.3
80%	30.8
84%	31.2
90%	31.8
98%	33.7

Depending on the audience for these estimates, you might heavily edit the entries in this table before you present them. In some circumstances, however, it might be quite useful to point out that although totaling the Best Case estimates yields a total of 20 staff weeks, it's only 2% likely that you'll beat 23.5 weeks and only 25% likely that you'll beat 26.9 weeks.

As always, you should consider the precision of the estimates before you present them—I would normally present 24 weeks instead of 23.5 and 27 weeks instead of 26.9.

Cautions About Percentage Confident Estimates

One general pitfall with the approach I just described is that the Expected Case estimates need to be accurate—that is, they need to be truly 50% likely. You should underrun those estimates just as often as you overrun them. If you find that you're overrunning them more often than you're underrunning them, they aren't really 50% likely and you shouldn't use them as your expected cases. If the expected cases aren't accurate, then the sum of the expected cases won't be accurate either.

Chapter 9 provides suggestions for making the individual estimates more accurate.

Tip #52	Focus on making your Expected Case estimates accurate. If the individual estimates are accurate, aggregation will not create problems. If the individual estimates are not accurate, aggregation will be problematic until you find a way to make them accurate.

Additional Resources

Humphrey, Watts S. *A Discipline for Software Engineering*. Reading, MA: Addison-Wesley, 1995. Appendix A of Humphrey's book contains a short, readable summary of statistical techniques that are useful for software estimation.

Stutzke, Richard D. *Estimating Software-Intensive Systems*, Upper Saddle River, NJ: Addison-Wesley, 2005. Chapter 5 of Stutzke's book goes into more detail on some of the statistics presented in this chapter. Chapter 20 describes how to create a WBS.

Gonick, Larry and Woollcott Smith. *The Cartoon Guide to Statistics*. New York, NY: Harper Collins, 1993. Despite the silly title, this is a respectable (and fun) introduction to statistical techniques. Many readers will find the extensive illustrations help them learn the statistical concepts. Some readers might find that the focus on pictures rather than text makes the concepts harder to understand.

Larsen, Richard J. and Morris L. Marx. *An Introduction to Mathematical Statistics and Its Applications, Third Edition*. Upper Saddle River, NJ: Prentice Hall, 2001. This book is a fairly readable, traditional introduction to mathematical statistics; at least it's readable when you consider the subject matter. It's an unavoidable fact that if you want to use statistical techniques, sooner or later you'll have to do some math!

Chapter 11
Estimation by Analogy

Applicability of Techniques in This Chapter

	Estimation by Analogy
What's estimated	Size, Effort, Schedule, Features
Size of project	S M L
Development stage	Early–Late
Iterative or sequential	Both
Accuracy possible	Medium

Gigacorp (a fictional corporation) was about to begin work on Triad 1.0, a companion product to its successful AccSellerator 1.0 sales-presentation software. Mike had been appointed project manager of Triad 1.0, and he needed a ballpark estimate for an upcoming sales planning meeting. He called his staff meeting to order.

"As you know, we're embarking on development of Triad 1.0," he said. "The technical work is very similar to AccSellerator 1.0. I see this project as being a little bigger overall than AccSellerator 1.0, but not much bigger."

"The database is going to be quite a bit bigger," Jennifer volunteered. "But the user interface should be about the same size."

"It will have a lot more graphs and reports than AccSellerator 1.0 had, too, but the foundation classes should be very similar; I think we'll end up with the same number of classes." Joe said.

"That all sounds right to me," Mike said. "I think this gives me enough to do a back-of-the-envelope calculation of project effort. My notes indicate that the total effort for the last system was 30 staff months. What do you think is a reasonable ballpark estimate for the effort of the new system?"

What do *you* think is a reasonable ballpark estimate for the effort of the new system?

11.1 Basic Approach to Estimating by Analogy

The basic approach that Mike is using in this example is estimation by analogy, which is the simple idea that you can create accurate estimates for a new project by comparing the new project to a similar past project.

I've had several hundred estimators create estimates for the Triad project. Using the approach implied in the example, their estimates have ranged from 30 to 144 staff months, with an average of 53 staff months. The standard deviation of their estimates is 24, or 46% of the average answer. That is not very good! A little bit of structure on the process helps a lot.

Here is a basic estimation by analogy process that will produce better results:

1. Get detailed size, effort, and cost results for a similar previous project. If possible, get the information decomposed by feature area, by work breakdown structure (WBS) category, or by some other decomposition scheme.

2. Compare the size of the new project piece-by-piece to the old project.

3. Build up the estimate for the new project's size as a percentage of the old project's size.

4. Create an effort estimate based on the size of the new project compared to the size of the previous project.

5. Check for consistent assumptions across the old and new projects.

Tip #53	Estimate new projects by comparing them to similar past projects, preferably decomposing the estimate into at least five pieces.

Let's continue using the Triad case study to examine these steps.

Step 1: Get Detailed Size, Effort, and Cost Results for a Similar Previous Project

After the first meeting, Mike asked the Triad staff to gather more specific information about the sizes of the old system and the relative amount of functionality in the old and new systems. When their work was completed, Mike asked how they had done. "Did you get the data on the project I outlined last week?" he asked.

"Sure, Mike," Jennifer replied. "AccSellerator 1.0 had 5 subsystems. They stacked up like this:

Database	5,000 lines of code (LOC)
User interface	14,000 LOC
Graphs and reports	9,000 LOC
Foundation classes	4,500 LOC
Business rules	11,000 LOC
TOTAL	**43,500 LOC**

"We also got some general information about the number of elements in each subsystem. Here's what we found:

Database	10 tables
User interface	14 Web pages
Graphs and reports	10 graphs + 8 reports
Foundation classes	15 classes
Business rules	???

"We've done a fair amount of work to scope out the new system. It looks like this:

Database	14 tables
User interface	19 Web pages
Graphs and reports	14 graphs + 16 reports
Foundation classes	15 classes
Business rules	???

"The comparison to most of the old system is pretty straightforward, but the business rules part is a little tough," Jennifer said. "We think it's going to be more complicated than the old system, but we're not sure how to put a number on it. We've talked it over, and our feeling is that it's at least 50% more complicated than the old system."

"That's great work," Mike said. "This gives me what I need to compute an estimate for my sales meeting. I'll crunch some numbers this afternoon and run them by you before the meeting."

Step 2: Compare the Size of the New Project to a Similar Past Project

The Triad details give us what we need to create a meaningful estimate by analogy. The Triad team has already performed Step 1, "Get detailed size, effort, cost results for a similar previous project." We can perform Step 2, "Compare the size of the new project piece-by-piece to the old project." Table 11-1 shows that detailed comparison.

Table 11-1   **Detailed Size Comparison Between AccSellerator 1.0 and Triad 1.0**

Subsystem	Actual Size of AccSellerator 1.0	Estimated Size of Triad 1.0	Multiplication Factor
Database	10 tables	14 tables	1.4
User interface	14 Web pages	19 Web pages	1.4
Graphs and reports	10 graphs + 8 reports	14 graphs + 16 reports	1.7
Foundation classes	15 classes	15 classes	1.0
Business rules	???	???	1.5

Writing down the numbers in columns 2 and 3 is the easy part. The tricky part is what to do in the Multiplication Factor entry in column 4. The main principle here is the Count, Compute, Judge principle. If we can find something to count, we're better off than if we insert subjective judgment.

The factors of 1.4 for database, 1.4 for user interface, and 1.0 for foundation classes seem straightforward.

The factor of 1.7 for graphs and reports is a little tricky. Should graphs be weighted the same as reports? Maybe. Graphs might require more work than reports, or vice versa. If we had access to the code base for AccSellerator 1.0, we could check whether graphs and reports should be weighted equally or whether one should be weighted more heavily than the other. In this case, we'll just assume they're weighted equally. We should document this assumption so that we can retrace our steps later, if we need to.

The business rules entry is also problematic. The team in the case study didn't find anything they could count, so our estimate is on shakier ground in that area than in the other areas. For sake of the example, we'll just accept their claim that the business rules for Triad will be about 50% more complicated than the business rules were in AccSellerator.

Step 3: Build Up the Estimate for the New Project's Size as a Percentage of the Old Project's Size

In Step 3, we convert the size measures from the different areas to a common unit of measure, in this case, lines of code. This will allow us to perform a whole-system size comparison between AccSellerator and Triad. Table 11-2 shows how this works.

Table 11-2 **Computing Size of Triad 1.0 Based on Comparison to AccSellerator 1.0**

Subsystem	Code Size of AccSellerator 1.0	Multiplication Factor	Estimated Code Size of Triad 1.0
Database	5,000	1.4	7,000
User interface	14,000	1.4	19,600
Graphs and reports	9,000	1.7	15,300
Foundation classes	4,500	1.0	4,500
Business rules	11,000	1.5	16,500
TOTAL	**43,500**	-	**62,900**

The code sizes for AccSellerator are carried down from the information that was generated in Step 1. The multiplication factors are carried down from the work we did in Step 2. The estimated code size for Triad is simply AccSellerator's code size multiplied by the multiplication factors. The total size in lines of code becomes the basis for our effort estimate, which will in turn become the basis for schedule and cost estimates.

Step 4: Create an Effort Estimate Based on the Size of the New Project Compared to the Previous Project

We now have enough background to compute an effort estimate, which is shown in Table 11-3.

Table 11-3   **Final Computation of Effort for Triad 1.0**

Term	Value
Size of Triad 1.0	62,900 LOC
Size of AccSellerator 1.0	÷ 43,500 LOC
Size ratio	= 1.45
Effort for AccSellerator 1.0	× 30 staff months
Estimated effort for Triad 1.0	= 44 staff months

Dividing the size of Triad by the size of AccSellerator gives us a ratio of the sizes of the two systems. We can multiply that by AccSellerator's actual effort, and that gives us the estimate for Triad of 44 staff months.

The estimate you compute and the estimate you present are two different matters. In this computation, you ended up with a single-point estimate. When you present the estimate, you might well decide to present it as a range, as discussed in Chapter 22, "Estimate Presentation Styles."

I've had the same several hundred estimators who created the original rolled-up estimates for Triad follow this approach, and their results are more accurate and consistent. The standard deviation of their results is only 7% rather than the 46%, even with the uncertainty surrounding graphs, reports, and business rules.

Step 5: Check for Consistent Assumptions Across the Old and New Projects

You should be checking your assumptions at each step. Some assumptions aren't completely checkable until you've computed the estimate. Look for the following major sources of inconsistency:

- Significantly different sizes between the old and new projects—that is, more than the factor of 3 difference described in Section 5.1, "Project Size." In this case, the sizes are different, but only by a factor of 1.45, which is not enough of a difference to cause any worry about diseconomies of scale.

- Different technologies (for example, one project in C# and the other in Java).

- Significantly different team members (for small teams) or team capabilities (for large teams). Small differences are OK and often unavoidable.

- Significantly different kinds of software. For example, an old system that was an internal intranet system and a new system that's a life-critical embedded system would not be comparable.

11.2 Comments on Uncertainty in the Triad Estimate

The information available to create the business rules estimate was pretty fuzzy. Should we fudge the business rules number upward to be conservative in our estimate? For estimation purposes, the answer is no. The focus of the estimate should be on *accuracy*, not conservatism. Once you move the estimate's focus away from accuracy, bias can creep in from many different sources and the value of the estimate will be reduced. The best estimation response to uncertainty is not to bias the estimate but to be sure that the estimate accurately expresses any underlying uncertainty. If you were completely confident in the business rules number, you might consider the effort estimate to be accurate to ±10%. Considering the uncertainty in the business rules, perhaps you would fudge the uncertainty number to something like +25%, −10%.

A better way to address the uncertainty arising from the business rules part of the estimate could be to carry a range for the business rules factor through your computations rather than using a single number. You might estimate the factor with a 50% variation (in other words, a range of 0.75 to 2.25) instead of using a single point factor of 1.5. That would produce an effort range of 38 to 49 staff months rather than the single-point estimate of 44 staff months.

One contrast between the estimate created using this approach and the estimate created using a rolled-up (undecomposed) approach is that, in the rolled-up approach, uncertainty in one area can spread to other areas. If there is a 50% uncertainty in the business rules, the estimator might apply that uncertainty to the whole estimate, rather than just to the quarter of the estimate related to business rules. If you applied that same 50% variation to the whole estimate, the estimate would range from 22 to 66 staff months rather than from 38 to 49 staff months. Identifying what specifically is uncertain and how much effect that should have on the estimate helps narrow the overall estimation range.

| Tip #54 | Do not address estimation uncertainty by biasing the estimate. Address uncertainty by expressing the estimate in uncertain terms. |

Estimation Uncertainty, Plans, and Commitments

Ultimately, the impact of uncertainty in the estimate will flow through to the project *plans* and *commitments*. Because the focus of plans and commitments is on maximizing performance rather than on accuracy, it is appropriate to adjust your commitments in a conservative direction, based on uncertainty in the underlying estimate.

Chapter 12
Proxy-Based Estimates

Applicability of Techniques in This Chapter

	Fuzzy Logic	Standard Components	Story Points	T-Shirt Sizing
What's estimated	Size, Features	Size, Effort	Size, Effort, Schedule, Features	Effort, Cost, Schedule, Features
Size of project	- M L	S M L	S M L	- M L
Development stage	Early	Early–Middle	Early–Middle	Early
Iterative or sequential	Sequential	Both	Both	Sequential
Accuracy possible	Medium	Medium	Medium–High	N/A

Most estimators can't look at a feature description and accurately estimate, "That feature will require exactly 253 lines of code." Similarly, it's difficult to directly estimate how many test cases your project will need, how many defects to expect, how many classes you'll end up with, and so on.

A family of estimation techniques known as proxy-based techniques helps to overcome these challenges. In proxy-based estimation, you first identify a *proxy* that is correlated with what you really want to estimate and that is easier to estimate or count (or available earlier in the project) than the quantity you're ultimately interested in. If you want to estimate a number of test cases, you might find that the count of the number of requirements is correlated with the number of test cases. If you want to estimate size in lines of code (LOC), you might find that a feature count—stratified by size category—is correlated with size in lines of code.

Once you've found your proxy, you estimate or count the number of proxy items and then use a calculation based on historical data to convert from the proxy count to the estimate that you really want.

This chapter discusses some of the most useful proxy-based techniques. The point of each of these techniques is that the whole has a greater validity than the individual parts. Thus, these techniques are useful for creating whole-project or whole-iteration estimates and for providing whole-project or whole-iteration insights, but not for creating detailed task-by-task or feature-by-feature estimates.

12.1 Fuzzy Logic

You can use an approach known as *fuzzy logic* to estimate a project's size in lines of code (Putnam and Myers 1992, Humphrey 1995). Estimators are usually capable of classifying features as Very Small, Small, Medium, Large, and Very Large. We can then use historical data about how many lines of code the average Very Small feature requires, how many lines of code the average Small feature requires, and so on to compute the total lines of code. Table 12-1 shows an example of how such an estimate might be created.

Table 12-1   **Example of Using Fuzzy Logic to Estimate a Program's Size**

Feature Size	Average Lines of Code per Feature	Number of Features	Estimated Lines of Code
Very Small	127	22	2,794
Small	253	15	3,795
Medium	500	10	5,000
Large	1,014	30	30,420
Very Large	1,998	27	53,946
TOTAL	-	**104**	**95,955**

The entries in the Average Lines of Code per Feature column in the table should be based on your organization's historical data and are fixed before the estimation begins. The Number of Features column is a count of how many features you have classified into each size category. The Estimated Lines of Code column is computed from the other two columns. As shown, the estimate has 5 significant digits, which is well beyond the accuracy of the underlying numbers. If I were presenting this estimate, I would present it as "96,000 lines of code" or even "100,000 lines of code" (that is, to one or two significant digits) to avoid using too much precision and conveying a false sense of accuracy.

How to Get the Average Size Numbers

Fuzzy logic works best when the sizes are calibrated from your organization's historical data. As a rule of thumb, the differences in size between adjacent categories should be at least a factor of 2. Some experts recommend a factor of 4 difference (Putnam and Meyers 1992).

You should create the initial size averages by classifying completed work from one or more completed systems. Go through the past system and classify each feature as Very Small, Small, Medium, Large, or Very Large. Then count the total number of lines of code for the features in each classification and divide that by the number of features to arrive at the average lines of code for each feature classification. Table 12-2 shows an example of how this might work out.

Table 12-2   **Example of Creating Average LOC Numbers**

Size	Number of Features	Count of Total LOC	Average LOC
Very Small	117	14,859	127
Small	71	17,963	253
Medium	56	28,000	500
Large	169	171,366	1,014
Very Large	119	237,762	1,998

The numbers in this table are purely for purposes of illustration. You should work out your own numbers by using your own organization's historical data.

Tip #55	Use fuzzy logic to estimate program size in lines of code.

How to Classify New Functionality

When assigning new functionality to size categories, it's important that the assumptions about what constitutes a Very Small, Small, Medium, Large, or Very Large feature in the estimate are the same as the assumptions that went into creating the average sizes in the first place. You can accomplish this in any of three ways:

- Have the same people who are going to create the estimate create the original numbers for the sizes.

- Train the estimators so that they classify features accurately.

- Document the specific criteria for Very Small, Small, Medium, Large, and Very Large so that estimators can apply the size categories consistently.

How Not to Use Fuzzy Logic

One interesting aspect of statistics is that statistical summaries can have more validity than any of the individual data points that make up the summary. As discussed in Chapter 10, "Decomposition and Recomposition," the Law of Large Numbers gives the rolled-up estimate an accuracy above and beyond the accuracy of the individual estimates. The whole is truly greater than the sum of its parts.

When using fuzzy logic, it's important to remember this phenomenon, that the rolled-up number has a validity that the underlying numbers do not have. The reason fuzzy logic works is that we can safely assume that if 71 small features required an average of 253 lines of code in the past, 15 small features will each probably require approximately 253 lines of code in the future. However, the fact that the average is 253 lines of code *does not* mean that any specific feature will actually consist of 253 lines of code. The sizes of individual Small features could range from 50 lines of code to 1,000 lines of code. So, although the rolled-up estimate produced by fuzzy logic can be surprisingly accurate, you should not overextend the technique to make estimates of sizes of specific features.

By the same token, the fuzzy logic approach works well when you have about 20 features or more. If you don't have at least 20 total features to estimate, the statistics of this approach won't work properly, and you should look for another method.

Extensions of Fuzzy Logic

Fuzzy logic can also be used to estimate effort if you have the underlying data to support it. Table 12-3 shows an example of how that would work.

Table 12-3   **Example of Using Fuzzy Logic to Estimate Effort**

Size	Average Staff Days per Feature	Number of Features	Estimated Effort (Staff Days)
Very Small	4.2	22	92.4
Small	8.4	15	126
Medium	17	10	170
Large	34	30	1,020
Very Large	67	27	1,809
TOTAL	-	**104**	**3,217**

The numbers shown in the table are purely for purposes of illustration, and you would need to derive your own Average Staff Days per Feature from your organization's historical data.

The final estimate of 3,217 staff days is again too precise. You could simplify it to 3,200 staff days, 3,000 staff days, or 13 staff years (assuming 250 staff days per year). You can also always consider presenting the number as a range, such as 10 to 15 staff years, which would communicate an entirely different accuracy than would 3,217 staff days.

12.2 Standard Components

If you develop many programs that are architecturally similar to each other, you can use the *standard components* approach to estimate size. You first need to find relevant elements to count in your previous systems. The specifics will vary depending on the kind of work you do. Typical systems might include dynamic Web pages, static Web pages, files, database tables, business rules, graphics, screens, dialogs, reports, and so on. After you've identified what the standard components are, you compute the average lines of code per component for your past systems. Table 12-4 shows an example of historical data for standard components.

Table 12-4   **Example of Historical Data on Lines of Code per Standard Component**

Standard Component	LOC per Component
Dynamic Web pages	487
Static Web pages	58
Database tables	2,437
Reports	288
Business rules	8,327

Once you have your historical data, you estimate the number of standard components you'll have in the new program, and you compute the size of the new program based on past sizes. Table 12-5 shows one example.

Table 12-5   **Example of Using Standard Components to Create a Size Estimate**

Standard Component	LOC per Component	Minimum Possible Number	Most Likely Number	Maximum Possible Number	Estimated Number	Estimated LOC
Dynamic Web pages	487	11	25	50	26.8	13,052
Static Web pages	58	20	35	40	33.3	1,931
Database tables	2,437	12	15	20	15.3	37,286
Reports	288	8	12	20	12.7	3,658
Business rules	8,327	-	1	-	1	8,327
TOTAL	-	-	-	-	-	**64,254**

In this table, you enter your estimated counts in columns 3 through 5. In column 3, you enter the minimum number of components you can possibly imagine the project having. For the dynamic Web pages component in this example, that number is 11. In the next column, you enter the number you think is the most likely—25 for dynamic Web pages. Then, in the fifth column, you enter the maximum number of components you can imagine—in this case, 50. The estimated number in column 6 is then computed using the Program Evaluation and Review Technique (PERT) formula that was discussed in Chapter 9, "Individual Expert Judgment." Here's that formula adapted to estimate number of components:

Equation #7	EstimatedNumberOfComponents = [MinimumPossible + (4 × MostLikely) + MaximumPossible] / 6

In this example, the estimated number of dynamic Web pages works out to $[11 + (4 \times 25) + 50] / 6 = 26.8$.[1]

Once again, the numbers in this table are for purposes of illustration only, and you should derive your own numbers from your own historical data.

Using Standard Components with Percentiles

A variation on this approach is based on the use of percentiles rather than estimated number of components. In this approach, you again need to have enough historical projects to compute meaningful percentiles (in other words, at least 10 historical projects, and, ideally, closer to 20). But if you have that much historical data, rather than estimating a number, you can estimate how much different from average you believe each component will be. Table 12-6 provides an example of a reference table you could construct.

Table 12-6   **Example of Reference Table for Standard Components**

	LOC per Component (Percentile)				
Standard Components	**Very Small (10th)**	**Small (25th)**	**Average (50th)**	**Large (75th)**	**Very Large (90th)**
Dynamic Web pages	5,105	6,037	12,123	24,030	35,702
Static Web pages	1,511	1,751	2,111	2,723	3,487
Database tables	22,498	30,020	40,027	45,776	47,002
Reports	1,518	2,518	3,530	5,833	5,533
Business rules	7,007	7,534	8,509	10,663	12,111

The entries in this table give the size of the standard components relative to other projects your organization has done. According to this table, 10% of the organization's projects had 5,105 lines of code or fewer for their dynamic Web pages, 50% of projects had 2,111 lines of code or fewer for their static Web pages, 75% of projects had 10,663 lines of code or fewer for their business rules, and so on.

---

[1] Sometimes people are confused by whether they should be dividing by 6 or some other number. The discussion in Chapter 10 about not dividing by 6 applied to computation of standard deviations. This formula computes the expected value, not the standard deviation, so the caution about not dividing by 6 doesn't apply here.

Once you have a reference table, you can classify the size you expect in each standard component area and look up the lines of code estimated for each component in Table 12-6. Table 12-7 shows an example.

Table 12-7 **Example of Using Standard Components to Create a Size Estimate**

Standard Component	Size Classification	Estimated LOC (from Table 12-6)
Dynamic Web pages	Average	12,123
Static Web pages	Large	2,723
Database tables	Small	30,020
Reports	Very Small	1,518
Business rules	Average	8,509
TOTAL	-	**54,893**

The entries in this table imply that you expect the project you're estimating to have an average number of dynamic Web pages compared to other projects your organization has done, a larger than average number of static Web pages, a smaller than average number of database tables, and so on.

This approach yields a size estimate of 54,893 lines of code. When presenting that number, it would once again be accurate to simplify it to 55,000 or 60,000 LOC (that is, 1 or 2 significant digits).

Limitations of Standard Components

The standard components approach has the advantage of requiring very little effort other than using your instincts to assess the sizes that the standard components will be in the new system and looking up the corresponding entries in the reference table. It will take some effort to construct and maintain a reference table similar to Table 12-4 or Table 12-6.

The practice of standard components is not based on counting, and so it violates the general principle of *count, compute, judge*. It does, however, tie estimates back to something familiar, and so it can be useful at times.

Overall, while the use of standard components is probably not the best technique to use later in a project, it can support the goal of minimizing the effort to create an early-in-the-project estimate that is subject to a high degree of inaccuracy anyway because of the Cone of Uncertainty.

Tip #56	Consider using standard components as a low-effort technique to estimate size in a project's early stages.

12.3 Story Points

Another variation on fuzzy logic is *story points*, which were originally associated with Extreme Programming (Cohn 2006). The technique is similar to fuzzy logic, but there are some interesting and useful variations that make story points worth discussing separately.

When using story points, the team reviews the list of stories (or requirements or features) it is considering building and assigns a size to each story. In this sense, story points are similar to fuzzy logic, except that the stories are normally assigned a numeric value from one of the scales shown in Table 12-8.

Table 12-8   **Most Common Story Point Scales**

Story Point Scale	Specific Points on the Scale
Powers of 2	1, 2, 4, 8, 16
Fibonacci sequence	1, 2, 3, 5, 8, 13

The result of this estimation activity is the creation of a list like the one shown in Table 12-9.

Table 12-9   **Example of List of Stories and Assigned Story Points**

Story	Points
Story 1	2
Story 2	1
Story 3	4
Story 4	8
...	
Story 60	2
TOTAL	**180**

At this stage of their use, the story points are not terribly useful because they are a unitless measure—they don't translate into any specific number of lines of code, number of staff days, or calendar time. The critical idea behind story points is that the team has estimated all the stories at the same time, using the same scale, and in a way that is substantially free from bias.

Next, the team will plan an iteration, including planning to deliver some number of story points. The plan might be based on an assumption that a story point translates to a specific amount of effort, but that is just an assumption at that early point in the project.

After the iteration has been completed, the team will be in a position to have some real estimation capability. The team can look at how many story points it delivered, how much effort it expended, and how much calendar time elapsed, and it can then make a preliminary calibration of how story points translate to effort and calendar time. This is often called *velocity*. Table 12-10 shows an example of this.

Table 12-10   **Data from Iteration 1 and Initial Calibration**

Data for Iteration 1
27 story points delivered
12 staff weeks expended
3 calendar weeks expended
Preliminary Calibration
Effort = 27 story points ÷ 12 staff weeks = 2.25 story points/staff week
Schedule = 27 story points ÷ 3 calendar weeks = 9 story points/calendar week

This initial calibration allows the project manager to make a historical-data-based estimate of the remainder of the project, as shown in Table 12-11.

Table 12-11   **Initial Projection for Remainder of Project**

Data for Iteration 1
Assumptions (from Preliminary Calibration)
Effort = 2.25 story points/staff week
Schedule = 9 story points/calendar week
Project size = 180 story points
Preliminary Whole-Project Estimate
Effort = 180 story points ÷ 2.25 story points/staff week = 80 staff weeks
Schedule = 180 story points ÷ 9 story points/calendar week = 20 calendar weeks

Of course, the computations in Table 12-11 assume that the team will remain the same in future iterations, and the projection doesn't account for the planning considerations of holidays, vacations, and so on. But on iterative projects, it does provide for very early projections of whole-project outcomes based on historical data from the same project.

The initial whole-project estimates should be refined based on data from later iterations. The shorter your iterations are, the sooner you'll have data you can use to estimate the rest of the project and the more confident you can be in those estimates.

Tip #57	Use story points to obtain an early estimate of an iterative project's effort and schedule that is based on data from the same project.

Cautions About Ratings Scales

Fuzzy logic uses a verbal scale of Very Small, Small, Medium, Large, and Very Large. Story points use a scale based on powers of 2 or Fibonacci numbers. Which is better?

On a numeric scale, the ratios between the numbers on the scale suggest that the underlying quantities being measured bear a proportionate relationship. If your story points scale is a Fibonacci sequence, a scale of 1, 2, 3, 5, 8, 13 suggests that a story of 5 points will take 5/3 as much effort as a story of 3 points. It suggests that a story of 13 points will take more than 4 times as much effort as a story of 3 points.

These relationships turn out to be a double-edged sword. If the necessary care is taken to ensure that stories classified as 13 points really are about 4 times as much effort as stories classified as 3 points, that's great. That means you can compute an average effort per story point (as described earlier), multiply the total number of story points by the average, and get a meaningful result (also as described earlier).

Accomplishing this level of accuracy requires that great discipline be exercised in assigning story points to stories. It also requires checking actual project data to ensure that the ratios that are estimated are the ratios actually found in practice.

If care is not taken to ensure that the underlying numeric ratios implied by the Fibonacci sequence or by the powers of 2 are accurate, numeric story points have the potential to lead to computed results that are less valid than they appear. The use of a numeric scale implies that you can perform numeric operations on the numbers: multiplication, addition, subtraction, and so on. But if the underlying relationships aren't valid—that is, a story worth 13 points doesn't really require 13/3 as much effort as a story worth 3 points—then performing numeric operations on the "13" isn't any more valid than performing a numeric operation on "Large" or "Very Large."

Table 12-12 illustrates another way of describing this issue.

Table 12-12   Example of What Can Happen with a Numeric Scale That Isn't as Numeric as It Appears

Story Point Classification	Number of Stories	Apparent Story Points	Intended Ratio	Actual Ratio (from Data)	Real Story Points
"1"	4	"4"	1	2	4
"2"	7	"14"	2	2.5	18
"3"	5	"15"	3	3	15
"5"	5	"25"	5	7	35
"8"	12	"96"	8	11	132
"13"	2	"26"	13	17	34
TOTAL	**43**	**"180"**	-	-	**238**

In this example, the misleading numeric scale led us to believe that 180 points was a reasonable approximation of our total effort, but the real effort is about 30% higher.

Tip #58	Exercise caution when calculating estimates that use numeric ratings scales. Be sure that the numeric categories in the scale actually work like numbers, not like verbal categories such as small, medium, and large.

12.4 T-Shirt Sizing

Nontechnical stakeholders often want (and need) to make decisions about project scope during the wide part of the Cone of Uncertainty. A good estimator will refuse to provide highly precise estimates while the project is still in the wide part of the Cone. Sales and marketing staff will say, "How can I know whether I want that feature if I don't know how much it costs?" And a good estimator will say, "I can't tell you what it will cost until we've done more detailed requirements work." It would appear that the two groups are at an impasse.

This impasse can be broken by realizing that the goal of software estimation is not pinpoint accuracy but estimates that are accurate enough to support effective project control. In this case, nontechnical stakeholders are typically not asking for an estimate in staff hours. They are asking whether a specific feature is a mouse, rabbit, dog, or elephant. This observation leads to a very useful estimation approach called *t-shirt sizing*.

In this approach, the developers classify each feature's size relative to other features as Small, Medium, Large, or Extra Large. In parallel, the customer, marketing, sales, or other nontechnical stakeholders classify each feature's business value on the same scale. These two sets of entries are then combined, as shown in Table 12-13.

Table 12-13   **Example of Using T-Shirt Sizing to Classify Features by Business Value and Development Cost**

Feature	Business Value	Development Cost
Feature A	Large	Small
Feature B	Small	Large
Feature C	Large	Large
Feature D	Medium	Medium
Feature E	Medium	Large
Feature F	Large	Medium
Feature G	Small	Small
Feature H	Small	Medium
...		
Feature ZZ	Small	Small

Creating this sort of relationship between business value and development cost allows the nontechnical stakeholder to say things like, "If the cost of Feature B is Large, I don't want it, because the value is only Small." This is a tremendously useful decision to be able to make early in the life cycle of that feature. If you were instead to carry that feature through some amount of detailed requirements, architecture, design, and so on, you would be expending effort on a feature that ultimately isn't cost justified. In software, a quick "No" answer has great value. T-shirt sizing allows for early-in-the-project decisions to rule out features so that you don't need to carry those features further into the Cone of Uncertainty.

The discussion about what to carry and what to cut is easier if the feature list can be sorted into a rough cost/benefit order. Typically, that is done by assigning a *net business value* number (another unitless measure) based on the combination of development cost and business value. Table 12-14 shows one possible scheme for assigning net business value. You can use this scheme or come up with one that seems to more accurately reflect the values in your environment.

Table 12-14 **Net Business Value Based on Ratio of Development Cost to Business Value**

	Development Cost			
Business Value	**Extra Large**	**Large**	**Medium**	**Small**
Extra Large	0	4	6	7
Large	–4	0	2	3
Medium	–6	–2	0	1
Small	–7	–3	–1	0

This sort of net business value lookup table allows you to add a third column to the original value/cost table (Table 12-13) and to sort that table by net business value, as shown in Table 12-15.

Table 12-15 **Example of Sorting T-Shirt Sizing Estimates by Approximate Net Business Value**

Feature	Business Value	Development Cost	Approximate Net Business Value
Feature A	L	S	3
Feature F	L	M	2
Feature C	L	L	0
Feature D	M	M	0
Feature G	S	S	0
Feature ZZ	S	S	0
Feature H	S	M	–1
Feature E	M	L	–2
...			
Feature B	S	L	–3

Remember that the Approximate Net Business Value column is an approximation. I don't suggest just counting down the list and drawing a line. The value of sorting by approximate business value is that it supports getting some quick "definitely yes" answers for the features at the top of the list and some quick "definitely no" decisions for the features at the bottom. That allows discussion to focus on the middle of the list, which is where the discussion will be most productive anyway.

Tip #59	Use t-shirt sizing to help nontechnical stakeholders rule features in or out while the project is in the wide part of the Cone of Uncertainty.

12.5 Other Uses of Proxy-Based Techniques

The examples in this chapter have shown how to use proxy-based techniques to estimate lines of code and effort. You could apply the same techniques to estimate test cases, defects, pages of user documentation, or anything else that might be easier to estimate by proxy than to estimate directly.

Tip #60	Use proxy-based techniques to estimate test cases, defects, pages of user documentation, and other quantities that are difficult to estimate directly.

As Chapter 7, "Count, Compute, Judge," described, there is hardly any limit to what you might be able to count. This chapter has presented just a few specific examples. If you believe you have something else in your environment that would be a better indication of project size than fuzzy logic, standard components, or story points, you should count that instead.

Tip #61	Count whatever is easiest to count and provides the most accuracy in your environment, collect calibration data on that, and then use that data to create estimates that are well-suited to your environment.

12.6 Additional Resources

Cohn, Mike. *Agile Estimating and Planning.* Upper Saddle River, NJ: Prentice Hall Professional Technical Reference, 2006. Cohn's book contains a more extended discussion of story points, including planning considerations as well as estimation techniques.

Humphrey, Watts S. *A Discipline for Software Engineering.* Reading, MA: Addison-Wesley, 1995. Chapter 5 of Humphrey's book discusses proxy-based estimation, which he calls the PROBE method, and goes into detail on some supporting statistical techniques. Chapter 5 also discusses fuzzy logic.

Chapter 13

Expert Judgment in Groups

Applicability of Techniques in This Chapter

	Group Reviews	Wideband Delphi
What's estimated	Size, Effort, Schedule, Features	Size, Effort, Schedule, Features
Size of project	- M L	- M L
Development stage	Early–Middle	Early
Iterative or sequential	Both	Sequential
Accuracy possible	Medium	Medium

Group expert judgment techniques are useful when estimating early in a project or for estimating large unknowns. This chapter presents an unstructured group judgment technique (group reviews) and a structured technique called Wideband Delphi.

13.1 Group Reviews

A simple technique for improving the accuracy of estimates created by individuals is to have a group review the estimates. When I have groups review estimates, I require three simple rules:

- **Have each team member estimate pieces of the project individually, and then meet to compare your estimates** Discuss differences in the estimates enough to understand the sources of the differences. Work until you reach consensus on high and low ends of estimation ranges.

- **Don't just average your estimates and accept that** You can compute the average, but you need to discuss the differences among individual results. Do not just take the calculated average automatically.

- **Arrive at a consensus estimate that the whole group accepts** If you reach an impasse, you can't vote. You must discuss differences and obtain buy-in from all group members.

The improvement in accuracy from this simple technique is significant. Figure 13-1 illustrates the results across 24 groups of estimators I've worked with.

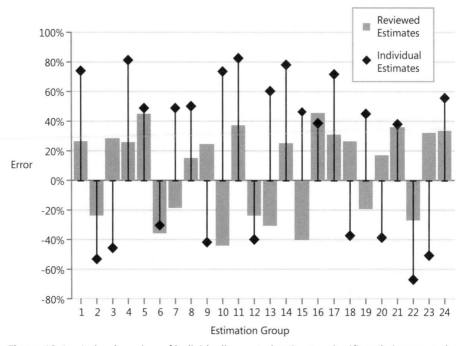

Figure 13-1   A simple review of individually created estimates significantly improves the accuracy of the estimates.

The individual estimates in Figure 13-1 average a Magnitude of Relative Error of 55%. The group-reviewed estimates average an error of only 30%. In this set of estimates, 92% of the group estimates were more accurate than the individual estimates and, on average, the reviews cut the error magnitude approximately in half.

Tip #62	Use group reviews to improve estimation accuracy.

How many experts are enough? Studies in other fields have found that the use of 3 to 5 experts with different backgrounds seems to be sufficient (Libby and Blashfield 1978, Jørgensen 2002).

In addition, it's useful to find experts with different backgrounds, different roles, or who use different techniques (Armstrong 2001, Jørgensen 2002).

13.2 Wideband Delphi

Wideband Delphi is a structured group-estimation technique. The original Delphi technique was developed by the Rand Corporation in the late 1940s for use in predicting trends in technology (Boehm 1981). The name Delphi comes from the ancient Greek oracle at Delphi. The basic Delphi technique called for several experts to create independent estimates and then to meet for as long as necessary to converge on, or at least agree upon, a single estimate.

An initial study on the use of Delphi for software estimation found that the basic Delphi technique was no more accurate than a less structured group meeting. Barry Boehm and his colleagues concluded that the generic Delphi meetings were subject to too much political pressure and were also likely to be dominated by the more assertive estimators in the group. Consequently, Boehm and his colleagues extended the basic Delphi technique into what has become known as Wideband Delphi. Table 13-1 describes the basic procedure.

Table 13-1   **Wideband Delphi Technique**

1. The Delphi coordinator presents each estimator with the specification and an estimation form.
2. Estimators prepare initial estimates individually. (Optionally, this step can be performed after step 3.)
3. The coordinator calls a group meeting in which the estimators discuss estimation issues related to the project at hand. If the group agrees on a single estimate without much discussion, the coordinator assigns someone to play devil's advocate.
4. Estimators give their individual estimates to the coordinator anonymously.
5. The coordinator prepares a summary of the estimates on an iteration form (shown in Figure 13-2) and presents the iteration form to the estimators so that they can see how their estimates compare with other estimators' estimates.
6. The coordinator has estimators meet to discuss variations in their estimates.
7. Estimators vote anonymously on whether they want to accept the average estimate. If any of the estimators votes "no," they return to step 3.
8. The final estimate is the single-point estimate stemming from the Delphi exercise. Or, the final estimate is the range created through the Delphi discussion and the single-point Delphi estimate is the expected case.

Source: Adapted from *Software Engineering Economics* (Boehm 1981).

Steps 3 through 7 can be performed either in person, in a group-meeting setting, or electronically via e-mail or chat software. Performing the steps electronically can help preserve anonymity. Iterations of steps 3 through 7 can be performed immediately or they can be performed in batch mode, depending on the time-criticality of the estimate and the availability of the estimators.

Figure 13-2   A Wideband Delphi estimating form.

The estimating form shown in Figure 13-2 can be a paper form or it can be drawn by the coordinator on a whiteboard. The form shown has a range of 0 to 20 staff months. The range you initially show on the form should be at least triple the range you expect the estimators to come up with so that the estimators don't feel constrained to a predefined range.

The coordinator should take care to prevent people with dominant personalities from unduly influencing the estimate. Software developers aren't known for their assertive personalities, and the most reserved person will sometimes have the best insights into the work being estimated.

It's also useful to show all the rounds of estimates on the same scale so that the estimators can observe how their estimates are converging (or, in some cases, diverging). Figure 13-3 gives an example of this.

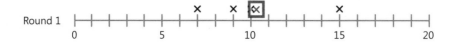

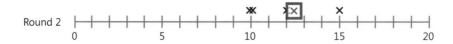

Staff Months

Figure 13-3   A Wideband Delphi estimating form after three rounds of estimates.

In this case, after Round 3, the group might decide to settle on a range of 12 to 14 staff months with an expected value of 13 staff months.

Effectiveness of Wideband Delphi

I've collected data on the use of Wideband Delphi with a very difficult estimation problem. For the first 25 groups I worked with, Figure 13-4 shows the error rate from a simple averaging of their initial estimates compared to the error rate from Wideband Delphi estimating.

My experience with Wideband Delphi suggests that it cuts estimation error by an average of approximately 40% compared to the initial group average. Of the groups in my study, about two-thirds produced a more accurate answer by using Wideband Delphi than by simply averaging their individual estimates.

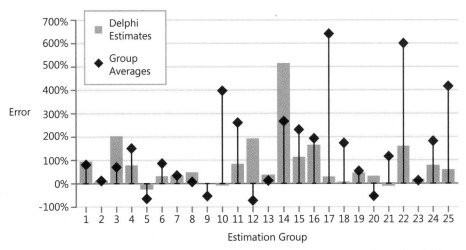

Figure 13-4   Estimation accuracy of simple averaging compared to Wideband Delphi estimation. Wideband Delphi reduces estimation error in about two-thirds of cases.

Of the 10 groups I've worked with that produced the *worst* initial estimates (shown in Figure 13-5), Wideband Delphi improved estimation accuracy in 8 out of 10 cases, with an average error reduction of about 60%.

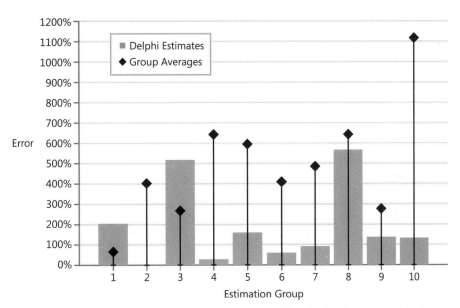

Figure 13-5   Wideband Delphi when applied to terrible initial estimates. In this data set, Wideband Delphi improved results in 8 out of 10 cases.

From this data, I conclude that Wideband Delphi improves accuracy in most cases, and it is especially useful in avoiding wildly erroneous results.

"The Truth Is Out There"

Implicit in estimation techniques that rely on averaging individual estimates is the idea that the correct answer lies somewhere in the range between the lowest estimate and the highest. In my Wideband Delphi data, however, 20% of the groups' initial estimation ranges do not include the correct answer. This means that averaging their initial estimates cannot possibly produce an accurate result.

Perhaps the most interesting phenomenon associated with Wideband Delphi is that one-third of the groups whose initial range does not include the correct answer ultimately settle on an estimate that is outside their initial range and closer to the correct answer. In other words, for these groups, the Wideband Delphi estimate turns out to be better than the best individual estimate. Figure 13-6 illustrates this dynamic. Notice that none of the groups settled on a final estimate that was worse than the worst individual estimate.

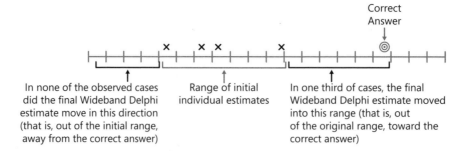

Figure 13-6   In about one-third of cases, Wideband Delphi helps groups that don't initially include the correct answer to move outside their initial range and closer to the correct answer.

When to Use Wideband Delphi

In the difficult group estimation exercise I've discussed in this chapter, Wideband Delphi reduced the average estimation error from 290% to 170%. Errors of 290% and 170% are very high, characteristic of estimates created in the wide part of the Cone of Uncertainty. Still, reducing error by 40% is valuable, whether the reduction is from 290% to 170% or from 50% to 30%.

Although my data seems to endorse the use of Wideband Delphi, industry studies on the question of how to combine estimates created by different estimators have been mixed. Some studies have found that group-based approaches to combining estimates work best, and others have found that simple averaging works best (Jørgensen 2002).

Because Wideband Delphi requires a meeting, it burns a lot of staff time, making it an expensive way to estimate. It is not appropriate for detailed task estimates.

Wideband Delphi is useful if you're estimating work in a new business area, work in a new technology, or work for a brand-new kind of software. It is useful for creating "order of magnitude" estimates at product definition or software concept time, before you've pinned down many of the requirements. It's also useful if a project will draw heavily from diverse specialties, such as a combined need for uncommon usability, algorithmic complexity, exceptional performance, intricate business rules, and so on. It also tends to sharpen the definition of the scope of work, and it's useful for flushing out estimation assumptions. In short, Wideband Delphi is most useful for estimating single, focused items that require input from numerous disciplines in the very wide part of the Cone of Uncertainty. In these uncertain situations, Wideband Delphi can be invaluable.

Tip #63	Use Wideband Delphi for early-in-the-project estimates, for unfamiliar systems, and when several diverse disciplines will be involved in the project itself.

Additional Resources

Boehm, Barry W. *Software Engineering Economics*. Englewood Cliffs, NJ: Prentice-Hall, Inc., 1981. Section 22.2 of Boehm's book describes the original Delphi method and Boehm's creation of Wideband Delphi.

NASA, "ISD Wideband Delphi Estimation," Number 580-PROGRAMMER-016-01, September 1, 2004, *http://software.gsfc.nasa.gov/AssetsApproved/PA1.2.1.2.pdf*. This document describes a Wideband Delphi technique used by the NASA Goddard Space Flight Center.

Wiegers, Karl. "Stop Promising Miracles," *Software Development*, February 2000. Wiegers's paper describes a variation on the Wideband Delphi technique.

Chapter 14

Software Estimation Tools

Applicability of Techniques in This Chapter

	Use of Software Estimation Tools
What's estimated	Size, Effort, Schedule, Features
Size of project	- M L
Development stage	Early–Middle
Iterative or sequential	Both
Accuracy possible	High

This book focuses on the art of estimation, but sometimes the best support for the art of estimation is the science of estimation—computationally intensive estimation methods that you can't easily do by hand, even with a good calculator.

14.1 Things You Can Do with Tools That You Can't Do Manually

Software estimation tools allow you to perform several kinds of estimation-related work that you can't readily perform manually.

Simulating project outcomes   Software estimation tools can perform sophisticated statistical simulations, and these simulations can help project stakeholders understand the scope of work. Figure 14-1 shows an example of simulated software project outcomes.

In the plot, the solid black lines indicate the 50/50, or median, schedule and effort. The dashed black lines represent the 25th percentile and 75th percentile outcomes.

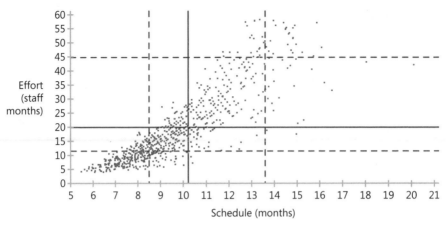

Figure 14-1   A tool-generated simulation of 1,000 project outcomes. Output from Construx Estimate.

The estimation software accounts for several sources of variability:

- Variation in productivity
- Variation in program size, possibly decomposed into multiple modules
- Variation in rates of staff buildup

For each simulated outcome, the software uses a statistical technique called Monte Carlo simulation to go through 100-point probability distributions and simulate one possible outcome each for productivity, size, and staff buildup. The software then computes one estimated point in the scatter plot from these three factors. To create the entire scatter plot, the software goes through this cycle 1,000 times. You can see why you wouldn't want to do this by hand!

Different tools use different approaches, and some of the tools that are more expensive than Construx Estimate will use more sophisticated techniques.

Probability analysis   Chapter 1, "What Is an 'Estimate'?" explained the fallacies of estimating with terms like "90% confident." When the estimates are created using judgment, such expressions are inherently error-prone. But when the estimates are generated using an estimation tool calibrated with historical data, numeric percentages are better supported and more meaningful. In Figure 14-1, for example, the effort of 45 staff months is 75% likely, because 75% of simulated projects took less than 45 staff months.

Table 14-1 shows an example of a tool-calculated probability analysis for project effort. The "nominal" mentioned in the third column refers to the 50% likely estimate of 20 staff months.

Table 14-1   **Example of Project Effort Probabilities Computed by Estimation Software**

Probability	Effort Will Be Less Than or Equal To	Difference from Nominal Effort Estimate
10%	7	−64%
20%	10	−50%
30%	13	−37%
40%	16	−20%
50%	20	0%
60%	26	30%
70%	37	84%
80%	58	189%
90%	142	611%

The most interesting aspects of this table are the very large increases in effort to move from 70% to 80% or 80% to 90% confidence. With judgment-based techniques, very few estimators would multiply their nominal estimate by a factor of 6 to compute the 90% confident estimate, but that is what's needed in this particular case. (These numbers can't be used generally; they are computed from the specific assumptions entered into the estimation software.)

Figure 14-2 shows a graphical depiction of the data in the table.

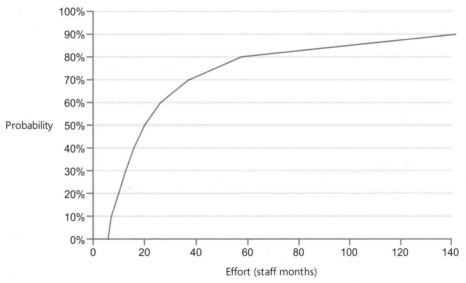

Figure 14-2   Example of probable project outcomes based on output from estimation software.

Accounting for diseconomies of scale   Estimation tools automatically account for differences in project sizes and the effect of size on productivity.

Accounting for creeping requirements   Requirements growth is such a common issue that most commercial estimation tools include an allowance for requirements growth over the course of a project.

Estimation of less common software issues   Estimation tools typically support estimating size of requirements documents, size of design documents, number of test cases, number of defects, mean time to failure, and numerous other quantities.

Calculation of planning options and integration with planning tools   Some software estimation tools will allow you to allocate effort across requirements, design, construction, test, and debugging activities, and they'll support dividing the project into as many iterations as you see fit. These sorts of calculations are tedious to perform by hand but easy to do with the right tool support. Some tools also integrate well with Microsoft Project and other project-planning tools.

What-if analysis   Estimation tools allow you to quickly revise your estimation assumptions and to see the effect on the estimate. The necessary computations can be performed instantly on a computer but would be time-consuming and error-prone if performed by hand.

Referee for unrealistic project expectations   Suppose that your boss has insisted that you complete a project in 50 staff months and 11 calendar months, and suppose that you've created the estimate shown in Figure 14-3. The blue rectangle in the lower left corner of the plot shows your boss's constraints on effort and schedule. The scatter plot of 1,000 simulated project outcomes shows that only 8 of 1,000 project outcomes fall within the specified constraints. This is a visually compelling argument against trying to complete this project within those constraints!

Acting as an objective authority when revising estimation assumptions   A common, unhealthy dynamic in software estimation occurs when a stakeholder rejects an initial estimate because it is too high. The stakeholder sometimes proposes a few minor feature cuts and then expects disproportionate reductions in the project's cost and schedule. A variation on this theme is slightly increasing the team size and then hoping for a large reduction in schedule.

Estimation software can serve as an impartial third party in arbitrating the effects of such changes. Without the tool, you are the person who must tell the stakeholder that his or her adjustments to the cost and schedule aren't supported by the feature cuts. With the tool, you can sit down on the same side of the table as the stakeholder and let the tool play the "bad cop" that tells the stakeholder that his or her changes don't produce as much reduction in the cost and schedule as was hoped for.

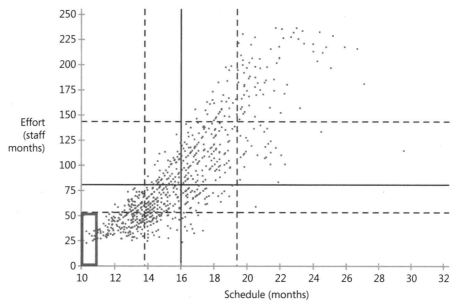

Figure 14-3   In this simulation, only 8 of the 1,000 outcomes fall within the desired combination of cost and schedule.

Figure 14-4 shows an example of the computed tradeoffs between project effort and schedule—that is, the amount of increased staff needed to shorten a schedule, or the savings in effort if the schedule can be lengthened. You might have better luck if the tool says that you need to increase staff from 20 staff months to 26 staff months to achieve a 1-month reduction in schedule than if *you* simply assert the same thing.

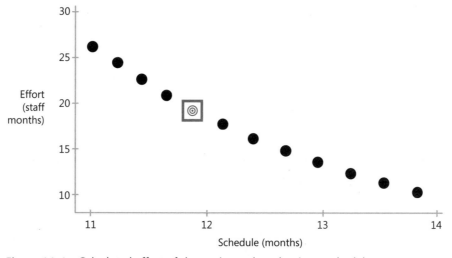

Figure 14-4   Calculated effect of shortening or lengthening a schedule.

Sanity-checking estimates created with the art of estimation   The best estimators use multiple estimation approaches and then look for convergence or spread among the estimates. An estimate created with a commercial tool can provide one of those estimates.

Estimating large projects   The larger the project being estimated, the less appropriate it is to rely solely on the art of estimation. Large projects should rely on a commercial software estimation tool to provide at least one of the estimates used to create and compare estimates.

Tip #64	Use an estimation software tool to sanity-check estimates created by manual methods. Larger projects should rely more heavily on commercial estimation software.

14.2 Data You'll Need to Calibrate the Tools

You don't need a lot of data to calibrate estimation tools to use your historical data. If you have data from one or more completed projects, including

- Effort, in staff months
- Schedule, in elapsed months
- Size, in lines of code

you can calibrate some of the models (including Construx Estimate) to use your historical data instead of industry-average data. Historical data from one project is better than nothing. Historical data from three or more projects is perfectly adequate.

The more expensive tools described in Section 14.4, "Summary of Available Tools," tend to use their large databases of historical-project results to justify their high price tags. But if you have historical data from three of your own projects, the estimate you create using your own data will usually be more accurate than an estimate created on the basis of a tool's generic data. Some of the more expensive tools are worth the money, but not for their large historical databases.

14.3 One Thing You Shouldn't Do with a Tool Any More than You Should Do Otherwise

The fact that an estimate comes out of a software estimation tool doesn't mean that it's accurate. The estimate's assumptions might be incorrect, or the estimate might have been calibrated with inappropriate or flawed calibration data. The tool's control knobs might have been used to insert bias. The tool's underlying estimation methodology might be questionable.

Tip #65	Don't treat the output of a software estimation tool as divine revelation. Sanity-check estimation tool outputs just as you would other estimates.

14.4 Summary of Available Tools

Numerous effective software estimation tools are available. Prices range from free to $20,000 per seat per year and up. Here are some of the more popular tools:

Angel, http://dec.bournemouth.ac.uk/ESERG/ANGEL/   The Analogy Software Tool is an interesting tool that supports estimating future projects by analogy to past projects.

Construx Estimate, www.construx.com/estimate   This is a freeware tool used to generate the estimation tool screen shots shown in this book. The underlying estimation methodology is based on the Putnam Estimation model (Putnam and Myers 1992). The tool also contains some functionality based on Cocomo II. I worked as the lead programmer on the first 2 versions of this tool.

Cocomo II, http://sunset.usc.edu/research/COCOMOII/   Several implementations of Cocomo II can be found on the Internet by searching for *Cocomo II*. The official versions can be found at the University of Southern California Web site listed above and are available for free.

Costar, www.softstarsystems.com   Costar is a low-priced, full implementation of Cocomo II offered by Softstar Systems.

KnowledgePLAN, www.spr.com   This tool is developed and sold by Software Productivity Research (Capers Jones's company) and emphasizes a high degree of integration with Microsoft Project.

Price-S, www.pricesystems.com   Price-S was originally developed by RCA and now consists of a suite of estimation products.

SEER, www.galorath.com   Like Price-S, SEER consists of several related products: SEER-SEM for estimation, planning, and control; SEER-SSM for in-depth software sizing; and SEER-AccuScope for simple software sizing.

SLIM-Estimate and Estimate Express, www.qsm.com   Quantitative Software Management's family of tools includes SLIM-Estimate, which is a full-featured and powerful estimation tool, and Estimate Express, which is less fully featured but still powerful.

Both tools are based on the Putnam estimation model. QSM is founded by Lawrence Putnam.

Additional Resources

For additional and updated pointers to estimation tools, please see my Web site at *www.construx.com/estimate/*.

Chapter 15
Use of Multiple Approaches

Applicability of Techniques in This Chapter

	Use of Multiple Estimation Approaches
What's estimated	Size, Effort, Schedule, Features
Size of project	S M L
Development stage	Early–Late
Iterative or sequential	Both
Accuracy possible	High

No single estimation technique is perfect, so using multiple approaches is useful in many contexts. The most sophisticated commercial software producers tend to use at least three different estimating approaches and then look for convergence or spread among their estimates. Convergence among the estimates tells you that you probably have a good estimate. Spread tells you that there are probably factors you have overlooked and need to understand better. This technique applies equally to estimates of size, effort, schedule, and features.

My first personal exposure to this idea was in creating the estimate for the first edition of my book *Code Complete* (McConnell 1993). I had spent about 2 years doing background research for the book, writing prototype chapters, and preparing in other ways to write the book. Throughout this 2-year period, I had the idea that I was writing a 250 to 300–page book. That idea didn't come from any analytical exercise—it was just a length that I had gotten stuck in my head.

Since I hadn't published a book before, I thought I should present a proposal to the publisher that made it look like I might be capable of actually finishing the book. So as I was nearing the completion of my proposal for the book, I created my first estimate by decomposition. I went through the detailed outline I'd planned for the book and estimated the length of each section individually. Table 15-1 shows what that estimate looked like.

Table 15-1   **Estimated Draft Pages in *Code Complete* Using Expert Judgment with Decomposition**

Chapter	Estimate #1: Original Whole-Book "Gut Feel" Estimate	Estimate #2: Expert Judgment with Decomposition
Preface	-	4
Welcome	-	5
Metaphors	-	11
Prerequisites	-	52
...	...	...
Character	-	20
Review of themes	-	20
TOTAL	**250–300**	**802**

Up to this point, I had essentially used two estimation techniques: gut instinct, which led to a 250 to 300–page estimate, and expert judgment with decomposition, which lead to an 802-page estimate. There was enough spread between these two estimates that I needed to understand why the estimates differed so much.

I was attached to my 250-page preconception of the book's length, so I thought, "That 802-page estimate can't possibly be right. I must have made an error in my estimate." I decided that I would reestimate the book a second time and get the "correct" estimate.

For the third estimate, I took the number of pages in each of the prototype chapters I'd written and I divided those page counts by the number of points in the outlines for those chapters. I had a ratio of 1.64 pages per outline point. I then went through my detailed outline for the whole book and counted the number of outline points per chapter. I multiplied those by 1.64. Table 15-2 shows the estimate obtained by using this method.

Table 15-2   **Estimated Draft Pages in *Code Complete* Using Outline Points and Historical Data**

Chapter	Estimate #1: Original Whole-Book "Gut Feel" Estimate	Estimate #2: Expert Judgment with Decomposition	Estimate #3: Outline Points and Historical Data
Preface	-	4	4
Welcome	-	5	5
Metaphors	-	11	11
Prerequisites	-	52	52
...	...	...	...
Life-cycle models	-	20	16
Review of themes	-	20	21
TOTAL	**250–300**	**802**	**759**

The third estimate of 759 pages was within 5% of the second estimate of 802 pages. Because of the convergence of those two estimates, I had a pretty clear picture that I wasn't writing a 250 to 300–page book, as I had thought for 2 years. I was writing a 750 to 800–page book.

My experience was representative of a more general finding: Estimation accuracy improves when results from multiple estimators or results from multiple estimation techniques are combined (Jørgensen 2002, Tockey 2004).

Tip #66	Use multiple estimation techniques, and look for convergence or spread among the results.

The software parallels of my book-related estimating are straightforward. People form ideas about possible project costs, durations, and features that are based on nothing in particular. They will keep those preconceived ideas until someone presents them with enough data to dislodge their preconceptions. Without data, I would not have believed that the scope of my project was three times as large as I had thought. With a little bit of data, I initially still needed more data before I was convinced.

Another parallel to software is that it's better to get bad news early than late. I adjusted my expectations about the size of my project at proposal time. I could have chosen to stop at that time. But I looked at the project scope and decided it was worth doing anyway, which gave me a more realistic view of the schedule I was planning and the commitment I was making.

The fact that two completely different approaches had produced similar estimates increased my confidence in those estimates. In software, be sure to use different kinds of estimation techniques to create your different estimates. For example, you might use estimation by proxy, expert judgment, estimation by analogy, and a software estimation tool.

Once I accepted the convergence of the estimates, I was suddenly able to see how other data confirmed that ballpark size as well. One of my prototype chapters was 72 pages long. That would have made up 29% of a 250-page book. I never believed that I was 29% done with the project just because I had completed that prototype chapter. Indeed, at the gut-instinct level I knew that chapter was no more than about 10% of the book. After my eyes were opened by the two convergent estimates, I realized that the length of the prototype confirmed that the real scope of the book was in the 750 to 800–page range, not the 250 to 300–page range.

Project-specific data usually provides the most accurate estimate. I ended up with 749 draft pages, which was only 10 pages (1%) different from the outline points estimate that had been created using historical data from the same project.

My original gut-instinct estimate was based on looking at other books in the 250 to 300–page range. Because I hadn't written a book before, I made what turned out to be a naïve assumption that I would need to write 250 to 300 pages to end up with a 250 to 300–page book. But page count from manuscript to published book expands because of blank pages between chapters, blank pages between book parts, the table of contents, perhaps a list of figures, the index, and other front and back matter. Page count is also affected by the choice of typeface, margins, line leading, and so on. All these elements are obvious once someone points them out, but as a rookie author it was easy for me to forget to account for them in my estimate. Even in my decomposed estimate I committed the classic estimating mistake of doing a good job of estimating the things I knew about but forgetting to estimate certain significant parts of the project.

Finally, my second two estimates converged to within about 5%. I didn't know it at the time, but that turns out to be a good target for convergence in general. (If you're in the wide part of the Cone of Uncertainty, you will sometimes need to settle for less convergence.).

Tip #67	If different estimation techniques produce different results, try to find the factors that are making the results different. Continue reestimating until the different techniques produce results that converge to within about 5%.

In a more software-specific context, I was later asked to estimate a project for one of my clients. The crosses in Figure 15-1 show the individual estimates I created for that project. The size of each cross represents the confidence I had in each estimate. The triangle shows my "most accurate estimate" of 75 staff months and 12 calendar months. Although the crosses look somewhat dispersed, the estimates in which I had the most confidence all converged to within 5% of the "most-accurate estimate." The square shows my client's business target of 25 staff months and 5 calendar months.

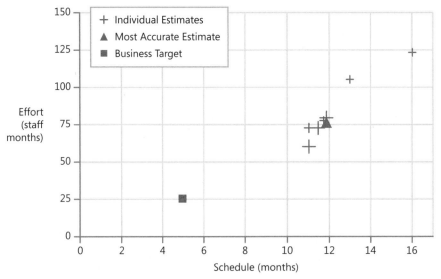

Figure 15-1   An example of multiple estimates for a software project.

In this particular case, the client chose to proceed on the basis of the business target of 5 calendar months and 25 staff months. This was unfortunate. The project was ultimately delivered after 14 calendar months and about 80 staff months' effort, and the team delivered far less functionality than originally planned.

Tip #68	If multiple estimates agree and the business target disagrees, trust the estimates.

Additional Resources

Tockey, Steve. *Return on Software*. Boston, MA: Addison-Wesley, 2005. Chapter 22 of Tockey's book discusses estimation with multiple methods, Chapter 23 discusses how to account for inaccuracy in estimates, and Chapters 24 and 25 discuss how to make decisions under conditions of risk and uncertainty.

Chapter 16

Flow of Software Estimates on a Well-Estimated Project

Applicability of Techniques in This Chapter

	Changing to More Accurate Estimation Techniques Later in the Project	Estimate Refinement Based on Project-Specific Data
What's estimated	Size, Effort, Schedule, Features	Size, Effort, Schedule, Features
Size of project	- M L	S M L
Development stage	Early–Late	Early–Late
Iterative or sequential	Sequential	Both
Accuracy possible	High	High

On poorly estimated projects, estimation focuses on directly estimating cost, effort, and schedule, with little or no focus on estimating the size of the software that will be built. Projects are reestimated many times, but usually in response to schedule slippages late in the project.

In a well-estimated project, the focus of estimation and the points at which the project is reestimated are different. This chapter describes the estimation flow of a well-estimated project. Chapter 17, "Standardized Estimation Procedures," describes how to create a standardized estimation approach that includes this healthy estimation flow.

16.1 Flow of an Individual Estimate on a Poorly Estimated Project

On poorly estimated projects, the creation of the estimate flows as shown in Figure 16-1.

The inputs, the estimation process, and the outputs are not well defined, and they are open to debate and scrutiny. Scrutinizing the estimation process would be beneficial if the objective were to obtain more accurate results. But the objective of the scrutiny is usually to make the estimate smaller. In other words, the scrutiny tends to put downward pressure on the estimate, which is not offset by any corresponding upward pressure.

Figure 16-1   Estimation on a poorly estimated project. Neither the inputs nor the process are well defined, and the inputs, process, and outputs are all open to debate.

Tip #69	Don't debate the output of an estimate. Take the output as a given. Change the output only by changing the inputs and recomputing.

16.2 Flow of an Individual Estimate on a Well-Estimated Project

If the estimation inputs and process are well-defined, arbitrarily changing the output is not a rational action. Project stakeholders might not like the output, but the appropriate corrective action is to adjust the inputs (for example, reduce the project's scope) and to recalculate the outputs, not just to change the output to a different answer.

Figure 16-2 shows the flow of an estimate on a well-estimated project.

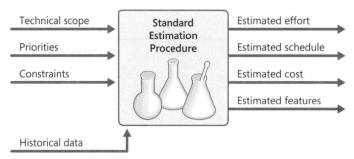

Figure 16-2   Estimation on a well-estimated project. The inputs and process are well defined. The process and outputs are not subject to debate; however, the inputs are subject to iteration until acceptable outputs are obtained.

In a well-estimated project, specific inputs of technical scope, priorities, and constraints are considered. These inputs can all be adjusted until the estimation process produces an acceptable outcome. Historical data is also an input to the estimate and is used to calibrate the productivity assumptions. Historical data is shown entering the bottom of the diagram because it shouldn't be adjusted in the context of a specific estimate—especially not to make the estimate come out to a specific result.

The estimation procedure itself is *standardized*. In other words, it is a procedure that is defined in advance of the need to create any specific estimate. Because it is standardized, it is not adjusted on an estimate-by-estimate basis—again, especially not for the purpose of moving the estimated results closer to the desired results. We'll discuss specific standardized estimation procedures in Chapter 17.

The outputs of estimated effort, schedule, cost, and features flow from following a defined process that uses defined inputs. On a well-estimated project, the outputs are not debated or scrutinized per se.

Differentiating between estimates, targets, and commitments is especially useful in this context. If the estimate is not what is desired, project leadership might nonetheless have good reasons to commit to achieving a target that is more aggressive than the estimate. But that doesn't change the estimate itself.

Within the estimation procedure, the only factor that ever needs to be estimated in the traditional sense (that is, by using judgment) is size. And you'll need to use judgment to estimate size only very early in a project, before you have requirements, stories, use cases, or something else you can count. Effort is computed from the size estimate by using historical productivity data. Schedule, cost, and features are computed from the effort estimate. Figure 16-3 shows this flow.

Figure 16-3 Flow of a single estimate on a well-estimated project. Effort, schedule, cost, and features that can be delivered are all computed from the size estimate.

Tip #70	Focus on estimating size first. Then compute effort, schedule, cost, and features from the size estimate.

16.3 Chronological Estimation Flow for an Entire Project

Because of the Cone of Uncertainty, most projects will benefit from being reestimated several times. Estimates created in the later days of a project can be more accurate than estimates created earlier. Project plans and controls can then be tightened up when the project is reestimated with better accuracy.

Tip #71	Reestimate.

Reestimation does not consist of simply doing the same estimation work again. It consists of converting to more accurate approaches as the project progresses. Figure 16-4 summarizes the most useful kinds of techniques for estimating at various points in a project for common kinds of projects.

Kind of Technique	Pre-Requirements	During Requirements	During Design	During Construction	During Initial Planning	During Construction	During Initial Planning	During Construction
Computing	●	●	●	●	●	●	●	●
Counting		○	●	●	○	●	○	●
Historical Data from Organization	●	●	○		●		●	
Historical Data from Same Project				●		●		●
Decomposition	○	●	●	●	●	●	●	●
Analogy	●	●	○		●		●	
Proxy-Based Estimation	●	●	●	○	●	○	●	○
Complex Algorithms	●	●	○		○		○	
Automated Estimation Tool	●	●	○		○		○	
Expert Judgment	○	○		●	○	●	○	●
Estimates by Skilled Estimators	●	●			○		○	
Estimates by Contributors		○	●	●	●	●	●	●
Bottom-Up, Task-Level Estimation			●	●	○	●	○	●
Group Estimates/Reviews	●	●	○		●		●	

● Primary Technique
○ Secondary Technique

Figure 16-4   Summary of applicability of different estimation techniques by kind of project and project phase.

Estimation Flow for Large Projects

Very early in a large project, counting won't be available, so you'll be using algorithms, software tools, and other macro techniques. You can still improve those early estimates with group reviews and by using multiple approaches.

As you move into later stages of a large project, you can move to more accurate, historical-data–based counting approaches and more toward micro techniques such as bottom-up task estimation, which will produce more accurate estimates (Symons 1991).

Tip #72	Change from less accurate to more accurate estimation approaches as you work your way through a project.

Estimation Flow for Small Projects

Small projects estimate from the beginning the same ways that larger projects estimate at the end. As soon as you know the specific people who will be working on your project and can start handing out specific task assignments (or work packages), it's time to switch from large-grain algorithmic approaches to bottom-up approaches based on individuals estimating their own assignments. On a small project, that might be on Day 1. On a large project, that can be several months into the project.

Tip #73	When you are ready to hand out specific development task assignments, switch to bottom-up estimation.

16.4 Estimate Refinement

When you miss a project milestone, there is a question about how to recalibrate the schedule. Suppose that you have a 6-month schedule. You planned to meet your first milestone in 4 weeks, but it actually took 6 weeks. Should you:

- Assume you can make up the lost two weeks later in the schedule?
- Add the two weeks to the total schedule?
- Multiply the whole schedule by the magnitude of the slip, in this case by 50 percent?

The most common approach is option #1. The reasoning usually goes like this: "Requirements took a little longer than we expected, but now they're solid, so we're bound to save time later. We'll make up the shortfall during coding and testing." But a 1991 survey of more than 300 projects found that projects hardly ever make up lost time—they tend to get further behind (van Genuchten 1991). Option #1 is seldom the best choice.

Option #2 assumes that the first milestone took two weeks longer than it should have but that the rest of the project will take the originally estimated amount of time. The Achilles' heel of option #2 is that estimation errors tend to be inaccurate for systemic reasons that pervade the whole project. It's unlikely that the whole estimate is accurate, except for the part that you've had real experience with. With rare exception, the correct response to actual results that diverge from estimated results is option #3.

Changing the estimate after missing or beating a milestone isn't the only option, of course. You can cut features, spend some of your project's risk buffer, or perform some combination of adjustments. You might also decide to delay and get more data by monitoring how you do meeting the next milestone. But if you're still off by 50 percent in meeting the next milestone, your corrective actions won't have as much time to work as they would have had when you first detected the estimation error.

Tip #74	When you reestimate in response to a missed deadline, base the new estimate on the project's actual progress, not on the project's planned progress.

16.5 How to Present Reestimation to Other Project Stakeholders

Estimators on poorly estimated projects allow themselves to be forced into providing a single-point estimate early on. They will then be held accountable for that estimate for the rest of the project. For example, suppose over the course of a project that you provide the set of estimates listed in Table 16-1.

Table 16-1   **Example of Estimation History of a Project Estimated Using Single-Point Estimates**

Point in Project	Estimate (Staff Months)
Initial concept	10
Approved product definition	10
Requirements complete	13
User interface design complete	14
First interim release	16
FINAL	**17**

With this set of estimates, the customer will consider the project to have slipped over budget and behind schedule the first time the estimate increases from 10 staff months to 13 staff months. Each time you reestimate the project after that, the project will seem to be slipping into ever more trouble. That's unfortunate, because what's really happening is that the first 10-month estimate was subject to a very high degree of inaccuracy. It's appropriate to reestimate several times after that. The final tally of 17 staff months might be the result of a well-run project, but the way the estimates were presented makes it seem otherwise.

Contrast that scenario with one in which you provide estimates in ranges that become narrower as the project progresses, as shown in Table 16-2.

Table 16-2   **Example of Estimation History of a Project Estimated Using Estimate Ranges**

Point in Project	Estimate (Staff Months)
Initial concept	3–40
Approved product definition	5–20
Requirements complete	9–20
User interface design complete	12–18
First interim release	15–18
FINAL	**17**

As you refine each estimate in this case, your customer will consider the project to be staying within expectations. Rather than losing the customer's confidence by taking one schedule slip after another, you build confidence by consistently meeting the customer's expectations and by tightening up the ranges as you go.

Another reason to use ranges rather than single-point estimates is that researchers have found that initial estimates tend to become "anchors" for future estimates, even when the original estimates are not well founded (Lim and O'Connor 1996, Jørgensen 2002). A poor, initial single-point estimate can thus contaminate the estimates for the whole project. Using ranges instead of single-point estimates helps avoid this problem.

Tip #75   Present your estimates in a way that allows you to tighten up your estimates as you move further into the project.

When to Present the Reestimates

There are no magic times to reestimate. Estimation accuracy improves continuously throughout the project. Projects commonly reestimate at major milestones, upon major releases, or when major project assumptions change, such as when a large influx of requirements changes are made.

Regardless of how many times you plan to reestimate, communicate your reestimation plan to other project stakeholders in advance. The Cone of Uncertainty frees you from making firm commitments in the early part of the project when you have a poor chance of ultimately meeting those commitments. But it obligates you to update project stakeholders regularly as your view of the project comes into focus.

Table 16-3 gives an example of an estimation schedule that you might publish on a sequentially run project.

Table 16-3   Example of an Estimation Schedule for a Sequential Project

After Milestone	Estimate Accuracy (for Remainder of Project)	Comments
Initial concept	−75%, +300%	For internal use only; do not publish outside of development group.
Approved product definition	−50%, +100%	*Exploratory Estimate.* For internal company use only; do not publish externally.
Requirements complete and user interface design complete (UIDC)	−20%, +25%	*Budget Estimate.* OK to publish the high end of the range externally. Do not publish the lower number or midpoint.
First interim release	−10%, +10%	Preliminary estimates fine-tuned with project data. Do not publish externally; these are just FYI. Available approximately UIDC + 45 days.
Second interim release	−10%, +10%	*Preliminary Commitment Estimate.* OK to publish the high end of the range externally. Do not publish the lower number.
Third interim release	−10%, +10%	*Final Commitment Estimate.* OK to publish the midpoint number externally.
Interim releases *4-X*	−10%, +10%	Estimates updated only when new requirements are approved by the Change Board.
Code complete	−5%, +5%	Same as above.

Depending on the needs of your project stakeholders, you might need to provide reestimates more or less frequently than illustrated in the table. You should adjust the details of this table to fit your environment. Chapter 17 extends this example and suggests an additional approach that's well suited to iterative projects.

Tip #76	Communicate your plan to reestimate to other project stakeholders *in advance*.

What If Your Management Won't Let You Reestimate?

Is it really true that your management won't let you reestimate? I doubt it. Your management might not allow you to change your *commitment*, but that is different from prohibiting you from reestimating. You should always plan to reestimate periodically, if only for your own internal project planning and project-control purposes, regardless of whether your management or customer will accept the result of the reestimation.

Many organizations do plan ahead for reestimation. I'll discuss that more in Section 17.2, "Fitting Estimation into a Stage-Gate Process."

16.6 A View of a Well-Estimated Project

It's difficult to know mid-stream how good your estimates are. The accuracy of a project's estimates is assessable only in hindsight. In hindsight, however, you can tell the difference between a well-estimated project and a poorly estimated one.

Once the project has been completed, review the project's estimation history to determine whether the project's estimates anticipated the project's eventual outcome. Figure 16-5 shows an example of a project that was well estimated.

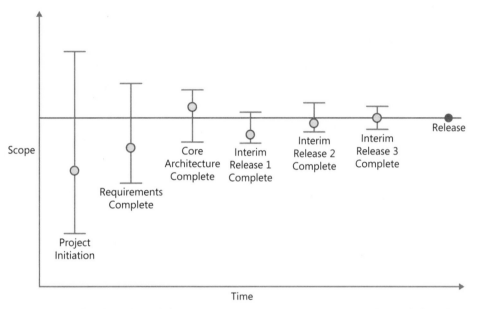

Figure 16-5   A well-estimated project. The single-point estimates miss the mark, but the ranges all include the eventual outcome.

The vertical bars in the figure represent the estimation ranges. The shaded blue dots represent the single-point Expected Case estimates. The solid blue dot represents the actual project outcome. In this project, the single-point estimates were different from the final outcome until the end of the project. But each of the ranges presented throughout the project included the eventual outcome, so I would consider this project to have been well estimated.

Figure 16-6 shows an example of a project that was systematically underestimated.

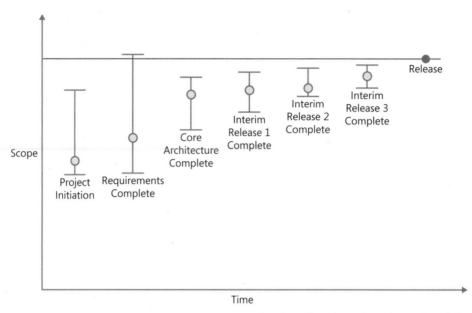

Figure 16-6   A poorly estimated project. The project is uniformly underestimated, and the estimation ranges are too narrow to encompass the eventual outcome.

In essence, this project has fallen prey to the same issue we discussed in Chapter 2 ("How Good an Estimator Are You?") with regard to unrealistically narrow ranges and "90% confident" claims. The project used estimation ranges, which is good, but the ranges were too narrow to include the project's eventual outcome, which is bad.

Chapter 17
Standardized Estimation Procedures

Applicability of Techniques in This Chapter

	Standardized Estimation Procedure	Assessing Effectiveness of an Estimation Procedure
What's estimated	Size, Effort, Schedule, Features	Size, Effort, Schedule, Features
Size of project	S M L	S M L
Development stage	Early–Late	Late
Iterative or sequential	Both	Both
Accuracy possible	High	High

A standardized estimation procedure is a well-defined process for creating estimates that is adopted at the organizational level and that provides guidance at the individual-project level. Standard procedures protect against poor estimation practices such as off-the-cuff estimation and guessing. They protect against changing estimates arbitrarily because a powerful stakeholder doesn't like a specific result. They encourage consistency of the estimation process. And, in the event of an especially poor estimate, they allow you to retrace your steps so that you can improve the procedure over time.

Standardized procedures are equally useful for large projects, small projects, iterative projects, and sequential projects, but the specifics will vary across these types of projects.

17.1 Usual Elements of a Standardized Procedure

Based on the typical estimation flow described in Chapter 16, "Flow of Software Estimates on a Well-Estimated Project," a standardized estimation procedure typically does the following:

- Emphasizes counting and computing when possible, rather than using judgment
- Calls for use of multiple estimation approaches and comparison of results
- Communicates a plan to reestimate at predefined points in the project

- Defines how the required estimation approach changes over the course of a project

- Contains a clear description of an estimate's inaccuracy

- Defines when an estimate can be used as the basis for a project budget

- Defines when an estimate can be used as the basis for internal and external commitments

- Calls for archiving estimation data and reviewing effectiveness of the procedure

For the standardized estimation procedure to do its job, it's important that the organization treat the procedure as a *standard*. Deviations from the procedure need to be justified in writing, and they should be rare.

The procedure itself should be documented in a "Software Engineering Standards" document or a "Standardized Estimation Procedure" document. The procedure itself is then subject to formal change control. The procedure can be changed at the end of a project, motivated by a desire to improve the procedure's accuracy for future projects. The procedure should not be changed "in flight." Such changes are too prone to bias that will undermine both the accuracy of the specific estimate in question and the effectiveness of the procedure for future projects.

Tip #77	Develop a Standardized Estimation Procedure at the organizational level; use it at the project level.

17.2 Fitting Estimation into a Stage-Gate Process

Many large, established organizations have a defined Software Development Life Cycle (SDLC). These life cycles tend to be part of "stage-gate processes," product life-cycle processes that are defined in terms of several "stages" and "gates" (Cooper 2001). Companies using stage-gate processes include 3M, Agilent, Corning, Exxon, GE, Guinness, Hewlett-Packard, Intel, Kodak, Proctor & Gamble, and many others.

Figure 17-1 shows a typical stage-gate process.

Figure 17-1 A typical stage-gate product development life cycle.

The SDLC identifies the software development activities that are normally performed during each stage. It also defines the exit criteria that determine whether the project is allowed to complete one stage and begin the next stage (that is, to proceed through the next gate). Details of SDLCs vary from one organization to another. Table 17-1 summarizes how an SDLC would coordinate with a typical product-oriented stage-gate process.

Table 17-1   **Typical Product-Oriented Stage-Gate SDLC (Abbreviated Version)**

Stage	Major Activities During Stage	Gate	Primary Exit Criteria
0. Discovery	■ Identify market opportunity ■ Assess high-level technical feasibility ■ Develop Preliminary Business Case	1	■ Approved Preliminary Business Case
1. Scoping	■ Define Product Vision ■ Develop Marketing Requirements ■ Validate concept with customers	2	■ Approved Product Vision ■ Approved Marketing Requirements
2. Planning	■ Develop detailed requirements ■ Develop detailed Software Development Plans ■ Develop budget estimates ■ Develop Final Business Case	3	■ Approved Software Development Plans ■ Approved Budget ■ Approved Final Business Case
3. Development	■ Execute main software development life cycle ■ Develop Marketing Launch Plan and Operations Plan ■ Develop final Test Plan	4	■ Approved Software Release Plan ■ Approved Marketing Launch Plan and Operations Plan ■ Approved Software Test Plan
4. Testing and validation	■ Execute final Test Plan ■ Decide to release	5	■ Pass release criteria
5. Launch	■ Execute Marketing Rollout Plan ■ Conduct project postmortem ■ Collect customer feedback and defect reports ■ Monitor business results	N/A	N/A

From an estimation point of view, stage-gate processes present both challenges and opportunities. The challenges tend to arise from the fact that many stage-gate processes were originally developed for hardware products, consumer goods, or other non-software products. While the basic frameworks of those processes are useful, they need to be tailored to software before they will be able to help software projects the way they help other kinds of product development.

One common challenge is that Development is often listed as a single stage (shown as Stage 3 in Table 17-1). The activities that occur during development represent 75% to 90% of the total work in a software project, and I would normally want to see more interim signs of progress during that stage than are implied by the single-gate review at the end of the stage. This is one situation in which you should feel free to revise your estimates periodically through such a stage to support effective project planning and control regardless of whether the organization encourages reestimation in the middle of the stage.

A second common issue is that the Scoping and Planning stages defined in Table 17-1 are often combined into a single stage. That essentially means that Gate 3 should occur at the point where the Cone of Uncertainty has narrowed to ±25%, which can be anywhere from 15% to 35% of the calendar time into the project. (Chapter 21, "Estimating Planning Parameters," discusses these percentages in more detail.) Nontechnical stakeholders often need to be educated about the extent of software development activities that must be completed to support a meaningful "Gate 3" review. The number and depth of activities are often greater than non-technical stakeholders expect.

Once you've educated nontechnical stakeholders about the mapping between the stage-gate process and the software life cycle, an SDLC provides powerful support for a standardized estimation procedure. It becomes natural to attach specific estimation ranges to the various gates of the SDLC, which helps to institutionalize the concept of estimation uncertainty.

Table 17-2 shows an example of how you might map estimation ranges onto an organization's SDLC.

Table 17-2   **Typical Correspondence Between SDLC Gates and Estimates**

SDLC Gate	Estimate Accuracy (for remainder of project)	Estimate Usage
1	−75%, +300%	*Vision Estimate.* For internal use only; do not publish outside of development group.
2	−50%, +100%	*Exploratory Estimate.* For internal company use only; do not publish externally.
3	−20%, +25%	*Budget Estimate.* OK to publish the high end of the range externally. Do not publish the lower number or midpoint.
4	−10%, +10%	*Final Commitment Estimate.* OK to publish the midpoint number externally.

Depending on the organization's focus, the Estimate Accuracy percentages might refer to variability in cost, effort, or features.

Tip #78	Coordinate your Standardized Estimation Procedure with your SDLC.

The next two sections provide examples of standardized estimation procedures. Section 17.3 provides an example of a procedure for use on sequential projects, and Section 17.4 provides an example of a procedure for iterative projects.

17.3 An Example of a Standardized Estimation Procedure for Sequential Projects

Table 17-3 shows an example of a standardized estimation procedure that could be used to estimate sequential software projects. This estimation procedure assumes that the organization's main priority is the software's feature set and that the main goal of estimation is to refine the accuracy of the cost and schedule estimates.

Table 17-3   Example Standardized Estimation Procedure for Sequential Projects— Emphasis on Estimating Cost and Schedule

I. Exploratory Estimate (Approved Product Definition)

A. Create at least one estimate using each of the following approaches:

1. One estimator shall estimate the project bottom-up, using a work breakdown structure.

2. One estimator shall estimate the project using standard components.

3. One estimator shall estimate the project top-down, using estimation by analogy with similar past projects.

B. Estimators shall use a Wideband Delphi process to converge to a single-point nominal estimate (N).

C. Estimates must always be presented as a range from 0.5N to 2.0N (i.e., −50%, +100%).

1. The single-point nominal developed for use in these calculations should not be presented.

2. These estimates may not be used for budgeting or external commitments, except to approve budget for completing the Product Design stage.

II. Budget Estimate (Product Design Complete)

A. Create new estimates using two of the approaches from step I:

1. Estimate the project bottom-up, using a work breakdown structure.

2. Estimate the project using standard components.

B. Create a function points estimate.

1. Compute function points based on requirements specification.

2. Calibrate estimation software using historical data from within our organization.

Table 17-3   Example Standardized Estimation Procedure for Sequential Projects—Emphasis on Estimating Cost and Schedule

3. Estimate the nominal effort and schedule using a commercial estimation software package.

C. Iterate estimates II.A(1), II.A(2), and II.B until the estimates converge to within 5% of each other. Use the average of these estimates as the nominal, N.

D. Compute estimate range as 0.8N to 1.25N.

1. Budget shall be allocated based on 1.0N.

2. Contingency budget shall be allocated as 0.25N.

3. Additional contingency may be allocated to allow for organization's historical rate of requirements growth.

4. Only the high end of the range (1.25N) should be published.

5. This estimate shall not be used for external commitments.

III. Preliminary Commitment Estimate (After Second Interim Release)

A. Build a bottom-up estimate.

1. Create a detailed task list.

(a) Task list shall be reviewed by the development lead, test lead, and documentation lead.

2. Have each developer, tester, and other individual contributors estimate the effort required to implement the requirements that he or she will be responsible for.

(a) Modules shall be estimated using best case, worst case, and expected case.

(b) Module nominals should be computed using the formula [BestCase + (4 x Expected Case) + WorstCase] / 6.

3. Add up the individual module nominals.

B. Compare II.D to III.A(3). Compute a nominal estimate, N, using the following formula: (2 x TheHigherEstimate + TheLowerEstimate) / 3

C. Compute estimate ranges as from 1.0 N to 1.1 N.

1. The high end of the range (1.1N) may be published externally.

2. External commitments may be made to 1.1N.

3. The range 1.0N to 1.1N may be published internally.

IV. Final Commitment Estimate (After Third Interim Release)

A. Compare estimated results to actual results from step III.

1. Compute a revised nominal based on the following formula: RemainingEffort = PlannedRemainingEffort / (ActualEffortToDate / PlannedEffortToDate)

2. Add any tasks that were omitted from step III.

B. The sum of IV.A.1 and IV.A.2 may be used as the new Nominal Effort, N.

1. The nominal (1.0N) may be published externally.

2. External commitments may be made to 1.0N.

3. The range 0.9N to 1.1N may be published internally.

V. Project Shall Be Reestimated at Any Time in Response to Major Changes in Project Assumptions

A. Changes in assumptions include but are not limited to increase in requirements, changes in definitions of major requirements, changes in staff availability, and changes in schedule targets.

Table 17-3   **Example Standardized Estimation Procedure for Sequential Projects— Emphasis on Estimating Cost and Schedule**

VI. Project Completion
A. Collect and archive data on actual project results for future use.
B. Review estimate accuracy of each estimate.
1. Analyze root causes of any major errors.
2. Assess whether the same accuracy could be produced with less effort.
3. Propose revisions to the standardized estimation procedure.

The estimation procedure shown in Table 17-3 illustrates all of the elements commonly found in estimation procedures:

Emphasizes counting and computing when possible, rather than using judgment   The estimates created for the Exploratory Estimate (Estimate I in Table 17-3) call for decomposition via a work breakdown structure, estimation by analogy, and estimation using standard components. None of these approaches is terribly accurate, but each involves at least some computation rather than just pure judgment.

Calls for use of multiple estimation approaches and comparison of results   The first three estimates (Estimates I, II, and III) call for multiple estimation approaches. More approaches are used early in the project, when computationally based approaches are not as available.

Communicates a plan to reestimate at predefined points in the project   The plan calls for Estimates I through V, which indicates an intent to reestimate periodically. Each estimate is linked to specific milestones in the project.

Defines how the required estimation approach changes over the course of a project   The details of each step are different, based on the improving project-generated data that becomes available later in the project. Late in the project, historical data from the same project becomes the primary basis for the estimate.

Contains a clear description of an estimate's inaccuracy   Each of the stages in the procedure contains an expression of inaccuracy. Estimate I.C calls for a range of –50% to +100%, narrowing to ±10% in Estimate IV.B.

Defines when an estimate can be used as the basis for a project budget   Estimate II is referred to as the "Budget Estimate." Estimate I states explicitly that it shall not be used becomes the basis for a budget.

Defines when an estimate can be used as the basis for internal and external commitments   Estimate III is called the "Preliminary Commitment Estimate," and Estimate IV is called the "Final Commitment Estimate." Earlier estimates explicitly state that they shall not be used as the basis for external commitments.

17.4 An Example of a Standardized Estimation Procedure for Iterative Projects

Table 17-4 shows an estimation procedure that's suitable for iterative software projects. This sort of procedure tends to be most useful in organizations that are on an annual budgeting cycle. The budget is fixed at the beginning of the cycle, which means staffing levels are also fixed. The estimation challenge is thus not to estimate cost (which is fixed by the budget) or schedule (which defaults to a year for annual budgeting cycles). The challenge is estimating the amount of functionality that can be delivered with fixed staff and within a fixed timeframe.

The procedure defined in Table 17-4 assumes that the iterations are well controlled—that is, that each iteration is brought to a releasable level of quality, "cleanup work" is performed within each release and does not accumulate off-plan, and so on.

Table 17-4 Example Standardized Estimation Procedure for Iterative Projects—Emphasis on Estimating Features

I. Exploratory Estimate (To Plan First Iteration)

A. Planned feature set shall be estimated using Story Points.

B. First iteration shall be planned using the organization's historical delivery rate.

    1. Iteration shall be no longer than 1 month.

    2. No estimate for the whole project shall be made.

    3. No commitments shall be made.

II. Planning Estimate (To Plan Second and Third Iterations)

A. Average Story Points per staff week shall be calculated (to calibrate effort).

B. Average Story Points per calendar week shall be calculated (to calibrate schedule).

C. Data from II.A and II.B shall be used to plan the second and third iterations.

    1. Iterations shall be no longer than 1 month each.

    2. A nominal estimate for the whole project shall be made in terms of number of Story Points that can be delivered in the amount of time and staffing level allowed (N).

        (a) Estimate may be published internally as 0.75N to 1.0N.

        (b) Estimate shall not be published externally.

        (c) No commitments shall be made.

III. Commitment Estimate (After Third Iteration)

A. Average story points per staff week shall be calculated based on first three iterations (to calibrate effort).

B. Average Story Points per calendar week shall be calculated based on first three iterations (to calibrate schedule).

C. Data from III.A and III.B shall be used to plan remainder of project.

    1. A nominal estimate for the whole project shall be made in terms of number of Story Points that can be delivered in amount of time and staffing level allowed (N).

        (a) Estimate may be published internally as 0.9N to 1.1N.

Table 17-4   **Example Standardized Estimation Procedure for Iterative Projects—Emphasis on Estimating Features**

(b) Estimate may be published externally as 0.9N to 1.0N.

(c) Commitments may be made based on 0.9N to 1.0N.

IV. Project Shall Be Reestimated at Any Time in Response to Major Changes in Project Assumptions

A. At a minimum, project estimation calibrations shall be updated after each third iteration to account for changes in staffing, increased productivity, and other factors.

V. Project Completion

A. Collect and archive data on actual project results for future use.

B. Review estimate accuracy of each estimate.

1. Analyze root causes of any major errors.

2. Assess whether the same accuracy could be produced with less effort.

3. Propose revisions to the standardized estimation procedure.

The procedure shown in Table 17-4 also illustrates many of the elements usually found in estimation procedures:

Emphasizes counting and computing when possible, rather than using judgment   In Estimate II, data from the project is fed back into the estimation process so that estimates from that point forward can be computed based on the project's historical data.

Calls for use of multiple estimation approaches and comparison of results   This procedure does not call for multiple approaches. If you were to use this procedure and you found that Story Points were not providing good predictive accuracy, you should amend the procedure to use additional estimation methods.

Communicates a plan to reestimate at predefined points in the project   The plan calls for Estimates I through III, which indicates an intent to reestimate periodically.

Defines how the required estimation approach changes over the course of a project   As with the sequential procedure, the details of each step in this procedure are different based on the historical data the project has generated.

Contains a clear description of an estimate's inaccuracy   Estimate I simply states that no whole-project estimate shall be made, and Estimate II provides an uncertainty range of 75% of intended functionality to 100% of intended functionality.

Defines when an estimate can be used as the basis for a project budget   In this case, the financial budget is assumed.

Defines when an estimate can be used as the basis for internal and external commitments   Estimate III is called the "Commitment Estimate." Earlier estimates explicitly state that they shall not be used as the basis of external commitments.

17.5 An Example of a Standardized Estimation Procedure from an Advanced Organization

Table 17-5 shows the estimation procedure used by the NASA Software Engineering Lab (SEL), one of the world's most advanced software development organizations.

Table 17-5   **NASA SEL Estimation Procedure**

Inputs		Outputs			
Project Phase	**Input Data for Estimate**	**Size Estimate**	**Effort Estimate**	**Schedule Estimate**	**Uncertainty Range[1]**
End of requirements analysis	Number of subsystems.	11,000 lines of code[2] per subsystem.	3,000 hours per sub-system.	Multiply number of subsystems by 83 weeks and divide by number of staff members.	+75% −43%
End of preliminary design	Number of functions and/or routines (units).	190 lines of code per unit.	52 hours per unit.	Multiply number of units by 1.45 weeks and divide by number of staff members.	+40% −29%
End of detailed design	Number of new and extensively modified units (N). Number of reused and slightly modified units (R)	Lines of code = 200 x (N + 0.2R)	0.31 hours per line of code.	Multiply lines of code by 0.0087 weeks and divide by number of staff members.	+25% −20%
End of implementation	Current size in lines of code. Effort expended to date. Schedule expended to date.	Add 26% to current size (for growth during testing).	Add 43% to effort already expended (to compute effort to complete).	Add 54% to schedule already expended.	+10% −9%

Table 17-5 **NASA SEL Estimation Procedure**

	Inputs	**Outputs**			
Project Phase	**Input Data for Estimate**	**Size Estimate**	**Effort Estimate**	**Schedule Estimate**	**Uncertainty Range**[1]
End of system testing	Effort expended to date.	Final software size has been reached.	Add 11% to effort already expended (to compute effort to complete).	Add 18% to schedule already expended.	+5% −5%

[1.] To allow for staff turnover, growth in requirements, and so on, conservative management practice calls for using estimates that lie between the predicted value and the upper bound.

[2.] "Lines of code" includes all source statements, including comments and blank lines.

Source: Adapted from *Manager's Handbook for Software Development, Revision 1* (NASA SEL 1990).

The most noteworthy aspect of the NASA SEL's estimation procedure is that it requires less work to create a more accurate estimate. This is representative of a more general rule that, the more sophisticated your estimates become, the less effort you will need to create accurate estimates.

The specific numbers in this estimation procedure are specific to the NASA SEL. They have been calibrated through decades of data collection and analysis and are for use by a highly sophisticated development organization. The specific numbers won't apply to other organizations.

The differences from the procedures that can be used by less advanced organizations are instructive, as are some of the similarities:

Emphasizes counting and computing when possible, rather than using judgment   The NASA SEL procedure is interesting in that even early-in-the-project estimates are based on counting and computing rather than judgment. Effort and schedule are never estimated directly.

Calls for use of multiple estimation approaches and comparison of results   This procedure is distinctive in that it does not call for the use of multiple approaches at any one point in time. The NASA SEL has been collecting and analyzing historical data long enough that it can produce accurate estimates with low effort.

Communicates a plan to reestimate at predefined points in the project   Table 17-5 indicates several points in the project at which new estimates will be created.

Defines how the required estimation approach changes over the course of a project   Each row in the table represents a different estimation approach for a different time in the project.

Contains a clear description of an estimate's inaccuracy   The right-most column in the table contains the plus and minus qualifiers used to adjust the nominal estimate. The first footnote presents a good general guideline: "Conservative management practice calls for using estimates that lie between the predicted value and the upper bound."

Defines when an estimate can be used as the basis for a project budget   That element is not expressed in this procedure.

Defines when an estimate can be used as the basis for internal and external commitments   That element is not directly expressed in this procedure. A noteworthy aspect of the table is that the first row in the table is for "End of requirements analysis." In the NASA SEL's terminology, "requirements analysis" is an activity that occurs after "requirements specification." Thus the table implies that the first time in the project an estimate can even be created is relatively deep into the Cone of Uncertainty.

17.6 Improving Your Standardized Procedure

When ad hoc estimation procedures are used, it's difficult to improve your estimates because you're never really sure which estimation practices produced the inaccurate estimates. When you use a standardized procedure, you'll know the steps that produced each estimate so that you can repeat the successes and prevent the failures.

After each project, you should assess the effectiveness of your estimates in several ways:

- How accurate were your estimates? Did your ranges include the final result, as discussed in Section 16.6, "A View of a Well-Estimated Project"?

- Were your ranges wide enough? Could they be made narrower and still account for the variability that you've observed?

- Did your estimates tend to be on the low side or the high side, or was the error tendency neutral?

- Were there sources of bias that affected the estimate?

- Which techniques produced the most accurate estimates? Do those techniques generally produce the most accurate estimates, or did they just happen to produce the best estimates in this case?

- Did you reestimate at the right times? Were there too many reestimates, too few, or the right number?

- Was the estimation process more elaborate than it needed to be? How could you streamline it without sacrificing accuracy?

Tip #79	Review your projects' estimates and estimation process so that you can improve the accuracy of your estimates and minimize the effort required to create them.

Additional Resources

Boehm, Barry W. *Software Engineering Economics*. Englewood Cliffs, NJ: Prentice-Hall, Inc., 1981. Chapter 21 describes a seven-step approach to estimating software projects.

Cooper, Robert G. *Winning at New Products: Accelerating the Process from Idea to Launch*. New York, NY: Perseus Books Group, 2001. Cooper is the father of stage-gate processes. This book describes how to develop your own stage-gate process.

McGarry, John, et al. *Practical Software Measurement: Objective Information for Decision Makers*, Boston, MA: Addison-Wesley, 2002. Section 5.1 discusses considerations to include in an estimation procedure.

NASA SEL. *Manager's Handbook for Software Development, Revision 1*. Document number SEL-84-101. Greenbelt, MD: Goddard Space Flight Center, NASA, 1990. This document describes the NASA SEL's estimation approach in more detail.

Part III
Specific Estimation Challenges

Chapter 18

Special Issues in Estimating Size

Applicability of Techniques in This Chapter

	Function Points	Dutch Method	GUI Elements
What's estimated	Size, Features	Size, Features	Size, Features
Size of project	S M L	S M L	S M L
Development stage	Early–Middle	Early	Early
Iterative or sequential	Sequential	Sequential	Sequential
Accuracy possible	High	Low	Low

Once you move from directly estimating effort and schedule to computing them from historical data, size becomes the most difficult quantity to estimate. Iterative projects might use a size estimate to help determine how many features can be delivered within an iteration, but they usually focus on techniques designed to estimate features more directly. Estimation in the later stages of sequential projects tends to focus on bottom-up effort estimates created by the people who will be doing the work. Estimating size is thus most applicable to the early and middle stages of sequential projects. The purpose of a size estimate is to support long-range predictability in the wide part of the Cone of Uncertainty.

The common size measures of lines of code and function points have different strengths and weaknesses, as do custom measures defined by organizations for their own use. Creating estimates by using multiple size measures and then looking for convergence or spread tends to produce the most accurate results.

This chapter describes how to create the size estimate. Chapter 19, "Special Issues in Estimating Effort," explains how to convert this chapter's size estimates into an effort estimate, and Chapter 20, "Special Issues in Estimating Schedule," describes how to convert the effort estimate into a schedule estimate.

18.1 Challenges with Estimating Size

Numerous measures of size exist, including the following:

- Features
- User stories

- Story points
- Requirements
- Use cases
- Function points
- Web pages
- GUI components (windows, dialog boxes, reports, and so on)
- Database tables
- Interface definitions
- Classes
- Functions/subroutines
- Lines of code

The lines of code (LOC) measure is the most common size measure used for estimation, so we'll discuss that first.

Role of Lines of Code in Size Estimation

Using lines of code is a mixed blessing for software estimation. On the positive side, lines of code present several advantages:

- Data on lines of code for past projects is easily collected via tools.
- Lots of historical data already exists in terms of lines of code in many organizations.
- Effort per line of code has been found to be roughly constant across programming languages, or close enough for practical purposes. (Effort per line of code is more a function of project size and kind of software than of programming language, as described in Chapter 5, "Estimate Influences." *What you get* for each line of code will vary dramatically, depending on the programming language.)
- Measurements in LOC allow for cross-project comparisons and estimation of future projects based on data from past projects.
- Most commercial estimation tools ultimately base their effort and schedule estimates on lines of code.

On the negative side, LOC measures present several difficulties when used to estimate size:

- Simple models such as "lines of code per staff month" are error-prone because of software's diseconomy of scale and because of vastly different coding rates for different kinds of software.

- LOC can't be used as a basis for estimating an individual's task assignments because of the vast differences in productivity between different programmers.

- A project that requires more code complexity than the projects used to calibrate the productivity assumptions can undermine an estimate's accuracy.

- Using the LOC measure as the basis for estimating requirements work, design work, and other activities that precede the creation of the code seems counterintuitive.

- Lines of code are difficult to estimate directly, and must be estimated by proxy.

- What exactly constitutes a line of code must be defined carefully to avoid the problems described in "Issues Related to Size Measures" in Section 8.2, "Data to Collect."

Some experts have argued against using lines of code as a measure of size because of problems associated with using them to analyze productivity across projects of different sizes, kinds, programming languages, and programmers (Jones 1997). Other experts have pointed out that variations of the same basic issues apply to other size measurements, including function points (Putnam and Myers 2003).

The underlying issue that's common to lines of code, function points, and other simple size measures is that measuring anything as multifaceted as software size using a single-dimensional measure will inevitably give rise to anomalies in at least a few circumstances (Gilb 1988, Gilb 2005).

We don't use single-dimensional measures to describe the economy or other complex entities. We can't even use a single measure to determine who the best hitter in baseball is. We consider batting average, home runs, runs batted in, on-base percentage, and other factors—and then we still argue about what the numbers mean. If we can't measure the best hitter using a simple measure, why would we expect we could measure something as complex as software size using a simple measure?

My personal conclusion about using lines of code for software estimation is similar to Winston's Churchill's conclusion about democracy: The LOC measure is a terrible way to measure software size, except that all the other ways to measure size are worse. For most organizations, despite its problems, the LOC measure is the workhorse technique for measuring size of past projects and for creating early-in-the-project estimates of new projects. The LOC measure is the *lingua franca* of software estimation, and it is normally a good place to start, as long as you keep its limitations in mind.

Your environment might be different enough from the common programming environments that lines of code are not highly correlated with project size. If that's true for you, find something that is more proportional to effort than lines of code, count that, and base your size estimates on that instead, as discussed in Chapter 8, "Calibration and Historical Data." Try to find something that's easy to count, highly correlated with effort, and meaningful for use across multiple projects.

Tip #80	Use lines of code to estimate size, but remember both the general limitations of simple measures and the specific hazards of the LOC measure.

18.2 Function-Point Estimation

One alternative to the LOC measure is function points. A function point is a synthetic measure of program size that can be used to estimate size in a project's early stages (Albrecht 1979). Function points are easier to calculate from a requirements specification than lines of code are, and they provide a basis for computing size in lines of code. Many different methods for counting function points exist. The standard for function-point counting is maintained by the International Function Point Users Group (IFPUG) and can be found on their Web site at *www.ifpug.org*.

The number of function points in a program is based on the number and complexity of each of the following items:

External Inputs   Screens, forms, dialog boxes, or control signals through which an end user or other program adds, deletes, or changes a program's data. They include any input that has a unique format or unique processing logic.

External Outputs   Screens, reports, graphs, or control signals that the program generates for use by an end user or other program. They include any output that has a different format or requires a different processing logic than other output types.

External Queries   Input/output combinations in which an input results in an immediate, simple output. The term originated in the database world and refers to a direct search for specific data, usually using a single key. In modern GUI and Web applications, the line between queries and outputs is blurry, but, generally, queries retrieve data directly from a database and provide only rudimentary formatting, whereas outputs can process, combine, or summarize complex data and can be highly formatted.

Internal Logical Files   Major logical groups of end-user data or control information that are completely controlled by the program. A logical file might consist of a single flat file or a single table in a relational database.

External Interface Files   Files controlled by other programs with which the program being counted interacts. This includes each major logical group of data or control information that enters or leaves the program.

Table 18-1 shows how the count of inputs, outputs, and so on gets converted to an Unadjusted Function Point count. You multiply the number of low-complexity inputs by 3, you multiply the number of low-complexity outputs by 4, and so on. The sum of those numbers gives you the Unadjusted Function Point count.

Table 18-1   **Multipliers for Computing an Unadjusted Function Point Count**

Program Characteristic	Function Points		
	Low Complexity	Medium Complexity	High Complexity
External Inputs	__ × 3	__ × 4	__ × 6
External Outputs	__ × 4	__ × 5	__ × 7
External Queries	__ × 3	__ × 4	__ × 6
Internal Logical Files	__ × 4	__ × 10	__ × 15
External Interface Files	__ × 5	__ × 7	__ × 10

Source: Adapted from *Applied Software Measurement, Second Edition* (Jones 1997).

After you've computed the Unadjusted Function Point total, you compute an Influence Multiplier based on the influence that 14 factors have on the program. These factors include data communications, online data entry, processing complexity, and ease of installation. The influence multiplier ranges from 0.65 to 1.35. When you multiply the unadjusted total by the Influence Multiplier, you get an Adjusted Function Point count.

If you've read my earlier comments about "subjective control knobs," you can probably guess what I think about the Influence Multiplier and its 14 control knobs. Two studies have found that Unadjusted Function Points are more strongly correlated with ultimate size than Adjusted Function Points are (Kemerer 1987, Gaffney and Werling 1991). Some experts also recommend eliminating the "low complexity" and "high complexity" judgments, and classifying all counted items as "medium," which eliminates another source of subjectivity (Jones 1997). The ISO/IEC 20926:2003 standard is based on Unadjusted Function Points.

Table 18-2 provides an example of how you would come up with the final Adjusted Function Point total. The specific number of inputs, outputs, queries, logical internal files, and external interface files shown in the table were chosen solely for purposes of illustration.

Table 18-2   **Example of Computing the Number of Function Points**

Program Characteristic	Function Points		
	Low Complexity	Medium Complexity	High Complexity
External Inputs	6 × 3 = 18	2 × 4 = 8	3 × 6 = 18
External Outputs	7 × 4 = 28	7 × 5 = 35	0 × 7 = 0
External Queries	0 × 3 = 0	2 × 4 = 8	4 × 6 = 24
Internal Logical Files	0 × 7 = 0	2 × 10 = 20	3 × 15 = 45
External Interface Files	2 × 5 = 10	0 × 7 = 0	7 × 10 = 70
Unadjusted Function Point total			284
Influence multiplier			1.0
Adjusted Function Point total			284

The example illustrated here works out to a size of 284 function points. You can convert that directly to an effort estimate (described in Chapter 19), or you can convert it first to a lines of code estimate, and then convert that to an effort estimate.

The terminology in the function-point approach is fairly database-oriented, but IFPUG has steadily updated the rules for counting function points, and the approach works well for all kinds of software. Studies have found that certified function-point counters will usually produce counts that are within about 10% of each other, so function-point counting presents a real possibility of narrowing the scope-related variability in the Cone of Uncertainty early in a project (Stutzke 2005).

| Tip #81 | Count function points to obtain an accurate early-in-the-project size estimate. |

Converting from Function Points to Lines of Code

If you want to convert to lines of code, Table 18-3 lists the conversion factors between function points and lines of code for several popular languages.

Table 18-3   **Programming Language Statements per Function Point**

Language	Programming Statements per Function Point		
	Minimum (Minus 1 Standard Deviation)	**Mode (Most Common Value)**	**Maximum (Plus 1 Standard Deviation)**
Ada 83	45	80	125
Ada 95	30	50	70
C	60	128	170
C#	40	55	80
C++	40	55	140
Cobol	65	107	150
Fortran 90	45	80	125
Fortran 95	30	71	100
Java	40	55	80
Macro Assembly	130	213	300
Perl	10	20	30
Second generation default (Fortran 77, Cobol, Pascal, etc.)	65	107	160
Smalltalk	10	20	40
SQL	7	13	15
Third generation default (Fortran 90, Ada 83, etc.)	45	80	125
Microsoft Visual Basic	15	32	41

Source: Adapted from *Estimating Software Costs* (Jones 1998), *Software Cost Estimation with Cocomo II* (Boehm 2000), and *Estimating Software Intensive Systems* (Stutzke 2005).

If your 284-function-point program were to be implemented in Java, you would take the range of 40 to 80 LOC per function point from the table and multiply that by 284 function points to arrive at a size estimate of 11,360 to 22,720 LOC, with an expected value of 55 times 284, or 15,675 LOC. To avoid conveying a false sense of accuracy, you might simplify these numbers to 11,000 to 23,000 LOC with an expected case of 16,000 LOC.

The conversion factors presented in the table use wide ranges, typically a factor of 2 to 3 between the high and low ends of the ranges. As with many other quantities you estimate, if you can collect historical data about how function points translate into lines of code in your organization, you will be able to estimate more accurately and probably with narrower ranges than if you use industry-average data.

This section's description of function-point counting just skims the surface of a sophisticated technique. While expert function-point counters can produce results that are within 10% of each other, counts of inexperienced function-point counters will vary by 20% to 25% (Kemerer and Porter 1992, Stutzke 2005). For more details on the technique, see the "Additional Resources" section at the end of this chapter.

18.3 Simplified Function-Point Techniques

Function-point counting requires going through a requirements specification line by line and literally counting each input, output, file, and so on. This can be time consuming.

Estimation experts have proposed a handful of simplified approaches to counting function points. Considering the other sources of variability that feed into a software project in the early stages when function points are relevant, a focus on minimizing the effort required to obtain a not-very-accurate estimate seems appropriate.

The Dutch Method

The Netherlands Software Metrics Association (NESMA) suggests an "Indicative" method for early-in-the-project function-point counting (Stutzke 2005). In its method, rather than counting all inputs, outputs, and queries, only Internal Logical Files and External Interface Files are counted. An Indicative Count is then computed using this equation:

Equation #8	$\text{IndicativeFunctionPointCount} = (35 \times \text{InternalLogicalFiles}) + (15 \times \text{ExternalInterfaceFiles})$

The numbers 35 and 15 have been derived through calibration, and you would ulti-mately want to come up with your own calibrations for use in your environment.

The function-point counts created using this method will be less accurate than counts created using the full function-point counting technique described in Sec-tion 18.2, "Function-Point Estimation." But the effort required is much lower, and so this sort of approximation can be useful for rough estimates.

Tip #82	Use the Dutch Method of counting function points to attain a low-cost ballpark estimate early in the project.

GUI Elements

As an alternative to counting function points directly, you might count GUI elements instead. This is an example of proxy-based estimation, as described in Chapter 12, "Proxy-Based Estimates." The process follows these steps:

1. Count the number of GUI elements according to the categories in Table 18-4.

2. Convert the GUI elements to an approximate function-point count by transfer-ring appropriate entries generated from Table 18-4 to the matrix shown in Table 18-1.

3. Calculate size in lines of code by using the relationships shown in Table 18-3.

Table 18-4   **Substituting GUI Elements for Function Points**

GUI Element	**Function-Point Equivalent**
Simple Client Window	1 Low Complexity External Input for add, change, and delete (if present), plus 1 Low Complexity External Query
Average Client Window	1 Average Complexity External Input for add, change, and delete (if present), plus 1 Average Complexity External Query
Complex Client Window	1 High Complexity External Input for add, change, and delete (if present), plus 1 High Complexity External Query
Average Report	1 Average Complexity External Output
Complex Report	1 High Complexity External Output
Any File	1 Low Complexity Internal Logical File
Simple Interface	1 Low Complexity External Input if coming in; 1 Low Complexity External Output if going out
Average Interface	1 Average Complexity External Input if coming in; 1 Average Complexity External Output if going out
Complex Interface	1 High Complexity External Input if coming in; 1 High Complexity External Output if going out
Message or Dialog Box	Not counted; are counted as part of the screen they connect to

If you use this approach, recognize how much uncertainty is feeding into your estimate. Some uncertainty likely exists in your original counts of the number of GUI elements or your estimates of them. You introduce additional uncertainty when you convert from GUI elements to function points. And you introduce still more uncertainty when you convert from function points to lines of code.

Tip #83	Use GUI elements to obtain a low-effort ballpark estimate in the wide part of the Cone of Uncertainty.

18.4 Summary of Techniques for Estimating Size

This chapter and other chapters in this book have presented numerous techniques for estimating size, including several techniques that can produce a size estimate in lines of code. Table 18-5 summarizes the techniques that have been presented so far.

Table 18-5   **Techniques for Estimating Size**

Technique	Chapter	Kind of Size That Can Be Estimated
Analogy	11	features, function points, Web pages, GUI components, database tables, interface definitions, lines of code
Decomposition	10	features, function points, Web pages, GUI components, database tables, interface definitions, lines of code
Dutch Method	18	function points, lines of code
Estimation Tools	14	function points, lines of code
Function Points	18	function points, lines of code
Fuzzy Logic	12	function points, lines of code
Group Reviews	13	features, user stories, story points, requirements, use cases, function points, Web pages, GUI components, database tables, interface definitions, classes, functions/subroutines, lines of code
GUI Elements	18	function points, lines of code
Standard Components	12	function points, lines of code
Story Points	12	story points, lines of code
Wideband Delphi	13	features, user stories, story points, requirements, use cases, function points, Web pages, GUI components, database tables, interface definitions, classes, functions/subroutines, lines of code

The entries in the table's "Kind of Size That Can be Estimated" column really depend on the calibration data you have. The most common kinds of size data—and the most generally usable—are function points and lines of code.

As Chapter 15, "Use of Multiple Approaches," discussed, the best estimators usually use multiple estimation techniques and then look for convergence or spread among the estimates. The different approaches listed in Table 18-5 provide numerous options for estimating size in different ways and then comparing your estimates.

Tip #84	With better estimation methods, the size estimate becomes the foundation of all other estimates. The size of the system you're building is the single largest cost driver. Use multiple size-estimation techniques to make your size estimate accurate.

Additional Resources

Garmus, David and David Herron. *Function Point Analysis: Measurement Practices for Successful Software Projects.* Boston, MA: Addison-Wesley, 2001. This book describes function-point counting and presents some simplified counting techniques.

Jones, Capers. *Applied Software Measurement: Assuring Productivity and Quality, 2d Ed.* New York, NY: McGraw-Hill, 1997. Jones discusses the history of function points in detail and presents the arguments against LOC measures.

Stutzke, Richard D. *Estimating Software-Intensive Systems.* Upper Saddle River, NJ: Addison-Wesley, 2005. Chapters 8 and 9 describe additional size-estimation techniques, including use case points, application points, Web objects, and simplified function-point techniques. Stutzke also discusses size estimation on COTS (commercial off the shelf) projects.

www.construx.com/resources/surveyor/. This site provides a free code-counting tool called Construx Surveyor.

www.ifpug.org. The International Function Point Users Group is the definitive source for current function point counting rules.

www.nesma.nl. The Netherlands Software Metrics Users Association Web site provides information on the Dutch counting method.

Chapter 19

Special Issues in Estimating Effort

Applicability of Techniques in This Chapter

	Informal Comparison to Past Projects	Estimation Software Tools	Industry-Average Effort Graphs	ISBSG Method
What's estimated	Effort	Effort	Effort	Effort
Size of project	S M -	S M L	S M -	S M -
Development stage	Early–Middle	Early–Middle	Early	Early
Iterative or sequential	Both	Both	Sequential	Sequential
Accuracy possible	Medium	High	Low–Medium	Low–Medium

Most projects eventually estimate effort directly from a detailed task list. But early in a project, effort estimates are most accurate when computed from size estimates. This chapter describes several means of computing those early estimates.

19.1 Influences on Effort

The largest influence on a project's effort is the size of the software being built. The second largest influence is your organization's productivity.

Table 19-1 illustrates the ranges of productivities between different software projects. The data in the table illustrates the hazards both of using industry-average data and of not considering the effect of diseconomies of scale. Embedded software projects, such as the Lincoln Continental and IBM Checkout Scanner projects, tend to generate code at a slower rate than shrink-wrapped projects such Microsoft Excel. If you used "average" productivity data from the wrong kind of project, your estimate could be wrong by a factor of 10 or more.

Within the same industry, productivity can still vary significantly. Microsoft Excel 3.0 produced code at about 10 times the rate that Lotus 123 v.3 did, even though both projects were trying to build similar products and were conducted within the same timeframe.

Even within the same organization, productivity can still vary because of diseconomies of scale and other factors. The Microsoft Windows NT project produced code at a much slower rate than other Microsoft projects did, both because it was a systems software project rather than an applications software project and because it was much larger.

Table 19-1   **Examples of Productivity Variation Among Different Kinds of Software Projects (* = Estimated)**

Product	New Lines of Code Equivalent	Staff Years	Year Built	Approximate Cost in 2006 Dollars	$/LOC	LOC/ Staff Year
IBM Chief Programmer Team Project	83,000	9	1968	1,400,000*	$17	9,200
Lincoln Continental	83,000	35	1989	2,900,000	$35	2,400
IBM Checkout Scanner	90,000	58	1989	4,900,000	$55	1,600
Microsoft Word for Windows 1.0	249,000	55	1989	8,500,000*	$34	4,500
NASA SEL Project	249,000	24	2002	3,700,000*	$15	10,000
Lotus 123 v. 3	400,000	263	1989	36,000,000	$90	1,500
Microsoft Excel 3.0	649,000	50*	1990	7,700,000	$12	13,000
Citibank Teller Machine	780,000	150	1989	22,000,000	$28	5,200
Windows NT 3.1 (first version)	2,880,000	2,000*	1994	200,000,000	$70	1,400
Space Shuttle	25,600,000	22,096	1989	2,000,000,000	$77	1,200

Sources: "Chief Programmer Team Management of Production Programming" (Baker 1972), "Microsoft Corporation: Office Business Unit" (Iansiti 1994), "How to Break the Software Logjam" (Schlender 1989), "Software Engineering Laboratory (SEL) Relationships, Models, and Management Rules" (NASA, 1991), *Microsoft Secrets* (Cusumano and Selby 1995).

The lowest rate of productivity in Table 19-1 on a line-of-code-per-staff-year basis is the Space Shuttle software, but it would be a mistake to characterize that development team as unproductive. For projects of that size, the odds of outright failure exceed 50% (Jones 1998). The fact that the project finished at all is a major accomplishment. Its productivity was only 15% less than the Windows NT project even though the Space Shuttle software was 10 times the size of the Windows NT project, which is impressive.

If you don't have historical data on your organization's productivity, you can approximate your productivity by using industry-average figures for different kinds of software: internal business systems, life-critical systems, games, device drivers, and so on. But beware of the factor of 10 differences in productivity for different organizations within the same industry. If you do have data on your organization's historical productivity, you should use that data to convert your size estimates to effort estimates instead of using industry-average data.

19.2 Computing Effort from Size

Computing an effort estimate from a size estimate is where we start to run into some of the weaknesses of the art of estimation and need to rely more on the science of estimation.

Computing Effort Estimates by Using Informal Comparison to Past Projects

If your historical data is for projects within a narrow size range (say, a factor of 3 difference from smallest to largest), you are probably safe using a linear model to compute the effort estimate for a new project based on the effort results from similar past projects. Table 19-2 shows an example of past-project data that could form the basis for such an estimate.

Table 19-2   **Example of Past Project Productivities for Use as the Basis of an Effort Estimate**

Project	Size (LOC)	Schedule (Calendar Months)	Effort (Staff Months)	Productivity (LOC/Staff Month)	Comments
Project A	33,842	8.2	21	1,612	
Project B	97,614	12.5	99	986	
Project C	7,444	4.7	2	3,722	Not used—too small for comparison
Project D	54,322	11.3	40	1,358	
Project E	340,343	24.0	533	639	Not used—too large for comparison

Suppose you're estimating the effort for a new business system, and you've estimated the size of the new software to be 65,000 to 100,000 lines of Java code, with a most likely size of 80,000 lines of code. Project C is too small to use for comparison purposes because it is less than one-third the size of the low end of your range. Project E is too large to use for comparison purposes because it is more than 3 times the top end of your range. Thus your relevant historical productivity range is 986 LOC per staff month (Project B) to 1,612 LOC per staff month (Project A). Dividing the lowest end of your size range by the highest productivity rate gives a low estimate of 40 staff months. Dividing the highest end of your size range by the lowest productivity gives a high estimate of 101 staff months. Your estimated effort is 40 to 101 staff months.

A good working assumption is that the range includes 68% of the possible outcomes (that is, ±1 standard deviation, unless you have reasons to assume otherwise). You can refer back to Table 10-6, "Percentage Confident Based on Use of Standard Deviation," to consider other probabilities that the 40 to 101 staff-month range might include.

What Kinds of Effort Are Included in This Estimate?

Because you're using historical data to create this estimate, it includes whatever effort is included in the historical data. If the historical data included effort only for development and testing, and only for the part of the project from end of requirements through system testing, that's what the estimate includes. If the historical data also included effort for requirements, project management, and user documentation, that's what the estimate includes.

In principle, estimates that are based on industry-average data usually include all technical work, but not management work, and all development work except requirements. In practice, the data that goes into computing industry-average data doesn't always follow these assumptions, which is part of why industry-average data varies as much as it does.

19.3 Computing Effort Estimates by Using the Science of Estimation

The science of estimation produces somewhat different results than the informal comparison to past projects does. If you plug the same assumptions into Construx Estimate (that is, using the historical data listed to calibrate the estimate), you get an expected result of 80 staff months, which is in the middle of the range produced by the less-formal approach. Construx Estimate gives a Best Case estimate (20% confident) of 65 staff months, and a Worst Case (80% confident) estimate of 94 staff months.

When Construx Estimate is calibrated with industry-average data instead of historical data, it produces a nominal estimate of 84 staff months and a 20% to 80% range of 47 to 216 staff months, which is a much wider range. This again highlights the benefit of using historical data, whenever possible.

Tip #85	Use software tools based on the science of estimation to most accurately compute effort estimates from your size estimates.

19.4 Industry-Average Effort Graphs

If you don't have your own historical data, you can look up a rough estimate of effort by using an effort graph, such as those contained in Figures 19-1 through 19-9. The bold blue lines in the figures represent a project's total technical effort (including development, quality assurance, and test) at the industry-average productivity level. The upper black line represents a level of effort that is one standard deviation higher than the average effort. I haven't shown the effort line that is one standard deviation below the average. If you don't have your own historical data and are using these graphs, that's a sign that your development organization is at best average. Prudent estimation practice calls for the assumption of industry-average productivity or worse.

The graphs show project sizes up to 250,000 lines of code, with maximum efforts on some of the graphs exceeding 10,000 staff months. For projects of that size, recognize that the use of more powerful and accurate estimation practices could easily improve project plans enough to save hundreds of thousands of dollars. Estimation guru Capers Jones has often commented that using manual methods to estimate projects larger than about 1,000 function points or 100,000 lines of code introduces significant error, and failure to use sophisticated estimation software for projects larger than about 5,000 function points or 500,000 lines of code constitutes management malpractice (Jones 1994, Jones 2005).

The math underlying these graphs is fairly involved, and so this book doesn't present the underlying formulas. The effort values on the graphs are presented using a logarithmic scale. The first line above 100 represents 200, the second represents 300, the first line above 1,000 represents 2,000, and so on.

The graphs appear similar to each other, but if you closely examine specific data points, you'll find they're quite different. For example, compare both the average and plus-one-standard-deviation values at 100,000 lines of code, and you'll see that the estimated staff months vary widely.

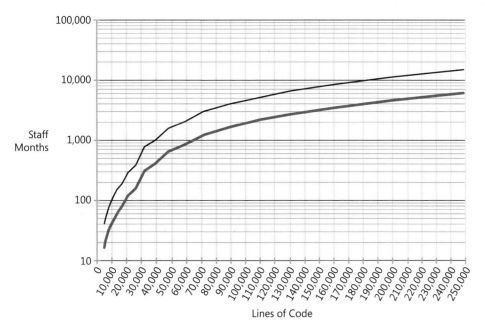

Figure 19-1   Industry-average effort for real-time projects.

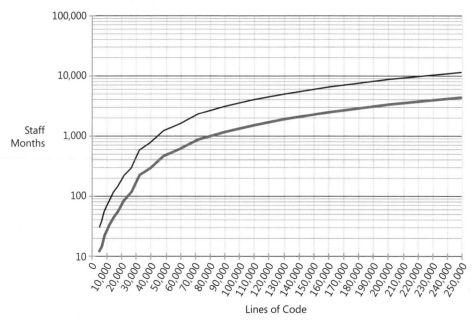

Figure 19-2   Industry-average effort for embedded systems projects.

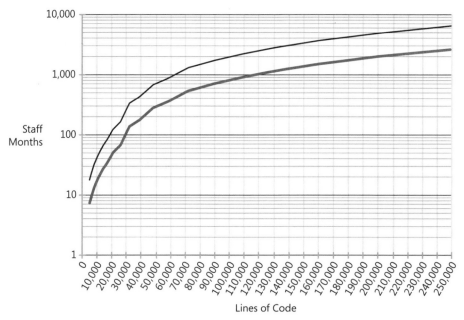

Figure 19-3   Industry-average effort for telecommunications projects.

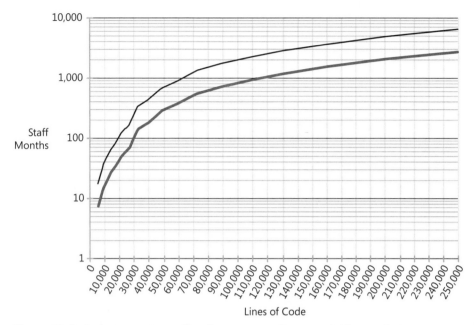

Figure 19-4   Industry-average effort for systems software and driver projects.

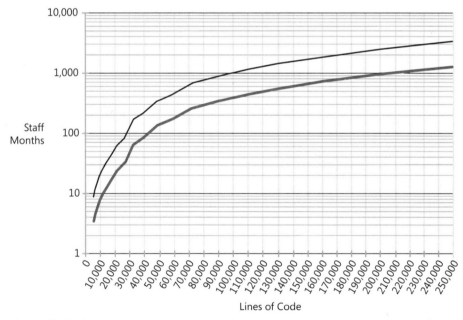

Figure 19-5   Industry-average effort for scientific systems and engineering research projects.

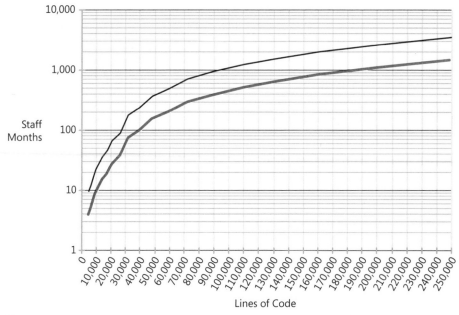

Figure 19-6 Industry-average effort for shrink-wrap and packaged software projects.

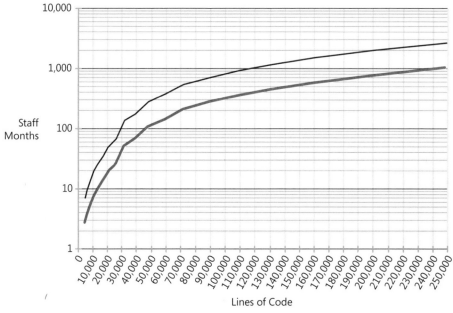

Figure 19-7 Industry-average effort for public internet systems projects.

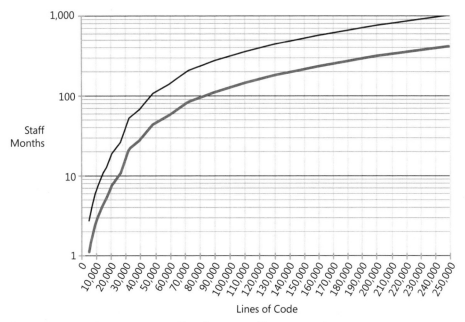

Figure 19-8   Industry-average effort for internal intranet projects.

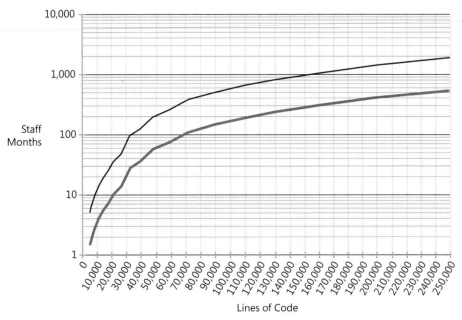

Figure 19-9   Industry-average effort for business systems projects.

Using the industry-average graphs, we can reestimate the example that began in Section 19.2, "Computing Effort from Size." That was a business-systems project with a size estimated between 65,000 and 100,000 lines of code. According to Figure 19-9, the average effort for a 65,000-LOC business system would be about 85 staff months. The average effort for a 100,000-LOC system would be about 170 staff months. If we had to use the upper line rather than the average line, the estimate would range from 300 to 600 staff months.

Tip #86	Use industry-average effort graphs to obtain rough effort estimates in the wide part of the Cone of Uncertainty. For larger projects, remember that more powerful estimation techniques are easily cost-justified.

19.5 ISBSG Method

The International Software Benchmarking Standards Group (ISBSG) has developed an interesting and useful method of computing effort based on three factors: the size of a project in function points, the kind of development environment, and the maximum team size (ISBSG 2005). Presented by project type, the following eight equations are the ones you'd use to estimate effort using this approach. The equations produce an estimate in staff months, assuming 132 project-focused hours per staff month (that is, excluding vacations, holidays, training days, company meetings, and so on). The General formula is a general-purpose formula for use on all project types and is based on calibration data from about 600 projects. The other categories are calibrated with data from 63 to 363 projects.

Kind of project: General

Equation #9	$\text{StaffMonths} = 0.512 \times \text{FunctionPoints}^{0.392} \times \text{MaximumTeamSize}^{0.791}$

Kind of project: Mainframe

Equation #10	$\text{StaffMonths} = 0.685 \times \text{FunctionPoints}^{0.507} \times \text{MaximumTeamSize}^{0.464}$

Kind of project: Mid-Range

Equation #11	$\text{StaffMonths} = 0.472 \times \text{FunctionPoints}^{0.375} \times \text{MaximumTeamSize}^{0.882}$

Kind of project: Desktop

Equation #12	$\text{StaffMonths} = 0.157 \times \text{FunctionPoints}^{0.591} \times \text{MaximumTeamSize}^{0.810}$

Kind of project: Third Generation Language

Equation #13	$\text{StaffMonths} = 0.425 \times \text{FunctionPoints}^{0.488} \times \text{MaximumTeamSize}^{0.697}$

Kind of project: Fourth Generation Language

Equation #14	$\text{StaffMonths} = 0.317 \times \text{FunctionPoints}^{0.472} \times \text{MaximumTeamSize}^{0.784}$

Kind of project: Enhancement

Equation #15	$\text{StaffMonths} = 0.669 \times \text{FunctionPoints}^{0.338} \times \text{MaximumTeamSize}^{0.758}$

Kind of project: New Development

Equation #16	$\text{StaffMonths} = 0.520 \times \text{FunctionPoints}^{0.385} \times \text{MaximumTeamSize}^{0.866}$

Suppose you were creating an effort estimate for a desktop business application of 1,450 function points in Java (the same system we've been estimating throughout this chapter) and you have a maximum team size of 7 people. The Desktop equation suggests you will have an effort of 56 staff months:

$$0.157 \times 1,450^{0.591} \times 7^{0.810}$$

You could also use the Third Generation Language equation to get an estimate of 58 staff months:

$$0.425 \times 1,450^{0.488} \times 7^{0.697}$$

An interesting aspect of the ISBSG method is that the formulas for effort depend on the maximum size of the project team, with smaller teams producing smaller total effort estimates. Varying the maximum team size in the example from 5 to 10 people causes the effort estimate to vary from 43 to 75 staff months. From an estimation point of view, this introduces uncertainty. From a *project control* point of view, this difference might lead you to use a smaller team size rather than a larger one. (This topic is addressed further in "Schedule Compression and Team Size" in Section 20.6, "Tradeoffs Between Schedule and Effort.")

Tip #87	Use the ISBSG method to compute a rough effort estimate. Combine it with other methods, and look for convergence or spread among the different estimates.

19.6 Comparing Effort Estimates

To provide a reality check on these estimates, you might compare the four different approaches to effort estimates in this chapter:

- Doing informal comparisons to past projects
- Using estimation software
- Using industry-average graphs
- Using the ISBSG method

If you graphed the estimate ranges from these techniques, they would look like those shown in Figure 19-10.

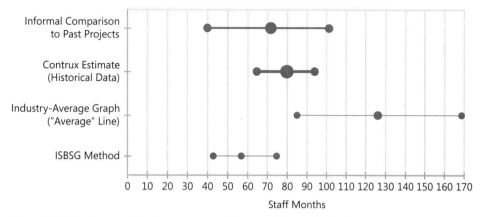

Figure 19-10   Ranges of estimates derived by using the methods discussed in this chapter. The relative dot sizes and line thicknesses represent the weight I would give each of the estimation techniques in this case.

The graph shows a range of estimates from about 40 to 110 staff months. The ISBSG method and the industry-average graphs are both using industry-average data, so I would weight them less heavily than the methods that are based on historical data. With the informal comparison to past projects, I would weight the projects that are most similar (including closest in size) the most heavily.

All things considered, in this case I would present a range of 65 to 100 staff months with an expected outcome of 80 staff months. You might think the expected outcome should fall in the middle of the range of 65 to 100, but the effort will often fall toward the low end of the range because of the issues discussed in Section 1.4, "Estimates as Probability Statements."

Tip #88	Not all estimation methods are equal. When looking for convergence or spread among estimates, give more weight to the techniques that tend to produce the most accurate results.

Additional Resources

Boehm, Barry, et al. *Software Cost Estimation with Cocomo II*. Reading, MA: Addison Wesley, 2000. The Cocomo II estimation model described in this book provides formulas for converting size estimates in lines of code into effort. Keep in mind the warnings about the "control knobs" involved.

ISBSG. *Practical Project Estimation, 2nd Edition: A Toolkit for Estimating Software Development Effort and Duration.* Victoria, Australia: International Software Benchmarking Standards Group, February 2005. This book contains numerous useful formulas for computing effort estimates from size estimates. The book is refreshingly candid about the accuracy of its formulas; it includes sample size and r-squared values you can use to assess the validity of its formulas.

Putnam, Lawrence H. and Ware Myers. *Measures for Excellence: Reliable Software On Time, Within Budget.* Englewood Cliffs, NJ: Yourdon Press, 1992. The Putnam model described in this book converts size estimates in lines of code into effort.

Chapter 20

Special Issues in Estimating Schedule

Applicability of Techniques in This Chapter

	The Basic Schedule Equation	Informal Comparison to Past Projects	Jones's First-Order Estimation Practice	Estimation Software Tools
What's Estimated	Schedule	Schedule	Schedule	Schedule
Size of project	- M L	S M L	- M L	- M L
Development stage	Early	Early	Early	Early
Iterative or sequential	Sequential	Both	Sequential	Both
Accuracy possible	Medium	Medium	Low	High

The need to meet customer deadlines, trade show deadlines, seasonal sales-cycle deadlines, regulatory deadlines, and other calendar-oriented deadlines seems to put much of the estimation pressure on the schedule. The schedule estimate seems to produce most of the heat in estimation discussions.

Ironically, once you move from intuitive estimation approaches to approaches based on historical data, the schedule estimate becomes a simple computation that flows from the size and effort estimates. If T.S. Eliot had written poems about software, he might have written

This is the way the estimate ends
This is the way the estimate ends
This is the way the estimate ends
Not with a bang but a whimper

20.1 The Basic Schedule Equation

A rule of thumb is that you can estimate schedule early in a project using the Basic Schedule Equation:

Equation #17	$$\text{ScheduleInMonths} = 3.0 \times \text{StaffMonths}^{1/3}$$

In case your math is a little rusty, the 1/3 exponent in the equation works the same as taking the cube root of *StaffMonths*.

Sometimes the 3.0 is a 2.0, 2.5, 3.5, 4.0 or similar number, but the basic idea that schedule is a cube-root function of effort is almost universally accepted by estimation experts. (The specific number is one that can be derived through calibration with your organization's historical data.) Barry Boehm commented in 1981 that this formula was one of the most replicated results in software engineering (Boehm 1981). Additional analysis over the past few decades has continued to affirm the validity of the schedule equation (Boehm 2000, Stutzke 2005).

To use the equation, suppose you've estimated that you will need 80 staff months to build your project. The schedule computed from this formula ranges from 8.6 to 17.2 months depending on what coefficient from 2.0 to 4.0 is used. The nominal schedule will be $(3.0 \times 80^{1/3})$, which is 12.9 months. (I don't recommend presenting the schedule estimate with this much precision; I'm including it here to make the calculations easier to follow.)

Tip #89   Use the Basic Schedule Equation to estimate schedule early in medium-to-large projects.

The schedule equation has some interesting implications for the Cone of Uncertainty, as shown by the numbers on the right axis of Figure 20-1.

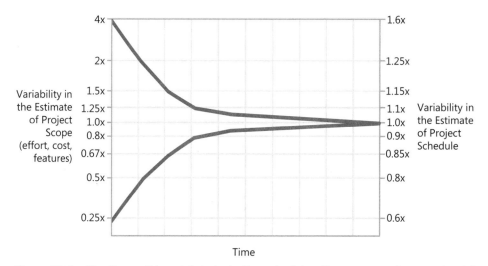

Figure 20-1   The Cone of Uncertainty, including schedule adjustment numbers on the right axis. The schedule variability is much lower than the scope variability because schedule is a cube-root function of scope.

The schedule equation is the reason that the uncertainty ranges in Figure 20-1 are much broader for efforts than they are for schedules. Effort increases in proportion to scope, whereas schedule increases in proportion to the cube root of effort.

The schedule equation implicitly assumes that you're able to adjust the team size to suit the size implied by the equation. If your team size is fixed, the schedule won't vary in proportion to the cube root of the scope; it will vary more widely based on your team-size constraints. Section 20.7, "Schedule Estimation and Staffing Constraints," will discuss this issue in more detail.

The Basic Schedule Equation is also not intended for estimation of small projects or late phases of larger projects. You should switch to some other technique when you know the names of the specific people working on the project.

20.2 Computing Schedule by Using Informal Comparisons to Past Projects

William Roetzheim proposes estimating schedules of new projects based on a ratio of schedule and effort from past projects (Roetzheim 1988, Stutzke 2005). We'll use the same projects that were used in Chapter 19, "Special Issues in Estimating Effort," which are repeated in Table 20-1 for reference.

Table 20-1   **Example of Past Project Efforts and Schedules for Estimating Future Schedules**

Project	Size (LOC)	Schedule (Calendar Months)	Effort (Staff Months)	Productivity (LOC/Staff Month)	Comments
Project A	33,842	8.2	21	1,612	
Project B	97,614	12.5	99	986	
Project C	7,444	4.7	2	3,722	Not used—too small for comparison
Project D	54,322	11.3	40	1,358	
Project E	340,343	24.0	533	639	Not used—too large for comparison

Roetzheim suggests estimating schedule in months by using the Informal Comparison to Past Projects formula:

Equation #18

$$\text{EstimatedSchedule} = \text{PastSchedule} \times (\text{EstimatedEffort} / \text{Past Effort})^{1/3}$$

The exponent of 1/3 is used for what this book calls medium-to-large projects (more than about 50 staff months). For smaller projects, you should use an exponent of 1/2.

Chapter 19's effort estimate of 65 to 100 staff months, with a most likely estimate of 80 staff months,gives us the estimated schedules from past projects shown in Table 20-2.

Table 20-2   **Example of Schedules Estimates Computed Using Informal Comparisons to Past Projects**

	Historical Data		Estimates		
Project	Past Schedule (Calendar Months)	Past Effort (Staff Months)	Low Estimate (65 Staff Months)	Nominal Estimate (80 Staff Months)	High Estimate (100 Staff Months)
Project A	8.2	21	12.0	12.8	13.8
Project B	12.5	99	10.8	11.6	12.5
Project D	11.3	40	13.2	14.2	15.3

Roetzheim's technique produces a best-case to worst-case range of 10.8 to 17.3 months. I would compute the Expected Case by simply averaging the three nominal estimates from the table. I would compute the low and high ends of the range by averaging the low estimates and the high estimates from the table. Those calculations produce a nominal schedule of 12.9 months with a range of 12.0 to 13.9 months.

Tip #90	Use the Informal Comparison to Past Projects formula to estimate schedule early in a small-to-large project.

20.3 Jones's First-Order Estimation Practice

If you have a function-point count, you can compute a rough schedule directly from function points by using what Capers Jones has described as the First-Order Estimation Practice (Jones 1996). To use it, take your function-point total and raise it to the appropriate power selected from Table 20-3. The Average exponents in the table are derived from Jones's analysis of several thousand projects. I've added approximate Better and Worse exponents to represent variations in performance.

Table 20-3   **Exponents for Computing Schedules from Function Points**

Kind of software	Better	Average	Worse
Object-oriented software	0.33	0.36	0.39
Client-server software	0.34	0.37	0.40
Business systems, internal intranet systems	0.36	0.39	0.42
Shrink-wrapped, scientific systems, engineering systems, public internet systems	0.37	0.40	0.43
Embedded systems, telecommunications, device drivers, systems software	0.38	0.41	0.44

Source: Loosely adapted from "Determining Software Schedules" (Jones 1995c) and *Estimating Software Costs* (Jones 1996).

If you estimate your project's total number of function points to be 1,450, and you're working in a business-systems organization with average productivity, you will raise 1,450 to the 0.39 power ($1,450^{0.39}$), for a rough schedule of 17 calendar months. If you are working in a best-in-class business-systems organization, you will raise 1,450 to the 0.36 power, for a schedule of 14 months. If you're developing an object-oriented business system, the object-oriented software exponents will give you a range of 11 to 17 months. Thus, it appears that the real schedule lies somewhere in the range of 11 to 17 months.

This practice isn't a substitute for more careful schedule estimation, but it does provide a simple means of getting a rough schedule estimate that's better than guessing. It can also provide a quick reality check. If you want to develop a 1,450-function-point business system in 9 months, you should think again. The best-in-class schedule would be 11 to 14 months, and most organizations aren't best in class. Jones's First-Order Estimation Practice allows you to know early on if you need to adjust your feature set expectations, schedule expectations, or both.

| **Tip #91** | Use Jones's First-Order Estimation Practice to produce a low-accuracy (but very low-effort) schedule estimate early in a project. |

20.4 Computing a Schedule Estimate by Using the Science of Estimation

In the final analysis, the art of estimation isn't very well equipped to take the last step in producing an accurate schedule. Schedules vary too much based on too many factors. The easiest and most accurate way to compute a schedule is to use a tool such as Construx Estimate.[1]

What happens when we use Construx Estimate to compute a schedule estimate for the case study? If we calibrate Construx Estimate with the historical effort and schedule data that was presented in Chapter 19, Construx Estimate calculates a schedule of 12.2 calendar months, with a 20% to 80% likely range of 11.6 to 12.9 months. With industry-average data, the nominal is 15.8 months and the range is 13.2 to 21.5 months!

The discrepancy between the nominals and ranges computed using historical data and industry-average data once again illustrates the benefits of using historical data.

---

[1] Construx Estimate can be downloaded for free from *www.construx.com/estimate.*

20.5 Schedule Compression and the Shortest Possible Schedule

After the nominal schedule has been computed, the question often arises, "How much can we shorten the schedule if we need to?" The answer depends on whether the feature set is flexible. If features can be cut, the schedule can be shortened as much as you want, subject to your willingness to cut features. This amounts to doing less work in less time, which is reasonable.

If the feature set is not flexible, shortening the schedule depends on adding staff to do more work in less time, which is also reasonable, up to a point.

Over the past several decades, numerous estimation researchers have investigated the effects of compressing a nominal schedule. Figure 20-2 summarizes the results of their investigations.

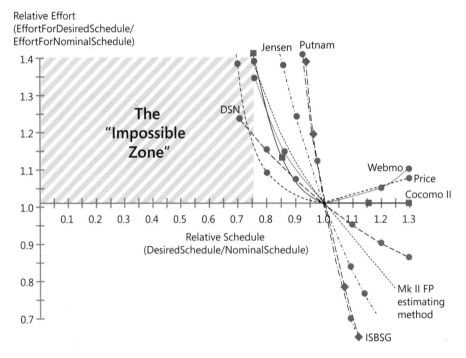

Source: *Adapted and extended from* Software Sizing and Estimating: Mk II *(Symons 1991),* Software Cost Estimation with Cocomo II *(Boehm et al 2000),* "Estimating Web Development Costs: There Are Differences" *(Reifer 2002), and* Practical Project Estimation, 2nd Edition *(ISBSG 2005).*

Figure 20-2   The effects of compressing or extending a nominal schedule and the Impossible Zone. All researchers have found that there is a maximum degree to which a schedule can be compressed.

The horizontal axis on the graph represents the relationship between the nominal schedule and the compressed schedule. A figure of 0.9 on that axis indicates a compressed schedule that takes 0.9 times as much time as the nominal schedule (that is, 90% of the nominal). The vertical axis represents the total effort required when the schedule is compressed or expanded compared to the effort required when the nominal schedule is used. A value of 1.3 on the vertical axis indicates that the compressed schedule requires 1.3 times as much total effort as the nominal schedule would require.

Several conclusions can be drawn from the graph in Figure 20-2:

Shortening the nominal schedule increases overall effort   All researchers have concluded that shortening the nominal schedule will increase total development effort. If the nominal schedule is 12 months with a team of 7 developers, you can't just use 12 developers to reduce the schedule to 7 months.

Shorter schedules require more effort for several reasons:

- Larger teams require more coordination and management overhead.

- Larger teams introduce more communication paths, which introduce more chances to miscommunicate, which introduce more errors, which then have to be corrected. Lawrence Putnam has observed that the shortest possible schedule is also the point at which error production is the highest (Putnam and Myers 2003).

- Shorter schedules require more work to be done in parallel. The more work that overlaps, the higher the chance both that one piece of work will be based on another incomplete or defective piece of work and that later changes will increase the amount of rework that must be performed.

Expert findings vary in the degree to which schedule reductions increase effort, but the experts all agree that it does. Specific tradeoffs between schedule and effort are discussed in Section 20.6.

Tip #92	Do not shorten a schedule estimate without increasing the effort estimate.

There is an Impossible Zone, and you can't beat it   If 8 people can write a program in 10 months, can 80 people write the same program in one month? Can 1,600 people write it in one day? The ineffectiveness of the extreme schedule compression in these examples is obvious. The endpoint–1,600 people working for one day–is absurd and easy to recognize.

Finding the limits of less-extreme schedule compression is a more subtle problem, but all researchers have concluded that there is an Impossible Zone, a point beyond which a nominal schedule cannot be compressed. The consensus of researchers is that schedule compression of more than 25% from nominal is not possible.

As Figure 20-2 illustrates, for a project of a particular size, there's a point beyond which the development schedule simply can't be shortened. Not by working harder. Not by working smarter. And not by finding creative solutions or by making the team larger. It simply can't be done (Symons 1991, Boehm 2000, Putnam and Myers 2003).

Tip #93	Do not shorten a nominal schedule more than 25%. In other words, keep your estimates out of the Impossible Zone.

Extending schedule beyond the nominal schedule usually reduces total effort, if you reduce team size   Experts have generally concluded that increasing the schedule beyond the nominal allows for a reduction in overall effort for the same reasons that shortening a schedule increases effort. A longer schedule allows for a smaller team, which reduces communication and coordination problems. It reduces overlap among activities, which allows more defects to be fixed "in phase" before they contaminate other work and cause more rework.

For an extended schedule to reduce effort, you must actually reduce the team size. If you simply allocate the same people to the same project fractionally instead of reducing the number of people on the team, you'll likely make matters worse instead of better, because of the issues discussed in Section 3.1, "Is it Better to Overestimate or Underestimate?"

Tip #94	Reduce costs by lengthening the schedule and conducting the project with a smaller team.

20.6 Tradeoffs Between Schedule and Effort

Lawrence Putnam's estimation model provides some rules of thumb for schedule compression and expansion, listed in Table 20-4.

Table 20-4   **Recommended Tradeoffs Between Effort and Schedule**

Schedule Compression/Expansion	Effort Increase/Reduction
−15%	+100%
−10%	+50%
−5%	+25%
Nominal	0%
+10%	−30%
+20%	−50%
+30%	−65%
More than +30%	Not practical

Source: Adapted from data in *Measures for Excellence* (Putnam and Myers 1992).

Putnam cautions that extending the schedule more than about 30% is likely to begin introducing different kinds of inefficiencies, which in turn begin increasing costs.

Some people have criticized Putnam's model for exaggerating the effect of schedule compression and expansion, but the International Software Benchmarking Standards Group's 2005 data produces very similar results (ISBSG 2005).

Schedule Compression and Team Size

One of the pitfalls of attempting to compress a schedule below the nominal, even if you avoid the Impossible Zone, is that you might increase team size above the economically effective maximum. Lawrence Putnam has conducted fascinating research on the relationship between team size, schedule, and productivity for medium-sized business systems. Figure 20-3 shows his results (Putnam and Myers 2003).

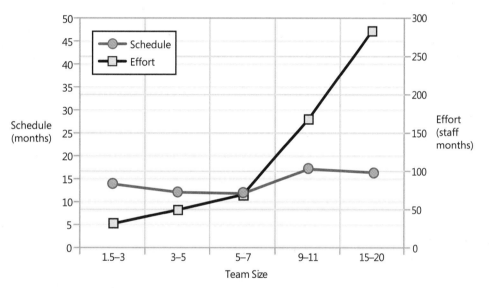

Figure 20-3   Relationship between team size, schedule, and effort for business-systems projects of about 57,000 lines of code. For team sizes greater than 5 to 7 people, effort and schedule both increase.

Putnam reviewed about 500 business projects that were in the range of 35,000 to 95,000 lines of code (LOC) and which averaged 57,000 LOC. He stratified these projects into 5 groups based on the sizes of the development teams. The average sizes of the projects for each team size were within 3,000 LOC of one another. Putnam found that, as team size increased from the 1.5 to 3 range to the 3 to 5 range, the schedule shortened and effort increased, which is what you would expect. As team size increased from 3–5 to 5–7, the schedule again decreased and effort again increased. But when team size increased from 5–7 to 9–11, *both the schedule and effort increased*. And when team size increased to 15 to 20, schedule stayed flat but effort increased dramatically.

I suspect (based on nothing but my own judgment) that Putnam's data is showing that software's diseconomy of scale is not a smooth, incremental function but is more like a step function that has large penalties that kick in at certain sizes.

Putnam has not yet generalized his findings to other kinds of software or other project sizes, but for the medium-sized business-systems domain, this is an important finding: A team size of 5 to 7 people appears to be economically optimal for medium-sized business-systems projects. For larger team sizes, both schedule and effort degrade.

Tip #95	For medium-sized business-systems projects (35,000 to 100,000 lines of code) avoid increasing the team size beyond 7 people.

20.7 Schedule Estimation and Staffing Constraints

Nominally, you can compute the average team size by taking the effort estimate and dividing it by the schedule. If you've estimated a 12-month schedule for a project of 80 staff months, your average team size is just the staff months divided by the schedule, 80 divided by 12, which is 6 to 7 team members.

The schedule estimates produced in this chapter produce the nominal schedule for a project at a particular level of effort. These techniques assume that, whatever the nominal schedule is, you'll be able to adjust your team size to fit the level indicated. If you're in a position to apply an average of 6 to 7 people to the project estimated in this chapter, you should be able to achieve the combination of 80-staff-month effort and 12-calendar-month schedule that's been estimated.

What if you have only 4 people to work on the project? What if you're already at a point in the project where you're assigning specific tasks? What if you have 10 people who are each available two-thirds of the time? What if the team is already intact and doesn't need any ramp-up time? The formulas in this chapter don't account for such factors: these formulas are macro estimation techniques that are appropriate only in the early stages of medium-to-large projects.

Medium and large projects typically experience some ramp up of team members from the beginning to the middle of the project, and some ramp down in the final stages. A medium-sized project might average 15 people, but it might start with 5, peak at 20, and end with 10.

Smaller projects more often use "flat staffing"—the whole team starts on Day 1 and continues through the end of the project. If your schedule estimate is 12 months but your plans show that, based on people's availability, you will need 15 months to actually apply 80 staff months of effort, your plans should take precedence over the original schedule estimate.

The purpose of the schedule estimates in this chapter is not to predict your final schedule to the day but to provide a sanity check on your schedule-related plans.

Once you've used schedule estimation to ensure that your plans are reasonable, detailed planning considerations (such as who is available when) will take precedence over the initial schedule estimation described.

Tip #96	Use schedule estimation to ensure your plans are plausible. Use detailed planning to produce the final schedule.

20.8 Comparison of Results from Different Methods

Here are the five schedule estimation methods we've used in this chapter:

- Basic Schedule Equation
- The Informal Comparison to Past Projects formula
- Jones's First-Order Estimation Practice
- Software tool calibrated with industry-average data
- Software tool calibrated with historical data

Figure 20-4 shows graphically how these different schedule estimates compare.

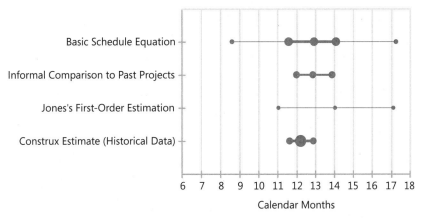

Figure 20-4   Ranges of schedule estimates produced by the methods discussed in this chapter. The relative dot sizes and line thicknesses represent the weights I would give each of these estimates. Looking at all the estimates, including those that aren't well founded, hides the real convergence among these estimates.

At first glance, the schedule estimates in this example don't seem to converge very well. One refinement that could be made is based on the Basic Schedule Equation used to generate the top line. The total range shown in Figure 20-4 is for coefficients in the Basic Schedule Equation that range from 2.0 to 4.0. If you review your historical data, you can assess how much that coefficient should actually vary. The past projects' coefficients in this chapter's example have ranged only from 2.7 to 3.7, which narrows the schedule range produced by the Basic Schedule Equation to 11.6 to 14.1 months.

In this case, I would again heavily weight the estimate produced with Construx Estimate both because it is an estimation-science approach and, more important, because it's based on historical data. I would weight the Basic Schedule Equation and the Informal Comparison to Past Projects formulas second. I would not use Jones's First-Order Estimation Practice approach at all for a situation in which I have better data.

Figure 20-5 shows the convergence of the schedule estimates when we remove the overly generic data.

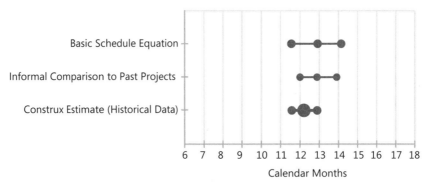

Figure 20-5   Ranges of schedule estimates produced by the most accurate methods. Once the estimates produced by overly generic methods are eliminated, the convergence of the estimates becomes clear.

Based on this convergence, I would present a range of 11.5 to 14 months, and I would probably not provide an Expected Case within that range. The schedule techniques in this chapter are all early-in-the-Cone-of-Uncertainty techniques, so not providing a single-point number would normally be acceptable at this early stage of a project.

Tip #97	Remove the results of overly generic estimation techniques from your data set before you look for convergence or spread among your estimates.

Additional Resources

Putnam, Lawrence H. and Ware Myers. *Five Core Metrics*. New York, NY: Dorset House, 2003. Chapter 11 goes into detail about the efficiency penalty for exceeding 7 people on a medium-sized business-systems project.

Stutzke, Richard D. *Estimating Software-Intensive Systems*. Upper Saddle River, NJ: Addison-Wesley, 2005. Stutzke provides several additional methods for estimating schedule, most of which are more mathematically intensive than the techniques described in this chapter.

Chapter 21
Estimating Planning Parameters

The line between project estimation and project planning is wide and blurry. Numerous planning parameters need to be estimated, including how much effort to allocate to construction, testing, requirements, and design; how many testers to have for each developer; how many effort hours you can expect to apply to a specific project in a calendar week or month; how large the risk buffer should be; and many other figures that are needed for planning purposes.

When a project gets to the level of planning discussed in this chapter, the goals of planning tend to be antagonistic toward the goals of estimation. For example, once you estimate the amount of risk buffer you need, the purpose of risk management planning from that point forward will be to minimize the amount of the risk buffer that you actually use, essentially invalidating your estimate.

Estimation of planning parameters is estimation at its least pure: the interplay between fine-grained target setting and fine-grained estimation should be intense and highly iterative. The goal of estimation in this context is to make sure your initial plans are realistic. From that point forward, planning and project control, rather than estimation, should prevail.

In short, planning addresses "how" to conduct a project, and estimation addresses "how much" of a quantity to plan for, which is the focus of this chapter.

21.1 Estimating Activity Breakdown on a Project

One important planning decision is how much effort to allocate to the activities of requirements, architecture, construction, system test, and management. This choice will need to be made regardless of whether the project is sequential or iterative. In other words, the issue is not how much time to allocate to phases, it is how much effort to allocate to activities, whenever they will be performed.

Estimating Allocation of Effort to Different Technical Activities

Please note that the rolled-up (undecomposed) effort estimate described in Chapter 19, "Special Issues in Estimating Effort," beginning in Section 19.2, "Computing Effort from Size," forms the basis for the activity allocations made in this section.

Table 21-1 lists the percentages of the total effort estimate that you would allocate to the basic activities of architecture, construction, and system test. (*KLOC* stands for "1,000 lines of code.") Because of the diseconomy of scale described in Chapter 5, "Estimate Influences," the proportion of effort allocated to each activity depends on the size of the project. Requirements and management work are usually treated as special cases and are discussed later.

Table 21-1   Approximate Technical Effort Breakdown for Projects of Different Sizes

	Activity		
Size	Architecture	Construction	System Test
1 KLOC	11%	70%	19%
25 KLOC	16%	57%	27%
125 KLOC	18%	53%	29%
500 KLOC	19%	44%	37%

Sources: Albrecht 1979; Boehm 1981; Glass 1982; Boehm, Gray, and Seewaldt 1984; Boddie 1987; Card 1987; Grady 1987; McGarry, Waligora, and McDermott 1989; Putnam and Myers 1992; Brooks 1995; Jones 1998; Jones 2000; Boehm et al, 2000; Putnam and Myers 2003; Boehm and Turner 2004; Stutzke 2005.

The entries listed in Table 21-1 are *approximate*. They depend on the specific technical practices you use, the life-cycle model you use, effectiveness of your quality assurance work, and many other factors. Ultimately, you should develop your own table based on your organization's historical data. Until you've done that, you can use Table 21-1 as a starting point and then use the factors presented in Table 21-5 to adjust your estimate for the specific type of project you're estimating.

Estimating Requirements Effort

Table 21-1 does not include effort allocated to requirements. If you created your effort estimate using industry-average productivity data, that data is normally assumed not to include requirements activity. (That isn't always true, which is one reason that industry-average data varies as much as it does.)

If you create your estimate using your own historical data, your estimate might or might not include requirements data, depending on whether the historical data you use contains requirements data.

Estimation models, including Cocomo II and the Putnam model, assume that the rolled-up, "main build" estimates they produce do not include requirements work. One reason is that the percentage of requirements effort varies more than the percentages of the other activities do. You can quickly rush through requirements, defining a large requirements set only very loosely, which will then require

Herculean effort to implement. Or you can invest more time and define a smaller set of high-quality requirements, which will allow a lower effort implementation.

With these caveats in mind, Table 21-2 lists the approximate proportion of effort you should plan for requirements work on projects of different sizes. You would add the percentage of effort from the table to your base effort estimate to compute total technical effort, including requirements work.

Table 21-2   **Approximate Requirements-Effort Proportions for Projects of Different Sizes**

Size	Amount to Add to Base Effort
1 KLOC	5%
25 KLOC	5%
125 KLOC	8%
500 KLOC	10%

Sources: same as for Table 21-1.

Estimating Management Effort

As with requirements effort, the rolled-up effort estimate won't include management effort unless you're using your own historical data and your historical data includes management effort. Table 21-3 lists approximate management effort for projects of different sizes. As with the requirements effort, you add the percentage of effort from the table, including management work, to your base effort estimate to compute total technical effort.

Table 21-3   **Approximate Management-Effort Proportions for Projects of Different Sizes**

Size	Amount to Add to Base Effort from Table 21-1 (Not Including Requirements Effort)
1 KLOC	10%
25 KLOC	12%
125 KLOC	14%
500 KLOC	17%

Sources: same as for Table 21-1.

Estimating Total Activity

For ease of computation, Table 21-4 lists the effort to allocate to requirements, architecture, construction, system test, and management for projects of different sizes.

This table is useful when the data you use to calibrate your rolled-up effort estimate includes both requirements and management effort.

Table 21-4   **Total Effort Breakdown for Projects of Different Sizes**

		Activity			
Size	**Requirements**	**Architecture and Planning**	**Construction**	**System Test**	**Management**
1 KLOC	4%	10%	61%	16%	9%
25 KLOC	4%	14%	49%	23%	10%
125 KLOC	7%	15%	44%	23%	11%
500 KLOC	8%	15%	35%	29%	13%

Sources: same as for Table 21-1.

Adjustments Due to Project Type

As Chapter 5 discussed, the type of project influences the total effort on a project. It also influences the percentage of effort that will be allocated to different kinds of activities. Table 21-5 lists the adjustments you should make to your nominal activity-percentage estimate based on the kind of project you're working on.

Table 21-5   **Approximate Adjustments in Activity Proportions Based on Kind of Project**

Activity	**Business Systems, Internal Intranet Systems**	**Embedded Systems, Telecommunications, Device Drivers, Systems Software**	**Shrink-Wrap, Scientific Systems, Engineering Systems, Public Internet Systems**
Requirements	–3%	+20%	–20%
Architecture	–7%	+10%	–5%
Construction	+5%	–10%	+2%
System Test	–7%	+6%	+9%
Management	+3%	+3%	–15%

Sources: Putnam and Myers 1992; Jones 1998; Jones 2000; Boehm et al, 2000; Putnam and Myers 2003; Boehm and Turner 2004; Stutzke 2005.

Tip #98   When allocating project effort across different activities, consider project size, project type, and the kinds of effort contained in the calibration data used to create your initial rolled-up estimate.

Example of Allocating Effort to Activities

Suppose you're developing a business system that you've estimated will consist of about 80,000 lines of code (1,450 function points) and will require about 80 staff months total effort. The basic technical activity breakdown from Table 21-1 provides percentages for projects of 25 KLOC and 125 KLOC. An 80-KLOC project is about halfway between those two sizes, so we'll use the average of the table's 25 KLOC and 125 KLOC entries. Based on those percentages, you'll need to allocate 17% of your effort to architecture (13.6 staff months), 55% to construction (44.0 staff months), and 28% to system test (22.4 staff months). Table 21-2 suggests that you add 6.5% for requirements work (5.2 staff months), and Table 21-3 suggests you add 13% for project management (10.4 staff months). Table 21-6 then shows how you multiply your base effort allocation by the adjustment factors for business-systems projects to compute a final effort estimate.

Table 21-6 **Example of Adjusting a Nominal Effort Allocation Based on Project Type**

Activity	Nominal Effort Allocation (Staff Months)	Business-Systems Adjustment	Final Effort Allocation (Staff Months)	Final %
Requirements	5.2	–3%	5.0	4%
Architecture	13.6	–7%	12.6	13%
Construction	44.0	+5%	46.6	51%
System Test	22.4	–7%	20.8	22%
Management	10.4	+3%	10.7	10%
TOTAL	**95.6**	-	**95.7**	**100%**

In this example, the totals for nominal effort estimate and final effort estimate work out to 95.6 and 95.7 staff months. In these calculations, the two totals sometimes don't work out exactly the same because of rounding errors in the adjustment factors.

Recognize that these allocations of effort to phases are approximate. They represent useful starting points for planning. Once the estimates get you into the right planning ballpark, detailed planning considerations should take precedence over these initial estimates.

Developer-to-Tester Ratios

A common planning question is, "What should the ratio of developers to testers be?" Table 21-7 lists some common ratios.

Table 21-7   **Examples of Developer-to-Tester Ratios**

Environment	Commonly Observed Developer-to-Tester Ratios
Common business systems (internal intranet, management information systems, and so on)	3:1 to 20:1 (often no test specialists at all)
Common commercial systems (public internet, shrink wrap, and so on)	1:1 to 5:1
Scientific and engineering projects	5:1 to 20:1 (often no test specialists at all)
Common systems projects	1:1 to 5:1
Safety-critical systems	5:1 to 1:2
Microsoft Windows 2000	1:2
NASA Space Shuttle Flight Control Software	1:10

The data in this table is based on observations of organizations that my company and I have worked with during the past 10 years.

As you can see from the data in the table, ratios vary significantly even within specific kinds of software. This is appropriate, because the ratio that will work the best for a specific company or a specific project will depend on the development style of the project, the complexity of the specific software being tested, the ratio of legacy code to new code, the skill of the testers compared to the skill of the developers, the degree of test automation, and numerous other factors.

Ultimately, the developer-to-tester ratio is settled more by planning than by estimation—that is, it's determined more by what you think you *should* do than by what you predict you will do.

21.2 Estimating Schedule for Different Activities

Allocating calendar time to different activities and phases on a project tends again to be more a planning-related judgment than an estimate. Table 21-8 lists approximate schedule breakdowns for the core technical activities at different project sizes. It would be convenient if the numbers in the table weren't expressed as ranges. The schedule for these activities tends to be influenced by when specific people become available, how fragmented their effort is between the project you're estimating and their other responsibilities, and other factors. The schedule breakdown is thus subject to more variability than the effort breakdown is.

Table 21-8   **Approximate Schedule Breakdown At Different Project Sizes**

Size	Activity		
	Architecture	**Construction**	**System Test**
1 KLOC	15–25%	50–65%	15–20%
25 KLOC	15–30%	50–60%	20–25%
125 KLOC	20–35%	45–55%	20–30%
500 KLOC	20–40%	40–55%	20–35%

Sources: Boehm 1981; Putnam and Myers 1992; Boehm et al, 2000; Putnam and Myers 2003; Stutzke 2005.

As with effort, the schedule for requirements is typically estimated as an add-on to the base schedule estimate. Table 21-9 lists the amount to add to the base schedule for requirements work.

Table 21-9   **Approximate Schedule to Add for Requirements at Different Project Sizes**

Size	Amount to Add for Requirements
1 KLOC	10–16%
25 KLOC	12–20%
125 KLOC	13–22%
500 KLOC	24–30%

Sources: Boehm 1981; Putnam and Myers 1992; Boehm et al, 2000; Putnam and Myers 2003; Stutzke 2005.

If your project is highly iterative, you'll be allocating schedule within each iteration. If your project is more sequential, you'll be allocating schedule within whole-project phases.

Tip #99	Consider your project's size, type, and development approach in allocating schedule to different activities.

As with allocating effort to activities, allocating schedule to activities is easiest to do when you have your own historical data.

21.3 Converting Estimated Effort (Ideal Effort) to Planned Effort

Effort estimates are usually expressed in "staff months," "staff days," or similar terms. Such effort estimates represent *ideal* effort, in which each effort month corresponds to one calendar month.

Mike Cohn describes the difference between ideal time and planned time as akin to the difference between the minutes on the game clock vs. the minutes on the wall clock in an American football game (Cohen 2006). A normal game of American football lasts 60 minutes on the game clock. On the wall clock, a game can last anywhere from 2 to 4 hours.

Similarly, a software project planner shouldn't assume that one person can perform one staff month's worth of work in one calendar month's time. The "effort month" might be diluted by vacation, holidays, or training; it might be split across multiple projects; or it might be affected by other factors.

In considering how to convert ideal effort to planned effort, you should consider the following factors:

- What hours are included in the calibration data you used to create the effort estimate? Do they include management effort, requirements, and test, or just development effort? Do they include overtime? Whatever assumptions were baked into the calibration data will flow into the estimated effort.

- How many projects will the project's staff be spread across? If a programmer is divided between two projects, it can take two or more calendar months to accomplish one focused project-month of effort.

- Does your calibration data account for vacation, holidays, sick days, training time, trade show support, customer support, supporting systems that are in production, and so on? If not, you'll need to account for those dilutions in the effort as you convert estimated effort to planned effort.

These factors vary significantly from one organization to the next. If you work in an entrepreneurial organization in which the team can focus on a single project, you might be able to assume 40 to 50 hours per week of focused project time. In the companies I've seen achieve this, team members' internal motivation has been exceptionally strong; team sizes have been small; team members have been young with minimal family obligations; the company has offered significant financial incentives; and the work environment has no red-tape or corporate-overhead activities.

If you work in a large, established organization in which you have frequent corporate-overhead meetings and most people work about 40 hours per week, you might need to assume only 20 to 30 hours of project-focused time, and those hours might be spread across 2 or more projects.

Reports of the average time per day that staff are able to focus on a specific project vary. Capers Jones reports that, on average, technical workers apply about 6 hours of focused project time per day to their assigned projects, or 132 hours per month (Jones 1998). The Cocomo II model assumes 152 hours of focused project time per month (Boehm et al 2000). The specific number of hours varies significantly based on organizational specifics, so once again you should develop data based on your organization's track record if at all possible.

The "Additional Resources" section at the end of this chapter provides pointers to additional information on the planning aspects of this topic.

21.4 Cost Estimates

Estimating cost is nominally a straightforward function based on effort. However, numerous factors complicate the derivation of the cost estimate.

Overtime

Does your organization allow uncompensated overtime? If so, some percentage of the estimated effort might not contribute toward the cost estimate. Does your organization use hourly staff or contractors who are paid more for overtime hours? If so, some of your estimated effort might contribute more than average toward the cost estimate.

Is the Project Cost Based on Direct Cost, Fully Burdened Cost, or Some Other Variation?

Some organizations base their project costs on the employee's "direct costs," which are the costs directly attributable to a specific employee (payroll, payroll taxes, benefits, and so on). Other organizations base their project costs on "burdened costs," which include corporate overhead that isn't directly attributable to a specific employee (rent, corporate taxes, cost of human resources, sales, marketing, and so on). Depending on the size of the organization, amount of unbillable infrastructure, cost of office space, and other factors, the cost burden as a percentage of the employee's salary can range from 30% to 125% or higher.

Other Direct Costs

Some projects also incur costs for travel, specialized development tools, hardware, and other specific expenses. Those need to be included in the cost estimate as well.

The "Additional Resources" section at the end of this chapter provides pointers to additional information on this topic.

21.5 Estimating Defect Production and Removal

Defect production on a software project is a function of effort and project size, so it's possible to estimate defect production. Knowing how many defects are likely to be produced is useful information when you are planning how much effort you'll need to remove the defects.

Capers Jones provides one way of looking at defect production based on a program's size in function points (Jones 2000). As Table 21-10 indicates, Jones's data suggests that a typical project produces a total of about 5 defects per function point. This works out to about 50 defects per 1,000 lines of code (depending on the programming language used).

Table 21-10   Typical Defect-Production Rates by Activity

Activity	Average Defects Created
Requirements	1 defect per function point
Architecture	1.25 defects per function point
Construction	1.75 defects per function point
Documentation	0.60 defects per function point
Bad fixes	0.40 defects per function point
TOTAL	**5.0 defects per function point**

One factor that contributes to software's diseconomy of scale is that larger projects tend to produce more defects per line of code, which requires more defect-correction effort, which in turn drives up project costs. Table 21-11 presents a breakdown of defects based on project size.

Table 21-11   Project Size and Error Density

Project Size (in Lines of Code)	Typical Error Density
Smaller than 2K	0–25 errors per KLOC
2K–16K	0–40 errors per KLOC
16K–64K	0.5–50 errors per KLOC
64K–512K	2–70 errors per KLOC
512K or more	4–100 errors per KLOC

Source: "Program Quality and Programmer Productivity" (Jones 1977), *Estimating Software Costs* (Jones 1998).

The industry-average ranges of defect production vary by more than a factor of 10. Historical data about defect rates on your past projects will support more accurate estimates of defect production.

Tip #100	Use industry-average data or your historical data to estimate the number of defects your project will produce.

Estimating Defect Removal

Defect production is only part of the planning equation. Defect removal is the other part. The software industry has accumulated a fair amount of data about the defect-removal efficiency of the most common defect-removal techniques. Table 21-12 lists the defect-removal rates for inspections, reviews, unit testing, system testing, and other techniques.

Table 21-12   **Defect-Removal Rates**

Removal Step	Lowest Rate	Modal Rate	Highest Rate
Informal design reviews	25%	35%	40%
Formal design inspections	45%	55%	65%
Informal code reviews	20%	25%	35%
Formal code inspections	45%	60%	70%
Modeling or prototyping	35%	65%	80%
Personal desk checking of code	20%	40%	60%
Unit test	15%	30%	50%
New function (component) test	20%	30%	35%
Integration test	25%	35%	40%
Regression test	15%	25%	30%
System test	25%	40%	55%
Low-volume beta test (<10 sites)	25%	35%	40%
High-volume beta test (>1,000 sites)	60%	75%	85%

Source: Adapted from *Programming Productivity* (Jones 1986a), "Software Defect-Removal Efficiency" (Jones 1996), and "What We Have Learned About Fighting Defects" (Shull et al 2002).

The range from lowest rate to highest rate is significant, and, as usual, historical data from your own organization will support more accurate estimates.

An Example of Estimating Defect-Removal Efficiency

Combining the information from the defect-production and the defect-removal tables allows you to estimate the number of defects that will remain in your software at release time (and of course helps you assess the steps to take to remove more or less of the defects, depending on your quality goals).

Suppose you have a 1,000-function-point system. Using Jones's data from Table 21-10, you would estimate that the project would generate a total of 5,000 defects. Table 21-13 shows how those defects would be removed using a typical defect-removal strategy consisting of personal desk checking of code, unit testing, integration testing, system testing, and low-volume beta testing.

Table 21-13   **Example of Typical Defect Insertion and Defect Removal (Assuming a 1,000-Function-Point System)**

Activity	Effect on Defects	Total Defects Produced So Far	Defects Still Remaining
Requirements	+1,000 defects	1,000	1,000
Architecture	+1,250 defects	2,250	2,250
Construction	+1,750 defects	4,000	4,000
Personal desk checking of code	−40%	4,000	2,400

Table 21-13 **Example of Typical Defect Insertion and Defect Removal (Assuming a 1,000-Function-Point System)**

Activity	Effect on Defects	Total Defects Produced So Far	Defects Still Remaining
Documentation	+600 defects	4,600	3,000
Unit testing	−30%	4,600	2,100
Integration testing	−35%	4,600	1,365
System test	−40%	4,600	819
Bad fixes	+400 defects	5,000	1,219
Low-volume beta testing	−35%	5,000	792
Defects remaining at release	**−84%**	**5,000**	**792 (16%)**

This typical approach to defect removal is expected to remove only about 84% of defects from the software prior to its release, which is approximately the software industry average (Jones 2000). The specific numbers you obtain using this technique are, as usual, approximate.

Table 21-14 shows how a best-in-class organization might plan to remove defects. This example assumes the project team will produce the same total number of 5,000 defects. But defect-removal practices will include requirements prototyping, formal design inspections, personal desk-checking of code, unit testing, integration testing, system testing, and high-volume beta testing. As the data in the table shows, this combination of techniques is estimated to remove about 95% of defects prior to the software's release.

Table 21-14 **Example of Best-in-Class Defect Insertion and Defect Removal (Assuming a 1,000-Function-Point System)**

Activity	Effect on Defects	Total Defects Produced So Far	Defects Still Remaining
Requirements	+1,000 defects	1,000	1,000
Requirements prototyping	−65%	1,000	350
Architecture	+1,250 defects	2,250	1,600
Formal design inspections	−55%	2,250	720
Construction	+1,750 defects	4,000	2,470
Documentation	+600 defects	4,600	3,070
Personal desk checking of code	−40%	4,600	1,842
Unit testing	−30%	4,600	1,289
Integration testing	−35%	4,600	838
System test	−40%	4,600	503

Table 21-14   **Example of Best-in-Class Defect Insertion and Defect Removal (Assuming a 1,000-Function-Point System)**

Activity	Effect on Defects	Total Defects Produced So Far	Defects Still Remaining
Bad fixes	+400 defects	5,000	903
High-volume beta testing	–75%	5,000	226
Defects remaining at release	**–95%**	**5,000**	**226 (5%)**

As with the previous example, the specific estimate of 226 defects is more precise than is supported by the underlying data.

Tip #101	Use defect-removal-rate data to estimate the number of defects that your quality assurance practices will remove from your software before it is released.

Lawrence Putnam provides two additional rules of thumb for defect removal. If you want to move from 95% reliability to 99% reliability, you should plan to add 25% to the "main build" part of your schedule. You should plan to add another 25% to your schedule to improve from 99% to 99.9% reliability (Putnam and Myers 2003). (In Putnam's terminology, "reliability" and "pre-release defect removal" are synonymous.)

Further estimation of quality attributes can be an involved topic that relies heavily on the science of estimation. The "Additional Resources" section at the end of this chapter describes where to find more information.

21.6 Estimating Risk and Contingency Buffers

Intuitively, we all know that high-risk projects should allow larger buffers for risk contingency and low-risk projects can get by with smaller buffers. But how large should you make the buffers?

Risks are typically analyzed according to their severity (or impact) and probability. Table 21-15 shows an example of a table of risks, including the risks' probabilities, severities, and risk exposures.

Table 21-15   **Example of a Risk Lists Table for Project Schedule Risks**

Risk	Probability	Severity, Schedule	Risk Exposure, Schedule
#1	5%	15 weeks	0.75 weeks
#2	25%	2 weeks	0.5 weeks
#3	25%	8 weeks	2 weeks
#4	50%	2 weeks	1 week
TOTAL RE	-		**4.25 weeks**

The severity of a risk multiplied by its probability is usually referred to as the Risk Exposure, or RE. Statistically, the RE is the risk's "expected value," or the amount that the project should *expect* to add to its schedule because of its risks. For the risks listed in Table 21-15, the project should expect to add 4.25 weeks to its base schedule because of project risks. There is a 50% chance the project will add more than that and a 50% chance the project will add less than that.

Total RE makes a good place to begin quantitative buffer planning. If you want more certainty that you will deliver on time, you should plan for a buffer that's larger than the total RE. If you can live with a high risk of overrun, you might plan for a smaller buffer.

RE tells only part of the story. In Table 21-15, if risk #1 or #3 hits, the project will blow past its 4.25 week expected buffer. That isn't very likely, but you should consider the effects that specific risks would have before you settle on a final contingency buffer.

Table 21-15 showed a risk list from the point of view of schedule risks only. Any given risk might also pose a risk to effort, cost, features, quality, or revenue. Table 21-16 shows an example of a risks list table that includes risks to schedule, cost, and revenue.

Table 21-16   **Example of a Risk Lists Table for Project Schedule Risks**

Risk	Probability	Severity, Schedule (Weeks)	Risk Exposure, Schedule (Weeks)	Severity, Cost	Risk Exposure, Cost	Severity, Revenue	Risk Exposure, Revenue
#1	5%	15	0.75	$150,000	$7,500	$10,000,000	$500,000
#2	25%	2	0.5	$20,000	$5,000	$0	$0
#3	25%	8	2	$80,000	$20,000	$500,000	$125,000
#4	50%	2	1	$20,000	$10,000	$0	$0
TOTAL RE		-	**4.25**	-	**$42,500**	-	**$625,000**

For buffer planning, you'll need separate buffers for schedule, effort, cost, features, and quality. These buffers are only loosely related to each other.

Remember that the severities and probabilities are estimated and that the accuracy of the aggregate RE is only as accurate as the data that went into computing it in the first place.

Tip #102	Use your project's total Risk Exposure (RE) as the starting point for buffer planning. Review the details of your project's specific risks to understand whether you should ultimately plan for a buffer that's larger or smaller than the total RE.

The field of risk management is well advanced, and risk management is an area in which the science of estimation can play a significant role. The "Additional Resources" section that closes this chapter describes where to find more information on risk estimation.

21.7 Other Rules of Thumb

Here are some other rules of thumb that you can use for other planning issues:

- For administrative and clerical support, add 5% to 10% to the base effort estimate (Stutzke 2005).

- For IT support (lab setup, installing new software, and so on), add 2% to 4% to the base effort estimate (Stutzke 2005).

- For configuration management/build support, add 2% to 8% to the base effort estimate (Stutzke 2005).

- Allow for 1% to 4% increase in requirements per month (Jones 1998).

- To go from one-company, one-campus development to multiple-company, multiple-city development, allow for a 25% increase in effort (Boehm et al 2000).

- To go from one-company, one-campus development to international outsource development, allow for a 40% increase in effort (Boehm et al 2000).

- For first-time development with new language and tools compared to comparable development with familiar language and tools, allow for a 20% to 40% increase in effort (Boehm et al 2000).

- For first-time development in a new environment compared to comparable development with a familiar environment, allow for a 20% to 40% increase in effort (Boehm et al 2000).

21.8 Additional Resources

Boehm, Barry W. *Software Engineering Economics.* Englewood Cliffs, NJ: Prentice-Hall, Inc., 1981. Although this edition has been largely superseded by *Software Cost Estimation with Cocomo II* (below), this edition contains interesting, detailed reference tables for effort and schedule breakdowns across activities.

Boehm, Barry, et al. *Software Cost Estimation with Cocomo II.* Reading, MA: Addison-Wesley, 2000. Appendix A of Boehm's book describes effort and schedule breakdowns for waterfall projects, MBASE projects, and Rational Unified Process projects. Table A.10 (which is actually six tables) provides detailed breakdowns of effort and schedule across different activities.

Cohn, Mike. *Agile Estimating and Planning*. Englewood Cliffs, NJ: Prentice Hall PTR, 2006. Chapter 5 of Cohn's book contains a nice description of the differences between ideal effort and planned effort.

DeMarco, Tom and Timothy Lister. *Waltzing with Bears: Managing Risk on Software Projects*, New York, NY: Dorset House, 2003. This book presents a readable introduction to software risk management.

Fenton, Norman E. and Shari Lawrence Pfleeger. *Software Metrics: A Rigorous and Practical Approach*. Boston, MA: PWS Publishing Company, 1997. Chapter 10 contains a detailed discussion of estimating software reliability. If you don't like equations with symbols like α, β, Ψ, ϕ, λ, Π, Σ, Γ, and $\int$, this is not the book for you because all these symbols show up in this chapter.

Jones, Capers. *Estimating Software Costs*. New York, NY: McGraw-Hill, 1998. Chapter 14 of Jones's book contains a detailed discussion and examples of how cost buildups can vary between different kinds of organizations. Chapter 21 explains how unpaid overtime affects cost estimates.

Jones, Capers. *Software Assessments, Benchmarks, and Best Practices*. Reading, MA: Addison-Wesley, 2000. Jones's book provides some data that is updated or expanded from the data he presents in *Estimating Software Costs*.

Putnam, Lawrence H. and Ware Myers. *Measures for Excellence: Reliable Software On Time, Within Budget*. Englewood Cliffs, NJ: Yourdon Press, 1992. Putnam and Myers provide numerous useful rules of thumb for planning. The overall context of the book is a detailed, mathematical explanation of Putnam's estimation model.

Stutzke, Richard D. *Estimating Software-Intensive Systems*. Upper Saddle River, NJ: Addison-Wesley, 2005. Chapter 12 describes approaches to effort allocation that are based on Cocomo 81 and Cocomo II. Chapters 15 and 23 focus on detailed cost estimation issues. Cost estimation and other cost-related issues are a major focus of Stutzke's book, and various cost-related tips are sprinkled throughout. Sections 12.1 and 12.2 discuss the relationships between effort, duration, and staff availability.

Tockey, Steve. *Return on Software*. Boston, MA: Addison-Wesley, 2005. Chapter 15 of Tockey's book contains a good discussion of determining unit cost, including methods of allocating overhead by using different costing methods and hazards associated with some of the methods.

Tip #103	Planning and estimation are related, and planning is a much bigger topic than can be addressed in one chapter in a book that focuses on software estimation. Read the literature on planning.

Chapter 22

Estimate Presentation Styles

Applicability of Techniques in This Chapter

	Matching Presentation Style to Estimate Accuracy
What's estimated	Size, Effort, Schedule, Features
Size of project	S M L
Development stage	Early–Late
Iterative or sequential	Both
Accuracy possible	N/A

The way you communicate an estimate suggests how accurate the estimate is. If your presentation style implies an unfounded accuracy, you lay the groundwork for a difficult discussion about the estimate itself. This chapter presents several options for presenting estimates.

22.1 Communicating Estimate Assumptions

An essential practice in presenting an estimate is to document the assumptions embodied in the estimate. Assumptions fall into several familiar categories:

- Which features are required
- Which features are not required
- How elaborate certain features need to be
- Availability of key resources
- Dependencies on third-party performance
- Major unknowns
- Major influences and sensitivities of the estimate
- How good the estimate is
- What the estimate can be used for

Figure 22-1 shows an example of an estimate that's presented with documented assumptions. By documenting and communicating your assumptions, you help to set the expectation that your software project is subject to variability.

Project Estimate

The base schedule estimate is 6 calendar months, which we believe is accurate to within 25%. This estimate can be used as the basis for the project budget but not for making external commitments. The estimate is based on the following assumptions.

1) The three key technical leaders will be assigned 100% to project on March 15.

2) All development and test staff will be assigned 100% to this project by April 15.

3) Graphics-formatting subsystem will be delivered by subcontractor with acceptable quality by August 1.

4) No updates in the business rules will be required.

5) Extent of required integration with the FooBar system is unknown. This estimate has allocated 250 staff hours for that integration work. If more work than that is required, the whole-project estimate will need to be increased.

6) No more than 5 new reports will be required.

7) New development tools will produce an improvement in productivity of 20% or more compared to past projects.

8) Staff will use fewer sick days than average because most of the project occurs during the summer months.

9) After the availability dates listed in (1) and (2), staff will not be called back to support previous versions of the software.

10) The project will be able to reuse at least 80% of the database code from Version 2.0 without modifications.

If these assumptions change, this estimate will need to be revised.

Figure 22-1   Example of documenting estimate assumptions.

This approach can also be useful when you're forced to base an estimate on assumptions that you think are unrealistic (such as assumptions 7 through 9 in Figure 22-1). You can go ahead and make the estimate, but you should also document the assumptions. Then, if the project unfolds in a way that invalidates the assumptions, you can point back to the estimate assumptions as a basis for revising the estimate.

Tip #104	Document and communicate the assumptions embedded in your estimate.

22.2 Expressing Uncertainty

The key issue in estimate presentation is documenting the estimate's uncertainty in a way that communicates the uncertainty clearly and that also maximizes the chances that the estimate will be used constructively and appropriately. This section describes several ways to communicate uncertainty.

Plus-or-Minus Qualifiers

An estimate with a plus-or-minus qualifier is an estimate such as "6 months, ±2 months" or "$600,000, +$200,000, −$100,000." The plus-or-minus style indicates both the amount and the direction of uncertainty in the estimate. An estimate of 6 months, +1/2 month, −1/2 month says that the estimate is quite accurate and that there's a good chance of meeting the estimate. An estimate of 6 months, +4 months, −1 month says that the estimate isn't very accurate and that there is less chance of meeting the estimate.

When you express an estimate with plus-or-minus qualifiers, consider how large the qualifiers are and what they represent. A typical practice is to make the qualifiers large enough to include one standard deviation on each side of the core estimate. With this approach, you'll still have a 16% chance that the actual result will come in above the top of your estimate and a 16% chance that it will come in below the bottom. If you need to account for more than the 68% probability in the middle of the one-standard-deviation range, use qualifiers that account for more than one standard deviation of variability. (See Table 10-6, "Percentage Confident Based on Use of Standard Deviation," on page 121, for a list of standard deviations and associated probabilities.)

Be sure to consider whether the minus qualifier should be the same as the plus qualifier. If you're dealing with effort or schedule, typically the minus side will be smaller than the plus side for the reasons discussed in Section 1.4, "Estimates as Probability Statements."

A weakness of the plus-or-minus style is that, as the estimate is passed through the organization, it tends to get stripped down to just the core estimate. Occasionally, managers simplify such an estimate out of a desire to ignore the variability implied by the estimate. More often, they simplify the estimate because their manager or their corporate budgeting system can handle only estimates that are expressed as single-point numbers. If you use this technique, be sure you can live with the single-point number that's left after the estimate gets converted to a simplified form.

Risk Quantification

Risk quantification is a combination of plus-or-minus qualifiers and communication of the estimate's assumptions. With risk quantification, you attach specific impacts to specific risks, as shown in Table 22-1.

Table 22-1   Example of an Estimate With Risk Quantification

Estimate: 6 months, +5 months, −1 month	
Impact	**Description of Risk**
+1.5 months	This version needs more than 20% new features compared to Version 2.0
+1 month	Graphics-formatting subsystem delivered later than planned
+1 month	New development tools don't work as well as planned
+1 month	Can't reuse 80% of the database code from the previous version
+0.5 month	Average staff sickness during the summer months instead of less sickness
−0.5 month	All developers assigned 100% by April 1
−0.5 month	New development tools work better than planned

This is a comparatively simple example that focuses only on schedule risks. A more full-fledged example might enumerate major risks to effort and features as well as risks to the schedule. Keep in mind that this technique is an estimate *presentation* technique. The purpose of the technique is to communicate to nontechnical stakeholders that the project presents risks. The point is not to deluge nontechnical stakeholders with detailed risk information. Thus, you should try to focus on rolled-up, large-grained risks.

When you document the sources of uncertainty this way, you provide your project stakeholders with information they can use to reduce the risks to the project, and you lay the groundwork for explaining estimate changes in case any of the risks materialize.

If you're far enough into the project to have made a *commitment*, the risks listed in Table 22-1 might be risks to meeting the commitment rather than risks to the estimate.

This example does not present the generic uncertainty in the project that arises from the Cone of Uncertainty. If you haven't yet made a commitment, you might need to present the Cone-related uncertainty, too.

Tip #105	Be sure you understand whether you're presenting uncertainty in an estimate or uncertainty that affects your ability to meet a commitment.

Confidence Factors

One of the questions that people often ask about a schedule is, "What chance do we have of making this date?" If you use the confidence-factor approach, you can answer that question by providing an estimate that looks like the one in Table 22-2.

Table 22-2   **Example of a Confidence-Factor Estimate**

Delivery Date	Probability of Delivering on or Before the Scheduled Date
January 15	20%
March 1	50%
November 1	80%

You can approximate these confidence intervals by using your "most likely" estimate and the multipliers from Table 4-1, "Estimation Error by Software-Development Activity," on page 39, for the appropriate phase of your project.

As discussed in Chapter 2, "How Good an Estimator Are You?" and throughout the book, avoid presenting highly confident percentages like "90% confident" unless you have a quantitatively derived basis for such a high percentage.

Also, consider whether you really need to present low probability estimates. The fact that a result is remotely possible doesn't mean that you have to put it on the table. I doubt that you're currently presenting the options that are 1% likely or 0.0001% likely. Presenting only those options that are at least 50% likely is a legitimate estimation strategy.

Tip #106	Don't present project outcomes to other project stakeholders that are only remotely possible.

Some people more easily understand data presented in a visual form than in a table form, so you might also consider a more visual presentation, such as the one shown in Figure 22-2.

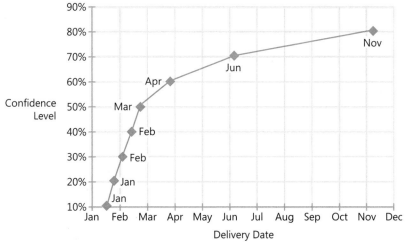

Figure 22-2   Example of presenting percentage-confident estimates in a form that's more visually appealing than a table.

Tip #107	Consider graphic presentation of your estimate as an alternative to text presentation.

Case-Based Estimates

Case-based estimates are a variation on confidence-factor estimates. Present your estimates for best case, worst case, and current case combined with your commitment, or planned case. You can use the gaps between the planned case and the best and worst cases to communicate the degree of variability in the project and the degree of optimism in the plan. If the planned case is much closer to the best case, that implies an optimistic plan. Table 22-3 shows an example of case-based estimates.

Table 22-3   **Example of Case-Based Estimates**

Case	Estimate/Commitment
Best case (estimate)	January 15
Planned case (commitment)	March 1
Current case (estimate)	April 1
Worst case (estimate)	November 1

The relationships between these different dates will be interesting. If the planned case and the best case are the same, and the current case and the worst case are the same, your project is in trouble!

If you use this technique, be prepared to explain to your project's stakeholders what would have to occur for you to achieve the best case or fall into the worst case. They will want to know about both possibilities.

Figure 22-3 provides an example of how you might present similar information visually.

Figure 22-3   Example of presenting case-based estimates in a visual form.

Depending on whether you're managing more to a schedule or to a feature set, the case-based estimate can be expressed in terms of feature delivery instead of dates. Table 22-4 shows an example of how you might present a case-based estimate for features.

Table 22-4   **Example of Case-Based Estimates for Features**

Case	Estimate/Commitment
Best case (estimate)	100% of Level 1 features
	100% of Level 2 features
	100% of Level 3 features
Planned case (commitment)	100% of Level 1 features
	100% of Level 2 features
	50% of Level 3 features
Current case (estimate)	100% of Level 1 features
	80% of Level 2 features
	0% of Level 3 features
Worst case (estimate)	100% of Level 1 features
	20% of Level 2 features
	0% of Level 3 features

Coarse Dates and Time Periods

Try to present your estimate in units that are consistent with the estimate's underlying accuracy. If your estimates are rough, use obviously coarse numbers, such as "We can deliver this in second quarter" or "This project will require 10 staff years," rather than misleadingly precise numbers, such as "We'll deliver this May 21" or "This project will require 15,388 staff hours." Consider using the following:

- Years
- Quarters
- Months
- Weeks

In addition to expressing the message that the estimate is an approximation, the advantage of coarse numbers is that you don't lose information when the estimate is simplified. An estimate of "6 months, +3 months, −1 month" can be simplified to "6 months." An estimate such as "second quarter" is immune to such simplification.

As you work your way into the Cone of Uncertainty, you should be able to tighten up your time units. Early in the Cone you might present your estimate in quarters. Later, when you're creating bottom-up estimates based on effort for individual tasks, you can probably switch to months or weeks and eventually to days.

22.3 Using Ranges (of Any Kind)

As discussed throughout this book, ranges are the most accurate way to reflect the inherent inaccuracy in estimates at various points in the Cone of Uncertainty. You can combine ranges with the other techniques described in this chapter (that is, ranges of coarse time periods, using ranges for a risk-quantified estimate instead of plus-or-minus qualifiers, and so on).

When you present an estimate as a range, consider the following questions:

What level of probability should your range include?   Should it include ±1 standard deviation (68% of possible outcomes), or does the range need to be wider?

How do your company's budgeting and reporting processes deal with ranges?   Be aware that companies' budgeting and reporting processes often won't accept ranges. Ranges are often simplified for reasons that have little to do with software estimation, such as "The company budgeting spreadsheet won't allow me to enter a range." Be sensitive to the restrictions your manager is working under.

Can you live with the midpoint of the range?   Occasionally, a manager will simplify a range by publishing the low end of the range. More often, managers will average the high and low ends and use that if they are not allowed to use a range.

Should you present the full range or only the part of the range from the nominal estimate to the top end of the range?   Projects rarely become smaller over time, and estimates tend to err on the low side. Do you really need to present the low end to high end of your estimate, or should you present only the part of the range from the nominal estimate to the high end?

Can you combine the use of ranges with other techniques?   You might want to consider presenting your estimate as a range and then listing assumptions or quantified risks.

Tip #108	Use an estimate presentation style that reinforces the message you want to communicate about your estimate's accuracy.

Usefulness of Estimates Presented as Ranges

Project stakeholders might think that presenting an estimate as a wide range makes the estimate useless. What's really happening is that presentation of the estimate as a wide range accurately conveys the fact that the estimate *is* useless! It isn't the presentation that makes the estimate useless; it's the uncertainty in the estimate itself. You can't remove the uncertainty from an estimate by presenting it without its uncertainty. You can only ignore the uncertainty, and that's to everyone's detriment.

The two largest professional societies for software developers—the IEEE Computer Society and the Association of Computing Machinery—have jointly decided that software developers have a professional responsibility to include uncertainty in their estimates. Item 3.09 in the IEEE-CS/ACM Software Engineering Code of Ethics reads as follows:

> *Software engineers shall ensure that their products and related modifications meet the highest professional standards possible. In particular, software engineers shall, as appropriate:*
>
> *3.09 Ensure realistic quantitative estimates of cost, scheduling, personnel, quality and outcomes on any project on which they work or propose to work* and provide an uncertainty assessment of these estimates. *[emphasis added]*

Including uncertainty in your estimates isn't just a nicety, in other words. It's part of a software professional's ethical responsibility.

Ranges and Commitments

Sometimes, when stakeholders push back on an estimation range, they're really pushing back on including a range in the commitment. In that case, you can present a wide estimation range and recommend that too much variability still exists in the estimate to support a meaningful commitment.

After you've reduced uncertainty enough to support a commitment, ranges are generally not an appropriate way to express the commitment. An estimation range illustrates what the nature of the commitment is—more or less risky—but the commitment itself should normally be expressed as a single-point number.

Tip #109	Don't try to express a commitment as a range. A commitment needs to be specific.

Additional Resources

Gotterbarn, Don, Keith Miller, and Simon Rogerson. "Computer Society and ACM Approve Software Engineering Code of Ethics," *IEEE Computer*, October 1999, pp. 84–88. Available from *www.computer.org/computer/code-of-ethics.pdf*. This article describes the adoption of the Software Engineering Code of Ethics and provides the full text of the Code.

Chapter 23
Politics, Negotiation, and Problem Solving

Applicability of Techniques in This Chapter

	Principled Negotiation
What's Estimated	Size, Effort, Features, Schedule
Size of Project	S M L
Development Stage	Early–Late
Iterative or Sequential	Both
Accuracy Possible	N/A

Philip Metzger observed decades ago that technical staff were fairly good at estimation but were poor at defending their estimates (Metzger 1981), and I haven't seen much evidence that technical staff have gotten better at defending their estimates in recent years. This chapter describes the reasons for the difficulty of getting an estimate accepted and an approach to help you negotiate estimates successfully.

23.1 Attributes of Executives

One issue in estimate negotiations arises from the personalities of the people doing the negotiating. Technical staff tend to be introverts. About three-quarters of technical staff are introverts, compared with about one-third of the general population (McConnell 2004b). Most technical workers get along with other people fine, but the realm of challenging social interactions is just not their strong suit.

Software negotiations typically occur between technical staff and executives or between technical staff and marketers. Gerald Weinberg points out that marketers and executives are often at least ten years older and more highly placed in the organization than technical staff. Plus, negotiation is part of their job descriptions (Weinberg 1994). In other words, estimate negotiations tend to be between introverted technical staff and seasoned professional negotiators.

With this as background, it's little wonder that technical staff look forward to software estimate negotiations about as much as they look forward to getting their wisdom teeth removed without anesthesia. The factors that make negotiating with executives challenging are not likely to change any time soon. Table 23-1 lists some of these factors.

Table 23-1   Ten Key Characteristics of Software Executives

1. Executives will always ask for what they want.
2. Executives will always probe to get what they want if they don't get it initially.
3. Executives will tend to probe until they discover your point of discomfort.
4. Executives won't always know what's possible, but they will know what would be good for the business if it were possible.
5. Executives will be assertive. That's how they got to be executives in the first place.
6. Executives will respect you when you are being assertive. In fact, they assume you will be assertive if you need to be.
7. Executives want you to operate with the organization's best interests at heart.
8. Executives will want to explore lots of variations to maximize business value.
9. Executives know things about the business, the market, and the company that you don't know, and they may prioritize your project's goals differently than you would.
10. Executives will always want visibility and commitment early (which would indeed have great business value, if it were possible).

For the most part, executives have these characteristics because *it's healthy for the organization for them to have them*. Don't expect these characteristics to change!

Tip #110	Understand that executives are assertive by nature and by job description, and plan your estimation discussions accordingly.

It might well be that estimate negotiations are a part of your job that you don't like much, but nobody ever said you get to enjoy 100% of your job. I've found that simply recognizing that negotiating is not my favorite activity helps me get through the negotiations more constructively.

23.2 Political Influences on Estimates

Several nontechnical factors influence management's response to software estimates.

External Constraints

In many cases management is concerned with significant external influences that require the delivery of the software by a specific date or at a certain cost. There might be an external, immovable deadline (such as the Christmas shopping season, a regulatory compliance date, or a trade show). Similarly, the cost of a project might be influenced by a competitive bidding environment in which management believes that your company won't get the work if it submits a bid high enough to cover your estimate.

The fact that an external requirement exists does not necessarily mean it's possible to meet that requirement. It does mean that you need to make it perfectly clear to the executives you're dealing with that you understand the requirement and that you take it seriously.

Tip #111	Be aware of external influences on the target. Communicate that you understand the business requirements and their importance.

Budgeting and Dates

A consideration for many businesses is that delivery dates tend to be influenced by quarter boundaries. Companies report expenses and revenues based on quarters. Sometimes it's easier to get a later date accepted than an earlier date because of the pressure to force the earlier date into the previous quarter. If you suggest a delivery date of July 15, you might well encounter pressure to deliver on June 30 instead— that is, in second quarter rather than third quarter. If you suggest a delivery date of September 15, a date deep into the third quarter, you might actually find that it's easier to get that delivery date approved than it would be to get the July 15 date accepted because there will be less pressure to push the delivery back into the previous quarter. This stickiness will tend to be even stronger for dates that cross fiscal year boundaries.

Negotiating an Estimate vs. Negotiating a Commitment

In some circumstances, negotiation is appropriate, and in others, it isn't. We don't negotiate questions of fact, such as the surface temperature of the Sun or the total volume of the Great Lakes. We look them up. Similarly, a software estimate is the result of an analytical activity, and it isn't rational to negotiate the estimate. It *is* rational to negotiate the commitment that is related to the estimate. Such a discussion might go something like this:

> TECHNICAL LEAD: *Our estimate for this project is that it will take 5 to 7 months. We're still pretty early in the Cone of Uncertainty, so we can tighten that up as we go.*
>
> EXECUTIVE: *Five to 7 months is too wide a range. How about if we just use an estimate of 5 months?*
>
> TECHNICAL LEAD: *We've found it really useful to distinguish between estimates and commitments. I can't change the estimate, because that's a result of a lot of computations. But I could possibly have my team commit to a delivery schedule of 5 months if we all agree that we want to take on that level of risk.*

EXECUTIVE: *That seems like semantics to me. What's the difference?*

TECHNICAL LEAD: *Our range of 5 to 7 months includes one standard deviation of variation on each side of our 50/50 estimate of 6 months. That means we have about an 84% chance that we'll deliver within 7 months. Our estimates suggest that we have only 16% chance of actually meeting a 5-month commitment.*

EXECUTIVE: *We need more than 50% confidence in the date we commit to, but 84% is more conservative than we need. What would the 75% confident date be?*

TECHNICAL LEAD: *According to the probabilities we estimated, that would be about 6.5 months.*

EXECUTIVE: *Let's commit to that then.*

TECHNICAL LEAD: *That sounds good.*

Many technical personnel view the kind of dialogue described here as a career-limiting move. In my experience, exactly the opposite is true. If you are willing to endure some uncomfortable dialogues—and if you always keep the best interests of your organization in mind—you are engaging in a career-*enhancing* move. The real career-limiting move is to sign up for unsupported, unrealistic commitments and then fail to deliver.

Tip #112	You can negotiate the commitment, but don't negotiate the estimate.

What to Do if Your Estimate Doesn't Get Accepted

Developers and managers sometimes worry that presenting an estimate that's too high will cause the project to be rejected. *That's OK.* Executive management has both the responsibility and the right to decide that a project is not cost-justified. When technical staff low-balls a project estimate, it denies the executives important information they need to make effective decisions, effectively undermining the executive's decision-making authority. This results in diverting company resources from projects that are cost-justified to projects that aren't cost-justified. Good projects aren't supported adequately, and bad projects are supported excessively. The whole scenario is incredibly unhealthy for the business, and it tends to end unpleasantly for the people involved in the projects that should not have been approved in the first place.

Responsibility of Technical Staff to Educate Nontechnical Stakeholders

If you want to ensure the success of your software projects, educate your nontechnical project stakeholders about the costs associated with arbitrarily cutting cost and schedule estimates without making corresponding cuts in the work that needs to be done. Educate them about the Cone of Uncertainty, and about the differences between estimates, targets, and commitments. In my experience, nontechnical stakeholders tend to be very receptive to these ideas when they're presented in the context of trying to do what's best for the organization.

Tip #113	Educate nontechnical stakeholders about effective software estimation practices.

In addition to educating nontechnical stakeholders about software, educating yourself about your business's objectives, priorities, and sensitivities will help support the most constructive estimation discussions possible.

23.3 Problem Solving and Principled Negotiation

In my 1996 book *Rapid Development*, I described estimation discussions as negotiations. As the years have gone by, I have become less and less convinced that negotiation is the most constructive way to view the discussions that occur around estimates of cost, schedule, and functionality.

Negotiation involves parties who have competing interests. The point is to divide a pie between two or more parties. In antagonistic negotiations, each side tries to get as much of the pie as possible, and every bit of pie that one side gets comes at the other side's expense. In collaborative negotiations, each side looks for ways to make the pie larger, but in the end, the pie still gets divided.

In software negotiations, there is no pie to divide. When we're negotiating with sales, marketing, or executives, we're all sitting on the same side of the table. Far from being a case of "they win and we lose," it's a case of "we all win" or "we all lose." Our interests are the same. We either lay the groundwork for the software project to succeed, which is a success for everyone, or we create the conditions for its failure, which is a failure for everyone. Thus, I can no longer see what is being *negotiated* in software estimate discussions.

A better model for the discussions between technical staff, sales, marketing, executives, and other stakeholders is collaborative problem solving. We all work together, share our expertise in different areas, and create a solution that will ultimately work for the best interests of the business.

Tip #114	Treat estimation discussions as problem solving, not negotiation. Recognize that all project stakeholders are on the same side of the table. Everyone wins, or everyone loses.

Once we, the technical staff, recognize that we are problem solving, we create a constructive frame of mind in which to have discussions about targets, estimates, and commitments. The trick now becomes how to get the other stakeholders into that frame of mind.

A Problem-Solving Approach to Negotiation

Even if we know that we are problem solving, the people we're discussing the estimate with might think they are negotiating. People negotiate in many different ways. Some strategies are based on strength of bargaining position, intimidation, friendship, or a desire to gain approval or curry favor. And some strategies rely on deception or other skillful psychological maneuvers.

Because estimation discussions tend to roam between estimates, targets, commitments, and plans, the discussions can't be tidily pigeonholed as pure negotiation or pure problem solving. You'll usually find yourself engaging in some elements of both problem solving and negotiation.

A good strategy that bridges the divide between negotiating and problem solving is the principled-negotiation method described in *Getting to Yes* (Fisher and Ury 1991). The method is called negotiation, but the participants are viewed as problem solvers. This method doesn't rely on negotiating tricks, and it explains how to respond to tricks when others use them. It's based on the idea of creating win-win alternatives. The method works well when only you are using it, and it works even better when the other side is using it too.

The strategy consists of four parts:

- Separate the people from the problem.
- Focus on interests, not positions.
- Invent options for mutual gain.
- Insist on using objective criteria.

Each of these is described in the following sections.

Separate the People from the Problem

Estimate discussions involve people first, interests and positions second. When the stakeholders' personalities are at odds—as, for example, the personalities of technical staff and marketers often are—discussions can get hung up on personality differences.

Begin by understanding the other side's position. Managers can be trapped by their organization's outdated policies. Some organizations fund software projects in ways that are essentially incompatible with the way software is developed. They don't allow managers to ask for funding just to develop the requirements and plans and come up with a good estimate. To get enough funding to do a meaningful estimate, managers have to get funding for the whole project. By the time they get a meaningful estimate, it can be embarrassing or even career-threatening to go back and ask for the right amount of funding. People at the highest levels of such organizations need to better understand software estimation so that they can institute funding practices that support effective software development.

In these discussions, you might think of yourself as an advisor on software estimation, and thereby avoid slipping into the role of adversary. Keep pulling the focus of the discussion back to what is best for the business.

It's also useful to try to take emotions out of the negotiating equation. Sometimes the easiest way to do that is to let the other people blow off steam. Don't react emotionally to their emotions. Invite them to express themselves fully. Say something like, "I can see that those are all serious concerns, and I want to be sure I understand our company's position. What else can you tell me about our business situation?" When they are done explaining, acknowledge what they've told you and reiterate your commitment to find a solution that's good for your organization. The other parts of principled negotiation will help you to follow through on that commitment.

Tip #115	Attack the problem, not the people.

Focus on Interests, Not Positions

Suppose you're selling your car in order to buy a new boat, and you've figured that you need to get $10,000 for your car to buy the boat you want. A prospective buyer approaches you and offers $9,000. You say, "There's no way I can part with this car for less than $10,000." The buyer says, "I can go to $9,000, but that's my limit."

When you negotiate in this way, you focus on positions rather than interests. Positions are bargaining statements that are so narrow that in order for one person to win, the other person has to lose.

Now suppose that the car buyer says, "I really can't go over $9,000, but I happen to know that you're in the market for a new boat, and I happen to be the regional distributor for a big boat company. I can get the boat you want for $2,000 less than you can get it from any dealer. Now what do you think about my offer?" Well, now the offer sounds pretty good because it will leave you with $1,000 more than you would have gotten if the buyer had just agreed to the price of your opening position.

Underlying interests are broader than bargaining positions, and focusing on them opens up a world of negotiating possibilities. Consider the following scenario:

EXECUTIVE: *We need Giga-Blat 4.0 in 6 months.*

TECHNICAL LEAD: *We've estimated the project carefully. Unfortunately, our estimates show that we can't deliver it in less than 8 months.*

EXECUTIVE: *That's not good enough. We really need it in 6 months.*

TECHNICAL LEAD: *Do we really need all the functionality that's currently required? If we could cut enough functionality, we could deliver it in 6 months.*

EXECUTIVE: *We can't cut functionality. We've already cut features to the bone on this release. We need all the features, and we need them within 6 months.*

TECHNICAL LEAD: *What's the major factor that's driving the 6-month schedule? Maybe we can find a creative solution.*

EXECUTIVE: *The annual trade show for our industry is in 6 months. If we miss the trade show, we've missed our chance to demo the software to many of our key accounts. That will effectively push back our sales cycle by a whole year.*

TECHNICAL LEAD: *I really can't commit to delivering the final software in time for the trade show. But I can commit to having a beta version ready for the trade show, and I can provide a tester who knows where all the problems are and who can run the software during the show so that it doesn't break. How does that sound?*

EXECUTIVE: *If you can promise the software won't crash, that will work fine.*

TECHNICAL LEAD: *No problem.*

One major difference between typical negotiating and problem solving via discussion of interests is that negotiations tend to get frozen into positions. The turning point in this dialogue came when the technical lead asked, "What's the major factor that's driving the six-month schedule?" That switched the dialogue from arguing about positions to trying to understand the company's interests and solve the underlying business problem.. When you focus on interests, you're more likely to find a win-win solution.

Invent Options for Mutual Gain

Your most powerful negotiating ally in estimate discussions is not your estimate; it's your ability to generate *planning options* that nontechnical stakeholders have no way of knowing about. You hold the key to a vault of technical knowledge, and that puts the responsibility for generating creative solutions more on your shoulders than anyone else's. It's your role to propose the full range of possibilities and tradeoffs.

Table 23-2 lists some of the planning options you might suggest to break a logjam in your discussion.

Table 23-2 Planning Options That Might Help Break a Discussion Deadlock

Feature-Related Options

- Move some of the desired functionality into version 2. Few people need all of what they asked for exactly when they asked for it.
- Use an iterative approach. Deliver the software in versions 0.2, 0.4, 0.6, 0.8, and 1.0, with the most important functionality coming first.
- Cut features altogether, with an emphasis on cutting the features that are most expensive.
- Use t-shirt sizing to focus on delivering the features with the highest net business value.
- Polish some features less. Implement them to some degree, but make them less fancy.
- Relax the detailed requirements for each feature. Define your mission as getting as close as possible to the requirements through the use of existing components.
- Build a feature-oriented Cone of Uncertainty. Define some features as "definitely in," some as "definitely out," and some as "possible." Propose a plan for tightening up the Feature Cone of Uncertainty as the project progresses.

Resource-Related Options

- Add more developers or testers, if it's early in the schedule.
- Add contract staff, if it's early in the project.
- Add higher-output technical staff (for example, subject-area experts or more senior developers).
- Add more administrative support.
- Increase the degree of developer support.
- Increase the level of end-user or customer involvement. Devote a full-time end-user to the project who is authorized to make binding decisions about the software's features.
- Increase the level of executive involvement to speed decision making.
- Suggest that another team do part of the work (but watch out for the extra integration issues this will create).
- Assign resources 100% to the project. Don't divide their attention between the new project and an old project or between multiple new projects.

Schedule-Related Options

- Provide an "estimate road map" that maps out a plan for reestimating and tightening up the estimates.
- Use estimation ranges or coarse estimates and refine them as the project progresses.
- Look for ways to plan toward specific cost, schedule, or feature goals as you refine the requirements and plans.
- Agree to delay making a specific commitment until you complete the next phase of the project (that is, the work required to narrow the Cone of Uncertainty).
- Do one or two short iterations to calibrate productivity, and then make a commitment based on the team's actual productivity.

The key is to prevent a shouting match like this one: *I can't do it.* "Yes you can." *No I can't.* "Can!" *Can't!* Lay out a set of options, and focus your discussion on those options. Don't include impossible options in the set you present. Avoid saying, "No, I can't do that"; instead, redirect the discussion toward what you can do. The more options you generate that support doing what's best for the organization, the easier it will be to show that you're on the same side of the table as the person you're problem solving with.

Tip #116	Generate as many planning options as you can to support your organization's goals.

One warning: In the cooperative, brainstorming atmosphere that arises from the free-wheeling problem-solving discussion, it's easy to agree to a solution that seems like a good idea at the time but by the next morning seems like a bad deal. The cautions in Section 4.8, "Off-the-Cuff Estimates," apply to this situation. Don't make any hard commitments to new options until you've had enough time to analyze them quietly by yourself.

Tip #117	As you foster an atmosphere of collaborative problem solving, don't make any commitments based on off-the-cuff estimates.

Insist on Using Objective Criteria

One of the oddest aspects of our business is that when careful estimation produces estimates that are notably larger than desired, the customer or manager will often simply disregard the estimate (Jones 1994). He or she might do that even when the estimate comes from an estimation tool or an outside estimation expert and even when the organization has a history of overrunning its estimates. Questioning an estimate is a valid and useful practice. Throwing it out the window and replacing it with wishful thinking is not.

When principled negotiation is infused with problem solving, you seek "a wise agreement as judged by any objective standard." You can reason with the other people about which objective standards are most appropriate, and you keep an open mind about standards they suggest. Most important, you don't yield to pressure, only to principle. To support discussions based on principle, it's important to recognize who is the most sensible owner for each specific part of the discussion.

Technical Staff and Technical Management Own the *Estimate*

You are in the best position to understand the technical scope of work and to create the estimates for it. Therefore, you should be the primary authority on the estimates.

Nontechnical Stakeholders Own the *Target*

Executives and sales and marketing people are usually in the best position to understand the needs and priorities of the business. Therefore, they should be the primary authorities on the business targets.

Technical Staff and Nontechnical Staff Jointly Own the *Commitment*

The commitment is where the targets and the estimates must ultimately be resolved. If you can reach agreement that you are the authority for the estimate and other stakeholders are the authority for the targets, most of the discussion will then naturally focus on the commitment. The overriding principle should be to reach agreement about what commitment will be best for the organization.

During these discussions, keep the following points in mind:

Don't negotiate the estimate itself   Clarify the difference between the estimate and the commitment. Keep moving the discussion back toward making a commitment that's in the organization's best interests.

Insist that the estimate be prepared by a qualified party   The most qualified estimator will often be you. In other cases, the qualified party might be an independent estimation group. Those groups are effective because they do not have a vested interest either in delivering the software in the shortest possible time or in avoiding hard work. If discussions become deadlocked on the topic of the estimate itself, propose submitting the estimate to a third party and pledge to accept the results. Ask other parties in the discussion to agree to do the same.

A variation on this theme is to bring in a consultant or outside expert to review your schedule. An unfamiliar expert sometimes has more credibility than a familiar one. Some organizations have also had success using software estimation tools. They've found that once technical staff calibrate the estimation tool for a specific project, the tool allows them to easily and objectively explore the effects of different options in an unbiased way.

Refer to your organization's standardized estimation procedure   You can avoid arguing about who creates the estimate most of the time if you've previously adopted a standardized estimation procedure. It's then easy to say, "Our procedure doesn't allow us to negotiate the estimate itself. Let's talk about the assumptions in the estimate (like project size) and the level of risk that it makes sense for the organization to take on in the commitment for this project."

Weather the storm   Although people have different tolerances for withstanding pressure, if your customers, managers, marketers, or other stakeholders want you to commit to impossible goals, I think the best approach is to politely and firmly stand by your principles. Batten down the hatches and endure the thunderstorm of an unwelcome estimate early in the project rather than the hurricane of schedule slips and cost overruns later.

No one really benefits from pretending that impossible goals can be met, even though sometimes people think they do. Improve your credibility by pushing for solutions that respond to the real business needs of your bosses and customers. Provide predictability and improve your organization's ability to meet its commitments.

Tip #118	Resolve discussion deadlocks by returning to the question of, "What will be best for our organization?"

Additional Resources

Fisher, Roger, William Ury, and Bruce Patton. *Getting to Yes, Second Edition.* New York, NY: Penguin Books, 1991. This book lays out the details of the principled negotiation strategy described in this chapter. The book is packed with memorable anecdotes and makes for interesting reading even if you're not very interested in negotiation.

Appendix A
Estimate Sanity Check

The following sanity check indicates how useful your current project estimate is likely to be in managing your project. For each Yes answer, give the estimate one point.

Yes

____ 1. Was a standardized procedure used to create the estimate?

____ 2. Was the estimation process free from pressure that would bias the results?

____ 3. If the estimate was negotiated, were only the inputs to the estimate negotiated, not the outputs or the estimation process itself?

____ 4. Is the estimate expressed with precision that matches its accuracy? (For example, is the estimate expressed as a range or coarse number if it's early in the project?)

____ 5. Was the estimate created using multiple techniques that converged to similar results?

____ 6. Is the productivity assumption underlying the estimate comparable to productivity actually experienced on past projects of similar sizes?

____ 7. Is the estimated schedule at least $2.0 \times \text{StaffMonths}^{1/3}$? (That is, is the estimate outside of the Impossible Zone?)

____ 8. Were the people who are going to do the work involved in creating the estimate?

____ 9. Has the estimate been reviewed by an expert estimator?

____ 10. Does the estimate include a nonzero allowance for the impact that project risks will have on effort and schedule?

____ 11. Is the estimate part of a series of estimates that will become more accurate as the project moves into the narrow part of the cone of uncertainty?

____ 12. Are *all* elements of the project included in the estimate, including creation of setup program, creation of data conversion utilities, cutover from old system to new system, etc.?

____ **TOTAL (see the next page for scoring information)**

Scoring

Scores of 10–12 indicate estimates that should be highly accurate. Scores of 7–9 indicate estimates that are good enough to provide project guidance but that are probably optimistic. Scores of 6 or below indicate estimates that are subject to significant bias, optimism, or both, and are not accurate enough to provide meaningful guidance to managing a project.

Answers to Chapter 2 Quiz, "How Good an Estimator Are You?"

Item	Answer
Surface temperature of the Sun	10,000°F/ 6,000°C
Latitude of Shanghai	31 degrees North
Area of the Asian continent	17,139,000 square miles
	44,390,000 square kilometers
The year of Alexander the Great's birth	356 BC
Total value of U.S. currency in circulation in 2004	$719.9 billion*
Total volume of the Great Lakes	5,500 cubic miles
	23,000 cubic kilometers
	2.4 x 10^22 cubic feet
	6.8 x 10^20 cubic meters
	1.8 x 10^23 U.S. gallons
	6.8 x 10^23 liters
Worldwide box office receipts for the movie *Titanic*	$1.835 billion*
Total length of the coastline of the Pacific Ocean	84,300 miles
	135,663 kilometers
Number of book titles published in the U.S. since 1776	22 million
Heaviest blue whale ever recorded	380,000 pounds
	190 English tons
	170,000 kilograms
	170 metric tons

* Billions are U.S. billions (that is, 10^9) rather than British billions (10^12)..

Appendix C
Software Estimation Tips

Chapter 1

Tip #1	Distinguish between estimates, targets, and commitments.

Tip #2	When you're asked to provide an estimate, determine whether you're supposed to be estimating or figuring out how to hit a target.

Tip #3	When you see a single-point "estimate," ask whether the number is an estimate or whether it's really a target.

Tip #4	When you see a single-point estimate, that number's probability is not 100%. Ask what the probability of that number is.

Chapter 2

Tip #5	Don't provide "percentage confident" estimates (especially "90% confident") unless you have a quantitatively derived basis for doing so.

Tip #6	Avoid using artificially narrow ranges. Be sure the ranges you use in your estimates don't misrepresent your confidence in your estimates.

Tip #7	If you are feeling pressure to make your ranges narrower, verify that the pressure actually is coming from an external source and not from yourself.

Chapter 3

Tip #8	Don't intentionally underestimate. The penalty for underestimation is more severe than the penalty for overestimation. Address concerns about overestimation through planning and control, not by biasing your estimates.

Tip #9	Recognize a mismatch between a project's business target and a project's estimate for what it is: valuable risk information that the project might not be successful. Take corrective action early, when it can do some good.

Tip #10	Many businesses value predictability more than development time, cost, or flexibility. Be sure you understand what your business values the most.

Chapter 4

Tip #11	Consider the effect of the Cone of Uncertainty on the accuracy of your estimate. Your estimate cannot have more accuracy than is possible at your project's current position within the Cone.

Tip #12	Don't assume that the Cone of Uncertainty will narrow itself. You must force the Cone to narrow by removing sources of variability from your project.

Tip #13	Account for the Cone of Uncertainty by using predefined uncertainty ranges in your estimates.

Tip #14	Account for the Cone of Uncertainty by having one person create the "how much" part of the estimate and a different person create the "how uncertain" part of the estimate.

Tip #15	Don't expect better estimation practices alone to provide more accurate estimates for chaotic projects. You can't accurately estimate an out-of-control process.

Tip #16	To deal with unstable requirements, consider project control strategies instead of or in addition to estimation strategies.

Tip #17	Include time in your estimates for stated requirements, implied requirements, and nonfunctional requirements—that is, *all* requirements. Nothing can be built for free, and your estimates shouldn't imply that it can.

| **Tip #18** | Include all necessary software-development activities in your estimates, not just coding and testing. |

| **Tip #19** | On projects that last longer than a few weeks, include allowances for overhead activities such as vacations, sick days, training days, and company meetings. |

| **Tip #20** | Don't reduce developer estimates—they're probably too optimistic already. |

| **Tip #21** | Avoid having "control knobs" on your estimates. While control knobs might give you a feeling of better accuracy, they usually introduce subjectivity and degrade actual accuracy. |

| **Tip #22** | Don't give off-the-cuff estimates. Even a 15-minute estimate will be more accurate. |

| **Tip #23** | Match the number of significant digits in your estimate (its precision) to your estimate's accuracy. |

Chapter 5

| **Tip #24** | Invest an appropriate amount of effort assessing the size of the software that will be built. The size of the software is the single most significant contributor to project effort and schedule. |

| **Tip #25** | Don't assume that effort scales up linearly as project size does. Effort scales up exponentially. |

| **Tip #26** | Use software estimation tools to compute the impact of diseconomies of scale. |

| **Tip #27** | If you've completed previous projects that are about the same size as the project you're estimating—defined as being within a factor of 3 from largest to smallest—you can safely use a ratio-based estimating approach, such as lines of code per staff month, to estimate your new project. |

| Tip #28 | Factor the kind of software you develop into your estimate. The kind of software you're developing is the second-most significant contributor to project effort and schedule. |

Chapter 6

| Tip #29 | When choosing estimation techniques, consider what you want to estimate, the size of the project, the development stage, the project's development style, and what accuracy you need. |

Chapter 7

| Tip #30 | *Count* if at all possible. *Compute* when you can't count. Use *judgment* alone only as a last resort. |

| Tip #31 | Look for something you can count that is a meaningful measure of the scope of work in your environment. |

| Tip #32 | Collect historical data that allows you to compute an estimate from a count. |

| Tip #33 | Don't discount the power of simple, coarse estimation models such as average effort per defect, average effort per Web page, average effort per story, and average effort per use case. |

| Tip #34 | Avoid using expert judgment to tweak an estimate that has been derived through computation. Such "expert judgment" usually degrades the estimate's accuracy. |

Chapter 8

| Tip #35 | Use historical data as the basis for your productivity assumptions. Unlike mutual fund disclosures, your organization's past performance really is your best indicator of future performance. |

| Tip #36 | Use historical data to help avoid politically charged estimation discussions arising from assumptions like "My team is below average." |

| **Tip #37** | In collecting historical data to use for estimation, start small, be sure you understand what you're collecting, and collect the data consistently. |

| **Tip #38** | Collect a project's historical data *as soon as possible* after the end of the project. |

| **Tip #39** | As a project is underway, collect historical data on a periodic basis so that you can build a data-based profile of how your projects run. |

| **Tip #40** | Use data from your current project (project data) to create highly accurate estimates for the remainder of the project. |

| **Tip #41** | Use project data or historical data rather than industry-average data to calibrate your estimates whenever possible. In addition to making your estimates more accurate, historical data will reduce variability in your estimate arising from uncertainty in the productivity assumptions. |

| **Tip #42** | If you don't currently have historical data, begin collecting it as soon as possible. |

Chapter 9

| **Tip #43** | To create the task-level estimates, have the people who will actually do the work create the estimates. |

| **Tip #44** | Create both Best Case and Worst Case estimates to stimulate thinking about the full range of possible outcomes. |

| **Tip #45** | Use an estimation checklist to improve your individual estimates. Develop and maintain your own personal checklist to improve your estimation accuracy. |

| **Tip #46** | Compare actual performance to estimated performance so that you can improve your individual estimates over time. |

Chapter 10

| **Tip #47** | Decompose large estimates into small pieces so that you can take advantage of the Law of Large Numbers: the errors on the high side and the errors on the low side cancel each other out to some degree. |

| **Tip #48** | Use a generic software-project work breakdown structure (WBS) to avoid omitting common activities. |

| **Tip #49** | Use the simple standard deviation formula to compute meaningful aggregate Best Case and Worst Case estimates for estimates containing 10 tasks or fewer. |

| **Tip #50** | Use the complex standard deviation formula to compute meaningful aggregate Best Case and Worst Case estimates when you have about 10 tasks or more. |

| **Tip #51** | Don't divide the range from best case to worst case by 6 to obtain standard deviations for individual task estimates. Choose a divisor based on the accuracy of your estimation ranges. |

| **Tip #52** | Focus on making your Expected Case estimates accurate. If the individual estimates are accurate, aggregation will not create problems. If the individual estimates are not accurate, aggregation will be problematic until you find a way to make them accurate. |

Chapter 11

| **Tip #53** | Estimate new projects by comparing them to similar past projects, preferably decomposing the estimate into at least five pieces. |

| **Tip #54** | Do not address estimation uncertainty by biasing the estimate. Address uncertainty by expressing the estimate in uncertain terms. |

Chapter 12

| **Tip #55** | Use fuzzy logic to estimate program size in lines of code. |

| Tip #56 | Consider using standard components as a low-effort technique to estimate size in a project's early stages. |

| Tip #57 | Use story points to obtain an early estimate of an iterative project's effort and schedule that is based on data from the same project. |

| Tip #58 | Exercise caution when calculating estimates that use numeric ratings scales. Be sure that the numeric categories in the scale actually work like numbers, not like verbal categories such as small, medium, and large. |

| Tip #59 | Use t-shirt sizing to help nontechnical stakeholders rule features in or out while the project is in the wide part of the Cone of Uncertainty. |

| Tip #60 | Use proxy-based techniques to estimate test cases, defects, pages of user documentation, and other quantities that are difficult to estimate directly. |

| Tip #61 | Count whatever is easiest to count and provides the most accuracy in your environment, collect calibration data on that, and then use that data to create estimates that are well-suited to your environment. |

Chapter 13

| Tip #62 | Use group reviews to improve estimation accuracy. |

| Tip #63 | Use Wideband Delphi for early-in-the-project estimates, for unfamiliar systems, and when several diverse disciplines will be involved in the project itself. |

Chapter 14

| Tip #64 | Use an estimation software tool to sanity-check estimates created by manual methods. Larger projects should rely more heavily on commercial estimation software. |

| Tip #65 | Don't treat the output of a software estimation tool as divine revelation. Sanity-check estimation tool outputs just as you would other estimates. |

Chapter 15

| Tip #66 | Use multiple estimation techniques, and look for convergence or spread among the results. |

| Tip #67 | If different estimation techniques produce different results, try to find the factors that are making the results different. Continue reestimating until the different techniques produce results that converge to within about 5%. |

| Tip #68 | If multiple estimates agree and the business target disagrees, trust the estimates. |

Chapter 16

| Tip #69 | Don't debate the output of an estimate. Take the output as a given. Change the output only by changing the inputs and recomputing. |

| Tip #70 | Focus on estimating size first. Then compute effort, schedule, cost, and features from the size estimate. |

| Tip #71 | Reestimate. |

| Tip #72 | Change from less accurate to more accurate estimation approaches as you work your way through a project. |

| Tip #73 | When you are ready to hand out specific development task assignments, switch to bottom-up estimation. |

| Tip #74 | When you reestimate in response to a missed deadline, base the new estimate on the project's actual progress, not on the project's planned progress. |

| Tip #75 | Present your estimates in a way that allows you to tighten up your estimates as you move further into the project. |

| Tip #76 | Communicate your plan to reestimate to other project stakeholders *in advance*. |

Chapter 17

Tip #77	Develop a Standardized Estimation Procedure at the organizational level; use it at the project level.

Tip #78	Coordinate your Standardized Estimation Procedure with your SDLC.

Tip #79	Review your projects' estimates and estimation process so that you can improve the accuracy of your estimates and minimize the effort required to create them.

Chapter 18

Tip #80	Use lines of code to estimate size, but remember both the general limitations of simple measures and the specific hazards of the LOC measure in.

Tip #81	Count function points to obtain an accurate early-in-the-project size estimate.

Tip #82	Use the Dutch Method of counting function points to attain a low-cost ballpark estimate early in the project.

Tip #83	Use GUI elements to obtain a low-effort ballpark estimate in the wide part of the Cone of Uncertainty.

Tip #84	With better estimation methods, the size estimate becomes the foundation of all other estimates. The size of the system you're building is the single largest cost driver. Use multiple size-estimation techniques to make your size estimate accurate.

Chapter 19

Tip #85	Use software tools based on the science of estimation to most accurately compute effort estimates from your size estimates.

Tip #86	Use industry-average effort graphs to obtain rough effort estimates in the wide part of the Cone of Uncertainty. For larger projects, remember that more powerful estimation techniques are easily cost-justified.

| Tip #87 | Use the ISBSG method to compute a rough effort estimate. Combine it with other methods, and look for convergence or spread among the different estimates. |

| Tip #88 | Not all estimation methods are equal. When looking for convergence or spread among estimates, give more weight to the techniques that tend to produce the most accurate results. |

Chapter 20

| Tip #89 | Use the Basic Schedule Equation to estimate schedule early in medium-to-large projects. |

| Tip #90 | Use the Informal Comparison to Past Projects formula to estimate schedule early in a small-to-large project. |

| Tip #91 | Use Jones's First-Order Estimation Practice to produce a low-accuracy (but very low-effort) schedule estimate early in a project. |

| Tip #92 | Do not shorten a schedule estimate without increasing the effort estimate. |

| Tip #93 | Do not shorten a nominal schedule more than 25%. In other words, keep your estimates out of the Impossible Zone. |

| Tip #94 | Reduce costs by lengthening the schedule and conducting the project with a smaller team. |

| Tip #95 | For medium-sized business-systems projects (35,000 to 100,000 lines of code) avoid increasing the team size beyond 7 people. |

| Tip #96 | Use schedule estimation to ensure your plans are plausible. Use detailed planning to produce the final schedule. |

| Tip #97 | Remove the results of overly generic estimation techniques from your data set before you look for convergence or spread among your estimates. |

Chapter 21

Tip #98	When allocating project effort across different activities, consider project size, project type, and the kinds of effort contained in the calibration data used to create your initial rolled-up estimate.

Tip #99	Consider your project's size, type, and development approach in allocating schedule to different activities.

Tip #100	Use industry-average data or your historical data to estimate the number of defects your project will produce.

Tip #101	Use defect-removal-rate data to estimate the number of defects that your quality assurance practices will remove from your software before it is released.

Tip #102	Use your project's total Risk Exposure (RE) as the starting point for buffer planning. Review the details of your project's specific risks to understand whether you should ultimately plan for a buffer that's larger or smaller than the total RE.

Tip #103	Planning and estimation are related, and planning is a much bigger topic than can be addressed in one chapter in a book that focuses on software estimation. Read the literature on planning.

Chapter 22

Tip #104	Document and communicate the assumptions embedded in your estimate.

Tip #105	Be sure you understand whether you're presenting uncertainty in an estimate or uncertainty that affects your ability to meet a commitment.

Tip #106	Don't present project outcomes to other project stakeholders that are only remotely possible.

Tip #107	Consider graphic presentation of your estimate as an alternative to text presentation.

| **Tip #108** | Use an estimate presentation style that reinforces the message you want to communicate about your estimate's accuracy. |

| **Tip #109** | Don't try to express a commitment as a range. A commitment needs to be specific. |

Chapter 23

| **Tip #110** | Understand that executives are assertive by nature and by job description, and plan your estimation discussions accordingly. |

| **Tip #111** | Be aware of external influences on the target. Communicate that you understand the business requirements and their importance. |

| **Tip #112** | You can negotiate the commitment, but don't negotiate the estimate. |

| **Tip #113** | Educate nontechnical stakeholders about effective software estimation practices. |

| **Tip #114** | Treat estimation discussions as problem solving, not negotiation. Recognize that all project stakeholders are on the same side of the table. Everyone wins, or everyone loses. |

| **Tip #115** | Attack the problem, not the people. |

| **Tip #116** | Generate as many planning options as you can to support your organization's goals. |

| **Tip #117** | As you foster an atmosphere of collaborative problem solving, don't make any commitments based on off-the-cuff estimates. |

| **Tip #118** | Resolve discussion deadlocks by returning to the question of, "What will be best for our organization?" |

Bibliography

Abdel-Hamid, T., and S. Madnick, 1986. "Impact of Schedule Estimation on Software Project Behavior," *IEEE Software*, 3, 4 (July 1986), pp. 70–75.

Albrecht, Allan J., 1979. "Measuring Application Development Productivity," *Proceedings of the Joint SHARE/GUIDE/IBM Application Development Symposium, October 1979*: 83–92.

Albrecht, A., and J. Gaffney, "Software Function, Source Lines of Code, and Development Effort Prediction: A Software Science Validation," *IEEE Transactions on Software Engineering*, SE-9 (6), 1983, pp. 639–648.

Armour, Phillip, 2002. "Ten Unmyths of Project Estimation," *Communications of the ACM*, November 2002, pp. 15–18.

Armstrong, J. Scott, ed., 2001. *Principles of forecasting: A handbook for researchers and practitioners.* Boston, MA: Kluwer Academic Publishers.

Arnone, Michael, 2005. "Azmi: Sentinel Won't Repeat Mistakes," *Federal Computer Week*, September 13, 2005.

Associated Press, 2003. "Boston's 'Big Dig' Opens to Public: Tunnel Project Is Five Years Behind Schedule, Billions Over Budget," MSNBC.com, December 20, 2003.

Baker, F. Terry, 1972. "Chief Programmer Team Management of Production Programming," *IBM Systems Journal*, vol. 11, no. 1, 1972, pp. 56–73.

Basili, V. R., and B. T. Perricone, 1984. "Software Errors and Complexity: An Empirical Investigation," *Communications of the ACM,* v. 27, 1984, pp. 42–52.

Bastani, Farokh, and Sitharama Iyengar, 1987. "The Effect of Data Structures on the Logical Complexity of Programs," *Communications of the ACM*, vol. 30, no. 3, pp. 250–259.

Beck, Kent, and Martin Fowler, 2001. *Planning Extreme Programming*, Boston, MA: Addison-Wesley.

Beck, Kent, 2004. *Extreme Programming Explained: Embrace Change*, 2d ed., Reading, MA: Addison-Wesley.

Bentley, Jon, 2000. *Programming Pearls*, 2d ed., Reading, MA: Addison-Wesley.

Boehm, Barry, and Richard Turner, 2004. *Balancing Agility and Discipline: A Guide for the Perplexed*, Boston, MA: Addison-Wesley.

Boehm, Barry, et al., 1995. "Cost Models for Future Software Life Cycle Processes: COCOMO 2.0," *Annals of Software Engineering, Special Volume on Software Process and Product Measurement*, J.D. Arthur and S.M. Henry Eds., Amsterdam, Netherlands: J.C. Baltzer AG, Science Publishers.

Boehm, Barry W., and Philip N. Papaccio, 1988. "Understanding and Controlling Software Costs," *IEEE Transactions on Software Engineering,* v. 14, no. 10, October 1988, pp. 1462–1477.

Boehm, Barry W., 1981. *Software Engineering Economics*, Englewood Cliffs, NJ: Prentice Hall.

Boehm, Barry W., 1987b. "Industrial software metrics top 10 list," *IEEE Software*, vol. 4, no. 9 (September 1987), pp. 84–85.

Boehm, Barry W., T. E. Gray, and T. Seewaldt, 1984. "Prototyping versus specifying: A multiproject experiment," *IEEE Transactions on Software Engineering*, vol. SE-10 (May 1984), pp. 290–303.

Boehm, Barry, et al., 2000. *Software Cost Estimation with Cocomo II*, Reading, MA: Addison-Wesley.

Brooks, Frederick P., Jr., 1975. *The Mythical Man-Month*, Reading MA: Addison-Wesley.

Brooks, Frederick P., Jr., 1995. *The Mythical Man-Month: Essays on Software Engineering, Anniversary Edition (2d Ed)*, Reading, MA: Addison-Wesley.

Car and Driver, 2004. "2005 Charting the Changes—BMW," *Car and Driver*, October 2004.

Card, David N., 1987. "A Software Technology Evaluation Program," *Information And Software Technology*, v. 29, no. 6, July/August 1987, pp. 291–300.

Cockburn, Alistair, 2001. *Agile Software Development*, Boston, MA: Addison-Wesley.

Cohn, Mike, 2005. *Agile Estimating and Planning*, Upper Saddle River, NJ: Prentice Hall PTR.

Conte, S. D., H. E. Dunsmore, and V. Y. Shen, 1986. *Software Engineering Metrics and Models*, Menlo Park, CA: Benjamin/Cummings.

Coombs, Paul, 2003. *IT Project Estimation: A Practical Guide to the Costing of Software*, Cambridge, United Kingdom: Cambridge Univeristy Press. This book is a short, conversational discussion of estimation. It is written mainly from the point of view of the author's personal experience and focuses roughly half on what I refer to "estimation" and half on what I refer to as "planning."

Cooper, Robert G., 2001. *Winning at New Products: Accelerating the Process from Idea to Launch*, New York, NY: Perseus Books Group.

Costello, Scott H., 1984. "Software engineering under deadline pressure," *ACM Sigsoft Software Engineering Notes*, 9:5 October 1984, pp. 15–19.

Crosstalk, June 2002. The whole issue of this magazine is devoted to the topic of cost estimation.

Crosstalk, April 2005. The whole issue of this magazine is devoted to the topic of cost estimation.

Curtis, Bill, 1981. "Substantiating Programmer Variability," *Proceedings of the IEEE*, vol. 69, no. 7, p. 846.

Curtis, Bill, et al., 1986. "Software Psychology: The Need for an Interdisciplinary Program," *Proceedings of the IEEE*, vol. 74, no. 8 (August 1986), pp. 1092–1106.

Cusumano, Michael, and Richard W. Selby, 1995. *Microsoft Secrets*, New York, NY: The Free Press.

Cusumano, Michael, et al., 2003. "Software Development Worldwide: The State of the Practice," *IEEE Software*, November/December 2003, pp. 28–34.

Davis, John Stephen, and Richard J. LeBlanc, 1988. "A Study of the Applicability of Complexity Measures," *IEEE Transactions on Software Engineering*, v. 14, no. 9, September 1988, pp. 1366–1372.

DeMarco, Tom, and Timothy Lister, 1985. "Programmer Performance and the Effects of the Workplace," in *Proceedings of the 8th International Conference on Software Engineering*, August 1985, pp. 268–272.

DeMarco, Tom, and Timothy Lister, 1999. *Peopleware: Productive Projects and Teams*, 2d ed., New York, NY: Dorset House.

DeMarco, Tom, and Timothy Lister, 2003. *Waltzing with Bears: Managing Risk on Software Projects*, New York, NY: Dorset House.

DeMarco, Tom, 1982. *Controlling Software Projects*, New York, NY: Yourdon Press.

Evangelist, Michael, 1984. "Program Complexity and Programming Style," *Proc. 1st Int. Conf. Data Engineering*, New York, NY: IEEE Computer Society Press, 534–541.

Fenton, Norman E., and Shari Lawrence Pfleeger, 1997. *Software Metrics: A Rigorous and Practical Approach*, Boston, MA: PWS Publishing Company.

Fisher, Roger, William Ury, and Bruce Patton, 1991. *Getting to Yes*, 2d ed., New York, NY: Penguin Books.

Gaffney, John. E., Jr., and Richard Werling, 1991. "Estimating Software Size from Counts of Externals, A Generalization of Function Points," Herndon, VA: Software Productivity Consortium document number SPC-91094-N.

Garmus, David, and David Herron, 2001. *Function Point Analysis: Measurement Practices for Successful Software Projects*, Boston, MA: Addison-Wesley.

Gilb, Tom, 1988. *Principles of Software Engineering Management*, Wokingham, England: Addison-Wesley.

Gilb, Tom, 2005. *Competitive Engineering: A Handbook for Systems Engineering, Requirements Engineering, an dSoftware Engineering Using Planguage*, Amsterdam, Netherlands: Elsevier.

Glass, Robert L., 1994, "IS Field: Stress Up, Satisfaction Down," *Software Practitioner*, Nov. 1994, pp. 1, 3.

Goldratt, Eliyahu M., 1997. *Critical Chain*, Great Barrington, MA: The North River Press.

Gorla, N., A. C. Benander, and B. A. Benander, 1990. "Debugging Effort Estimation Using Software Metrics," *IEEE Transactions on Software Engineering*, v. 16, no. 2, February 1990, pp. 223–231.

Gotterbarn, Don, Keith Miller, and Simon Rogerson. "Computer Society and ACM Approve Software Engineering Code of Ethics," *IEEE Computer*, October 1999, pp. 84–88. *Available from* www.computer.org/computer/code-of-ethics.pdf.

Grady, Robert B., 1992. *Practical Software Metrics For Project Management And Process Improvement*, Englewood Cliffs, NJ: Prentice Hall PTR.

Grady, Robert B., and Deborah L. Caswell, 1987. *Software Metrics: Establishing a Company-Wide Program*, Englewood Cliffs, NJ: Prentice Hall.

Gross, Neil, et al. "Software Hell," *Business Week*, Nov. 6, 1999, pp. 104ff.

Harvey, N., 2001. "Improving Judgment in Forecasting" in *Principles of forecasting: A handbook for researchers and practitioners*, Ed., J. S. Armstrong, Boston, MA: Kluwer Academic Publishers, pp. 59–80.

Heemstra, F. J. and R. J. Kusters, 1991. "Function Point Analysis: Evaluation of a Software Cost Estimation Model," *European Journal of Information Systems* 1(4): 223–237.

Heemstra, F.J., W.J.A. Siskens, and H. van der Stelt, 1989. "Kostenbeheersing Bij Automatiseringsprojecten: Een Empirisch Onderzoek," *Informatie*, vol. 31, no. 1 (1989) cited in (Putnam and Myers 2003).

Henry, Sallie, and Dennis Kafura, 1984. "The Evaluation of Software Systems' Structure Using Quantitative Software Metrics," *Software–Practice and Experience*, vol. 14, no. 6 (June 1984), pp. 561–73.

Herbsleb, James, et al., *Benefits of CMM Based Software Process Improvement: Initial Results*, Pittsburgh: Software Engineering Institute, Document CMU/SEI-94-TR-13, August 1994.

Hihn, J., and H. Habib-Agahi, 1991. "Cost Estimation of Software Intensive Projects: a Survey of Current Practices," International Conference on Software Engineering, IEEE Computer Society Press, Los Alamitos, CA: 276–287.

Höst, M., and C. Wohlin, 1998. "An Experimental Study of Individual Subjective Effort Estimations and Combinations of the Estimates," *International Conference on Software Engineering*, Kyoto, Japan, IEEE Computer Society, Los Alamitos, CA: 332–339.

Humphrey, Watts S., 1995. *A Discipline for Software Engineering.* Reading, MA: Addison-Wesley.

Iansiti, Marco, 1994. "Microsoft Corporation: Office Business Unit," Harvard Business School Case Study 9-691-033, Revised May 31, 1994, Boston, MA: Harvard Business School.

IEEE Software, Nov/Dec. 2001 Issue, focus on recent advances in software estimation with several papers on the topic.

IFPUG Web site: *www.ifpug.org.*

ISBSG 2001. *Practical Project Estimation: A Toolkit for Estimating Software Development Effort and Duration*, Australia: International Software Benchmarking Standards Group, March 2001.

ISBSG 2005. *Practical Project Estimation, 2nd Edition: A Toolkit for Estimating Software Development Effort and Duration*, Australia: International Software Benchmarking Standards Group, February 2005.

ISO/IEC 20926:2003. "Software engineering – IFPUG 4.1 Unadjusted functional size measurement method – Counting practices manual," International Organization for Standardization, 2003.

Jacobson, Ivar, Grady Booch, James Rumbaugh, 1999. *The Unified Software Development Process*, Reading, MA: Addison-Wesley.

Jones, Capers, 1996. "Software Defect-Removal Efficiency," *IEEE Computer*, April 1996.

Jones, Capers, 2005. "Software Engineering: The State of the Art in 2005," Version 5, Software Productivity Research Whitepaper, February 11, 2005.

Jones, Capers, 1986. *Programming Productivity,* New York, NY: McGraw-Hill.

Jones, Capers, 1994. *Assessment and Control of Software Risks*, Englewood Cliffs, NJ: Yourdon Press.

Jones, Capers, 1995c. "Determining Software Schedules," *IEEE Computer*, February 1995, pp. 73–75.

Jones, Capers, 1997. *Applied Software Measurement: Assuring Productivity and Quality*, 2d ed., New York, NY: McGraw-Hill.

Jones, Capers, 1998. *Estimating Software Costs*, New York NY: McGraw-Hill.

Jones, Capers, 2000. *Software Assessments, Benchmarks, and Best Practices*, Reading, MA: Addison-Wesley.

Jørgensen M., 2002. "A Review of Studies on Expert Estimation of Software Development Effort."

Jørgensen, M., and D. I. K. Sjøberg, 2002. "The Impact of Customer Expectation on Software Development Effort Estimates," *International Journal of Project Management*.

Josephs, R., and E. D. Hahn, 1995. "Bias and Accuracy in Estimates of Task Duration," *Organizational Behaviour and Human Decision Processes,* 61(2): 202–213.

Kemerer, C. F., 1987. "An Emprical Validation of Software Cost Estimation Models," *Communications of the ACM*, 30 (5), 1987, pp. 416–429.

Kemerer, Chris, and Benjamin Porter, 1992. "Improving the Reliability of Function Point Measurement: An Empirical Study," *IEEE Transactions on Software Engineering*, Vol. 18, No. 11, November 1992, Page 1011.

Kitchenham, B., S. L. Pfleeger, B. McColl, and S. Eagan, 2002. "A Case Study of Maintenance Estimation Accuracy," *Journal of Systems and Software*.

Knorr, Eric, 2005. "Anatomy of an IT Disaster: How the FBI Blew It," *InfoWorld*, March 21, 2005.

Krasner, Jerry, 2003. "Embedded Software Development Issues and Challenges," *Embedded Market Forecasters* whitepaper, www.embeddedforecast.com.

Lais, Sami, 2003. "Watch your step: Can major efforts avoid more slipups?" *Government Computer News*, Vol. 22, no. 34, 12/15/03.

Laranjeira, Luiz, 1990. "Software Size Estimation of Object-Oriented Systems," *IEEE Transactions on Software Engineering*, May 1990.

Larsen, Richard J., and Morris L. Marx, 2001. *An Introduction to Mathematical Statistics and Its Applications*, 3d ed., Upper Saddle River, NJ: Prentice Hall.

Lawlis, Dr. Patricia K., Capt. Robert M. Flowe, and Capt. James B. Thordahl, 1995. "A Correlational Study of the CMM and Software Development Performance," *Crosstalk*, September 1995.

Lederer, Albert L., and Jayesh Prasad, 1992. "Nine Management Guideliness for Better Cost Estimating," *Communications of the ACM*, February 1992, pp. 51–59.

Libby, R., and R. K. Blashfield, 1978. "Performance of a Composite as a Function of the Number of Judges," *Organizational Behaviour and Human Performance* 21(2): 121–129.

Lim, J. S., and M. O'Connor, 1996. "Judgmental Forecasting With Time Series and Causal Information," *International Journal of Forecasting* 12(1): 139–153.

McCabe, Tom, 1976. "A Complexity Measure," *IEEE Transactions on Software Engineering*, Volume SE-2, Number 12 (December 1976), pp. 308–320.

McConnell, Steve, 1993. *Code Complete*, Redmond, Wa.: Microsoft Press, 1993.

McConnell, Steve, 1996. *Rapid Development*, Redmond, WA: Microsoft Press.

McConnell, Steve, 1998. *Software Project Survival Guide*, Redmond, WA: Microsoft Press.

McConnell, Steve, 2000. "Sitting on the Suitcase," *IEEE Software*, May/June 2000.

McConnell, Steve, 2002. "Real Quality For Real Engineers," *IEEE Software*, March/April 2002.

McConnell, Steve, 2004a. *Code Complete*, 2d ed., Redmond, WA: Microsoft Press.

McConnell, Steve, 2004b. *Professional Software Development*, Boston, MA: Addison-Wesley.

McGarry, John, et al., 2002. *Practical Software Measurement: Objective Information for Decision Makers*, Boston, MA: Addison-Wesley.

McGraw, Gary, 2003. "From the Ground Up: The DIMACS Software Security Workshop," *IEEE Security & Privacy*, March/April 2003. Volume 1, Number 2. pp. 59–66.

Metzger, Philip W., 1981. *Managing a Programming Project*, 2d ed., Englewood Cliffs, NJ: Prentice Hall.

Mills, Harlan D., 1983. *Software Productivity*, Boston, MA: Little, Brown, pp. 71–81.

Mohanty, S. N., 1981. "Software Cost Estimation: Present and Future," *Software–Practice and Experience*, 11, pp. 103–121.

Mosemann, Lloyd K., II, 2002. "Did We Lose Our Religion?" *Crosstalk*, August 2002, pp. 22–25.

NASA SEL, 1990. *Manager's Handbook for Software Development, Revision 1*. Document number SEL-84-101. Greenbelt, MD: Goddard Space Flight Center, NASA.

NASA SEL, 1991. *Software Engineering Laboratory (SEL) Relationships, Models, and Management Rules*, SEL-91-001, February 1991.

NASA SEL, 1995. *Software Measurement Guidebook*, Document Number NASA-GB-001-94, Greenbelt, MD: Goddard Space Flight Center, NASA, June 1995.

NASA, "ISD Wideband Delphi Estimation," Number 580-PROGRAMMER-016-01, September 1, 2004, *http://software.gsfc.nasa.gov/AssetsApproved/PA1.2.1.2.pdf*.

Niessink, F., and H. van Vliet, 1997. "Predicting Maintenance Effort With Function Points," International conference on software maintenance, Bari, Italy, IEEE Computer Society, Los Alamitos, CA, pp. 32–39.

Park, R. E., 1996. "A Manager's Checklist for Validating Software Cost and Schedule Estimates," *American Programmer* 9(6), pp. 30–35.

Paynter, J., 1996. "Project Estimation Using Screenflow Engineering," International Conference on Software Engineering: Education and Practice, Dunedin, New Zealand, IEEE Computer Society. Press, Los Alamitos, CA, pp. 150–159.

Pehrson, Ron J., 1996. "Software Development for the Boeing 777," *CrossTalk*, January 1996.

Pfleeger, Shari Lawrence, Felicia Wu, and Rosalind Lews, 2005. "Software Cost Estimation and Sizing Methods," Santa, Monica, CA: The Rand Corporation.

Pietrasanta, Alfred M., 1990. "Alfred M. Pietrasanta on Improving the Software Process" *Software Engineering: Tools, Techniques, Practices*, vol. 1, no. 1 (May/June 1990), pp. 29–34.

Pitterman, Bill, 2000. "Telcordia Technologies: The Journey to High Maturity," *IEEE Software*, July 2000, pp. 89–96.

Prechelt, Lutz, 2000. "An Empirical Comparison of Seven Programming Languages," *IEEE Computer*, October 2000, pp. 23–29.

Putnam, Lawrence H., and Ware Myers, 1992. *Measures for Excellence: Reliable Software On Time, Within Budget*, Englewood Cliffs, NJ: Yourdon Press.

Putnam, Lawrence H., and Ware Myers, 1997. *Industrial Strength Software: Effective Management Using Measurement*, Washington, DC: IEEE Computer Society Press.

Putnam, Lawrence H., and Ware Myers, 1999. "Get the Estimate Right," *American Programmer*, July 1999, pp. 4–12.

Putnam, Lawrence H., and Ware Myers, 2003. *Five Core Metrics*, New York, NY: Dorset House.

Reifer, Donald J., 2002. "Estimating Web Development Costs: There Are Differences," *CrossTalk*, June 2002, pp. 13–17.

Roetzheim, William H., 1988. *Structured Computer Project Management*, Englewood Cliffs, NJ: Prentice Hall.

Rule, Grant, 1998. From Stutzke.

Rule, Grant, 2000. "Bees and the Art of Estimating," *IEEE Software*, November/December 2000.

Sackman, H., Erikson, W. J., Grant, E. E., 1968. "Exploratory Experimental Studies Comparing Online and Offline Programming Performance." *Communications of the ACM,* v. 11, no. 1, January 1968, pp. 3–11.

Sanchez Roberto, 1998. "UW Learns a Lesson," *Seattle Times,* April 12, 1998, page B1.

Schlender, Brenton, 1989. "How to Break the Software Logjam," *Fortune,* September 25, 1989.

Schneider, Geri, and Jason P. Winters, 2001. *Applying Use Cases,* 2d ed., Boston, MA: Addison Wesley Longman.

Schwaber, Ken, and Mike Beedle, 2002. *Agile Software Development with Scrum,* Englewood Cliffs, NJ: Prentice Hall.

Sheppard, S. B., et al., 1978. "Predicting Programmers' Ability to Modify Software," *TR 78-388100-3,* General Electric Company, May 1978.

Sheppard, S. B., et al., 1979. "Modern Coding Practices and Programmer Performance," *IEEE Computer,* no. 12, Dec 1979, pp. 41–49.

Shull, et al., 2002. "What We Have Learned About Fighting Defects," *Proceedings, Metrics 2002.* IEEE; pp. 249–258.

Smith, John, 1999. "The Estimation of Effort Based on Use Cases," Rational Software Whitepaper TP-171, October 1999.

Standish Group, The, 1994. "Charting the Seas of Information Technology," Dennis, MA: The Standish Group.

Stutzke, Richard D., 2005. *Estimating Software-Intensive Systems,* Upper Saddle River, NJ: Addison-Wesley.

Symons, Charles, 1991. *Software Sizing and Estimating: Mk II FPA (Function Point Analysis),* Chichester: John Wiley & Sons.

The Age, 2005. "Waiter, there's a bug in my Prius," *The Age,* www.theage.com.au, May 25, 2005.

The American Heritage Dictionary, Second College Edition, 1985.

The Irish Times, 2005. "HSE to suspend roll-out of 150m computer system," October 4, 2005.

Tockey, Steve, 2005. *Return on Software,* Boston, MA: Addison-Wesley.

Todd, P., and I. Benbasat, 2000. "Inducing Compensatory Information Processing Through Decision Aids That Facilitate Effort Reduction: an Experimental Assessment," *Journal of Behavioral Decision Making* 13(1): pp. 91–106.

University of Southern California, *Cocomo II Model Definition Manual, version 1.4,* undated (circa 1997).

Valett, J., and F. E. McGarry, 1989. "A Summary of Software Measurement Experiences in the Software Engineering Laboratory," *Journal of Systems and Software,* 9 (2), pp. 137–148.

Van Genuchten, Michiel, 1991. "Why Is Software Late? An Empirical Study of Reasons for Delay in Software Development." *IEEE Transactions on Software Engineering* SE-17, no. 6 (June), pp. 582–590.

Vu, John, 2004. "Lessons Learned in Process Improvement," SEPG 2004.

Walston, C. E., and C. P. Felix, 1977. "A Method of Programming Measurement and Estimation," *IBM Systems Journal,* v. 16, no. 1, 1977, pp. 54–73.

Ward, William T., 1989b. "Software Defect Prevention Using McCabe's Complexity Metric," *Hewlett Packard Journal*, April 1989, pp. 64–68.

Weinberg, Gerald M., and Edward L. Schulman, 1974. "Goals and Performance in Computer Programming," vol 16, no. 1, pp. 70–77.

Weinberg, Gerald M., 1994. *Quality Software Management, Vol. 3, Congruent Action*, New York, NY: Dorset House.

Weyuker, Elaine J., 1988. "Evaluating Complexity Measures," *IEEE Transactions on Software Engineering*, v. 14, no. 9, September 1988, pp. 1357–1365.

Wheeler, David A., 2001. "More than a Gigabuck: Estimating GNU/Linux's Size," http://www.dwheeler.com/sloc.

Wiegers, Karl, 2000. "Stop Promising Miracles," *Software Development*, February 2000.

Wiegers, Karl, 2003. *Software Requirements*, 2d ed. Redmond, WA: Microsoft Press.

Wiegers, Karl, 2006. *More About Software Requirements: Thorny Issues and Practical Advice*, Redmond, WA: Microsoft Press.

Withers, Bud, 1999. "Take Me Out to the Ballpark," *Seattle Times*, July 11, 1999, pp. S3–S4.

Zultner, Richard E., 1999. "Project Estimation with Critical Chain: Third-Generation Risk Management," *American Programmer*, July 1999, pp. 4–12.

Index

Steve McConnell

Steve McConnell is Chief Software Engineer at Construx Software where he oversees Construx's software engineering practices. Steve is the lead for the Construction Knowledge Area of the Software Engineering Body of Knowledge (SWEBOK) project. Steve has worked on software projects at Microsoft, Boeing, and other Seattle-area companies. Steve was the lead developer of Construx Estimate and of SPC Estimate Professional, winner of a *Software Development* magazine Productivity Award.

Steve is the author of *Rapid Development* (1996), *Software Project Survival Guide* (1998), *Professional Software Development* (2004) and *Code Complete, Second Edition* (2004). His books have twice won *Software Development* magazine's Jolt Product Excellence Award for outstanding software development book of the year. Steve was also the lead developer of SPC Estimate Professional, winner of a Software Development Productivity award. In 1998, readers of *Software Development* magazine named Steve one of the three most influential people in the software industry, along with Bill Gates and Linus Torvalds.

Steve earned a Bachelor's degree from Whitman College and a Master's degree in software engineering from Seattle University. He lives in Bellevue, Washington.

If you have any comments or questions about this book, please contact Steve at *steve.mcconnell@construx.com* or via *www.stevemcconnell.com*.

Additional Resources for Developers: Advanced Topics and Best Practices

Published and Forthcoming Titles from Microsoft Press

Code Complete, Second Edition
Steve McConnell ● ISBN 0-7356-1967-0

For more than a decade, Steve McConnell, one of the premier authors and voices in the software community, has helped change the way developers write code—and produce better software. Now his classic book, *Code Complete*, has been fully updated and revised with best practices in the art and science of constructing software. Topics include design, applying good techniques to construction, eliminating errors, planning, managing construction activities, and relating personal character to superior software. This new edition features fully updated information on programming techniques, including the emergence of Web-style programming, and integrated coverage of object-oriented design. You'll also find new code examples—both good and bad—in C++, Microsoft® Visual Basic®, C#, and Java, although the focus is squarely on techniques and practices.

More About Software Requirements: Thorny Issues and Practical Advice
Karl E. Wiegers ● ISBN 0-7356-2267-1

Have you ever delivered software that satisfied all of the project specifications, but failed to meet any of the customers expectations? Without formal, verifiable requirements—and a system for managing them—the result is often a gap between what developers think they're supposed to build and what customers think they're going to get. Too often, lessons about software requirements engineering processes are formal or academic, and not of value to real-world, professional development teams. In this follow-up guide to *Software Requirements*, Second Edition, you will discover even more practical techniques for gathering and managing software requirements that help you deliver software that meets project and customer specifications. Succinct and immediately useful, this book is a must-have for developers and architects.

Software Estimation: Demystifying the Black Art
Steve McConnell ● ISBN 0-7356-0535-1

Often referred to as the "black art" because of its complexity and uncertainty, software estimation is not as hard or mysterious as people think. However, the art of how to create effective cost and schedule estimates has not been very well publicized. *Software Estimation* provides a proven set of procedures and heuristics that software developers, technical leads, and project managers can apply to their projects. Instead of arcane treatises and rigid modeling techniques, award-winning author Steve McConnell gives practical guidance to help organizations achieve basic estimation proficiency and lay the groundwork to continue improving project cost estimates. This book does not avoid the more complex mathematical estimation approaches, but the non-mathematical reader will find plenty of useful guidelines without getting bogged down in complex formulas.

Debugging, Tuning, and Testing Microsoft .NET 2.0 Applications
John Robbins ● ISBN 0-7356-2202-7

Making an application the best it can be has long been a time-consuming task best accomplished with specialized and costly tools. With Microsoft Visual Studio® 2005, developers have available a new range of built-in functionality that enables them to debug their code quickly and efficiently, tune it to optimum performance, and test applications to ensure compatibility and trouble-free operation. In this accessible and hands-on book, debugging expert John Robbins shows developers how to use the tools and functions in Visual Studio to their full advantage to ensure high-quality applications.

The Security Development Lifecycle
Michael Howard and Steve Lipner ● ISBN 0-7356-2214-0

Adapted from Microsoft's standard development process, the Security Development Lifecycle (SDL) is a methodology that helps reduce the number of security defects in code at every stage of the development process, from design to release. This book details each stage of the SDL methodology and discusses its implementation across a range of Microsoft software, including Microsoft Windows Server™ 2003, Microsoft SQL Server™ 2000 Service Pack 3, and Microsoft Exchange Server 2003 Service Pack 1, to help measurably improve security features. You get direct access to insights from Microsoft's security team and lessons that are applicable to software development processes worldwide, whether on a small-scale or a large-scale. This book includes a CD featuring videos of developer training classes.

Software Requirements, Second Edition
Karl E. Wiegers ● ISBN 0-7356-1879-8

Writing Secure Code, Second Edition
Michael Howard and David LeBlanc ● ISBN 0-7356-1722-8

CLR via C#, Second Edition
Jeffrey Richter ● ISBN 0-7356-2163-2

For more information about Microsoft Press® books and other learning products, visit: **www.microsoft.com/mspress** *and* **www.microsoft.com/learning**

Additional Resources for Web Developers
Published and Forthcoming Titles from Microsoft Press

Microsoft® Visual Web Developer™ 2005 Express Edition: Build a Web Site Now!
Jim Buyens • ISBN 0-7356-2212-4

With this lively, eye-opening, and hands-on book, all you need is a computer and the desire to learn how to create Web pages now using Visual Web Developer Express Edition! Featuring a full working edition of the software, this fun and highly visual guide walks you through a complete Web page project from set-up to launch. You'll get an introduction to the Microsoft Visual Studio® environment and learn how to put the light-weight, easy-to-use tools in Visual Web Developer Express to work right away—building your first, dynamic Web pages with Microsoft ASP.NET 2.0. You'll get expert tips, coaching, and visual examples at each step of the way, along with pointers to additional learning resources.

Microsoft ASP.NET 2.0 Programming
Step by Step
George Shepherd • ISBN 0-7356-2201-9

With dramatic improvements in performance, productivity, and security features, Visual Studio 2005 and ASP.NET 2.0 deliver a simplified, high-performance, and powerful Web development experience. ASP.NET 2.0 features a new set of controls and infrastructure that simplify Web-based data access and include functionality that facilitates code reuse, visual consistency, and aesthetic appeal. Now you can teach yourself the essentials of working with ASP.NET 2.0 in the Visual Studio environment—one step at a time. With *Step by Step*, you work at your own pace through hands-on, learn-by-doing exercises. Whether you're a beginning programmer or new to this version of the technology, you'll understand the core capabilities and fundamental techniques for ASP.NET 2.0. Each chapter puts you to work, showing you how, when, and why to use specific features of the ASP.NET 2.0 rapid application development environment and guiding you as you create actual components and working applications for the Web, including advanced features such as personalization.

Programming Microsoft ASP.NET 2.0
Core Reference
Dino Esposito • ISBN 0-7356-2176-4

Delve into the core topics for ASP.NET 2.0 programming, mastering the essential skills and capabilities needed to build high-performance Web applications successfully. Well-known ASP.NET author Dino Esposito deftly builds your expertise with Web forms, Visual Studio, core controls, master pages, data access, data binding, state management, security services, and other must-know topics—combining defini-tive reference with practical, hands-on programming instruc-tion. Packed with expert guidance and pragmatic examples, this *Core Reference* delivers the key resources that you need to develop professional-level Web programming skills.

Programming Microsoft ASP.NET 2.0
Applications: *Advanced Topics*
Dino Esposito • ISBN 0-7356-2177-2

Master advanced topics in ASP.NET 2.0 programming—gaining the essential insights and in-depth understanding that you need to build sophisticated, highly func-tional Web applications success-fully. Topics include Web forms, Visual Studio 2005, core controls, master pages, data access, data binding, state management, and security considerations. Developers often discover that the more they use ASP.NET, the more they need to know. With expert guidance from ASP.NET authority Dino Esposito, you get the in-depth, comprehensive information that leads to full mastery of the technology.

Programming Microsoft Windows® Forms
Charles Petzold • ISBN 0-7356-2153-5

Programming Microsoft Web Forms
Douglas J. Reilly • ISBN 0-7356-2179-9

CLR via C++
Jeffrey Richter with Stanley B. Lippman
ISBN 0-7356-2248-5

Debugging, Tuning, and Testing Microsoft .NET 2.0 Applications
John Robbins • ISBN 0-7356-2202-7

CLR via C#, Second Edition
Jeffrey Richter • ISBN 0-7356-2163-2

For more information about Microsoft Press® books and other learning products,
visit: **www.microsoft.com/books** *and* **www.microsoft.com/learning**

Additional Resources for C# Developers

Published and Forthcoming Titles from Microsoft Press

Microsoft® Visual C#® 2005 Express Edition: Build a Program Now!
Patrice Pelland • ISBN 0-7356-2229-9

In this lively, eye-opening, and hands-on book, all you need is a computer and the desire to learn how to program with Visual C# 2005 Express Edition. Featuring a full working edition of the software, this fun and highly visual guide walks you through a complete programming project—a desktop weather-reporting application—from start to finish. You'll get an unintimidating introduction to the Microsoft Visual Studio® development environment and learn how to put the lightweight, easy-to-use tools in Visual C# Express to work right away—creating, compiling, testing, and delivering your first, ready-to-use program. You'll get expert tips, coaching, and visual examples at each step of the way, along with pointers to additional learning resources.

Microsoft Visual C# 2005 *Step by Step*
John Sharp • ISBN 0-7356-2129-2

Visual C#, a feature of Visual Studio 2005, is a modern programming language designed to deliver a productive environment for creating business frameworks and reusable object-oriented components. Now you can teach yourself essential techniques with Visual C#—and start building components and Microsoft Windows®–based applications—one step at a time. With *Step by Step*, you work at your own pace through hands-on, learn-by-doing exercises. Whether you're a beginning programmer or new to this particular language, you'll learn how, when, and why to use specific features of Visual C# 2005. Each chapter puts you to work, building your knowledge of core capabilities and guiding you as you create your first C#-based applications for Windows, data management, and the Web.

Programming Microsoft Visual C# 2005 Framework Reference
Francesco Balena • ISBN 0-7356-2182-9

Complementing *Programming Microsoft Visual C# 2005 Core Reference*, this book covers a wide range of additional topics and information critical to Visual C# developers, including Windows Forms, working with Microsoft ADO.NET 2.0 and Microsoft ASP.NET 2.0, Web services, security, remoting, and much more. Packed with sample code and real-world examples, this book will help developers move from understanding to mastery.

Programming Microsoft Visual C# 2005 *Core Reference*
Donis Marshall • ISBN 0-7356-2181-0

Get the in-depth reference and pragmatic, real-world insights you need to exploit the enhanced language features and core capabilities in Visual C# 2005. Programming expert Donis Marshall deftly builds your proficiency with classes, structs, and other fundamentals, and advances your expertise with more advanced topics such as debugging, threading, and memory management. Combining incisive reference with hands-on coding examples and best practices, this *Core Reference* focuses on mastering the C# skills you need to build innovative solutions for smart clients and the Web.

CLR via C#, Second Edition
Jeffrey Richter • ISBN 0-7356-2163-2

In this new edition of Jeffrey Richter's popular book, you get focused, pragmatic guidance on how to exploit the common language runtime (CLR) functionality in Microsoft .NET Framework 2.0 for applications of all types—from Web Forms, Windows Forms, and Web services to solutions for Microsoft SQL Server™, Microsoft code names "Avalon" and "Indigo," consoles, Microsoft Windows NT® Service, and more. Targeted to advanced developers and software designers, this book takes you under the covers of .NET for an in-depth understanding of its structure, functions, and operational components, demonstrating the most practical ways to apply this knowledge to your own development efforts. You'll master fundamental design tenets for .NET and get hands-on insights for creating high-performance applications more easily and efficiently. The book features extensive code examples in Visual C# 2005.

Programming Microsoft Windows Forms
Charles Petzold • ISBN 0-7356-2153-5

CLR via C++
Jeffrey Richter with Stanley B. Lippman
ISBN 0-7356-2248-5

Programming Microsoft Web Forms
Douglas J. Reilly • ISBN 0-7356-2179-9

Debugging, Tuning, and Testing Microsoft .NET 2.0 Applications
John Robbins • ISBN 0-7356-2202-7

For more information about Microsoft Press® books and other learning products,
visit: **www.microsoft.com/books** *and* **www.microsoft.com/learning**

Additional SQL Server Resources for Developers

Published and Forthcoming Titles from Microsoft Press

Additional Resources for Visual Basic Developers

Published and Forthcoming Titles from Microsoft Press

Microsoft® Visual Basic® 2005 Express Edition: Build a Program Now!
Patrice Pelland ● ISBN 0-7356-2213-2

Featuring a full working edition of the software, this fun and highly visual guide walks you through a complete programming project—a desktop weather-reporting application—from start to finish. You'll get an introduction to the Microsoft Visual Studio® development environment and learn how to put the lightweight, easy-to-use tools in Visual Basic Express to work right away—creating, compiling, testing, and delivering your first ready-to-use program. You'll get expert tips, coaching, and visual examples each step of the way, along with pointers to additional learning resources.

Microsoft Visual Basic 2005 *Step by Step*
Michael Halvorson ● ISBN 0-7356-2131-4

With enhancements across its visual designers, code editor, language, and debugger that help accelerate the development and deployment of robust, elegant applications across the Web, a business group, or an enterprise, Visual Basic 2005 focuses on enabling developers to rapidly build applications. Now you can teach yourself the essentials of working with Visual Studio 2005 and the new features of the Visual Basic language—one step at a time. Each chapter puts you to work, showing you how, when, and why to use specific features of Visual Basic and guiding as you create actual components and working applications for Microsoft Windows®. You'll also explore data management and Web-based development topics.

Programming Microsoft Visual Basic 2005 *Core Reference*
Francesco Balena ● ISBN 0-7356-2183-7

Get the expert insights, indispensable reference, and practical instruction needed to exploit the core language features and capabilities in Visual Basic 2005. Well-known Visual Basic programming author Francesco Balena expertly guides you through the fundamentals, including modules, keywords, and inheritance, and builds your mastery of more advanced topics such as delegates, assemblies, and My Namespace. Combining in-depth reference with extensive, hands-on code examples and best-practices advice, this *Core Reference* delivers the key resources that you need to develop professional-level programming skills for smart clients and the Web.

Programming Microsoft Visual Basic 2005 Framework Reference
Francesco Balena ● ISBN 0-7356-2175-6

Complementing *Programming Microsoft Visual Basic 2005 Core Reference*, this book covers a wide range of additional topics and information critical to Visual Basic developers, including Windows Forms, working with Microsoft ADO.NET 2.0 and ASP.NET 2.0, Web services, security, remoting, and much more. Packed with sample code and real-world examples, this book will help developers move from understanding to mastery.

Programming Microsoft Windows Forms
Charles Petzold ● ISBN 0-7356-2153-5

Programming Microsoft Web Forms
Douglas J. Reilly ● ISBN 0-7356-2179-9

Debugging, Tuning, and Testing Microsoft .NET 2.0 Applications
John Robbins ● ISBN 0-7356-2202-7

Microsoft ASP.NET 2.0 *Step by Step*
George Shepherd ● ISBN 0-7356-2201-9

Microsoft ADO.NET 2.0 *Step by Step*
Rebecca Riordan ● ISBN 0-7356-2164-0

Programming Microsoft ASP.NET 2.0 *Core Reference*
Dino Esposito ● ISBN 0-7356-2176-4

For more information about Microsoft Press® books and other learning products,
visit: **www.microsoft.com/books** *and* **www.microsoft.com/learning**

Additional SQL Server Resources for Administrators

Published and Forthcoming Titles from Microsoft Press

Microsoft® SQL Server™ 2005 Reporting Services *Step by Step*

Hitachi Consulting Services ● ISBN 0-7356-2250-7

SQL Server Reporting Services (SRS) is Microsoft's customizable reporting solution for business data analysis. It is one of the key value features of SQL Server 2005: functionality more advanced and much less expensive than its competition. SRS is powerful, so an understanding of how to architect a report, as well as how to install and program SRS, is key to harnessing the full functionality of SQL Server. This procedural tutorial shows how to use the Report Project Wizard, how to think about and access data, and how to build queries. It also walks the reader through the creation of charts and visual layouts to enable maximum visual understanding of the data analysis. Interactivity (enhanced in SQL Server 2005) and security are also covered in detail.

Microsoft SQL Server 2005 Administrator's Pocket Consultant

William R. Stanek ● ISBN 0-7356-2107-1

Here's the utterly practical, pocket-sized reference for IT professionals who need to administer, optimize, and maintain SQL Server 2005 in their organizations. This unique guide provides essential details for using SQL Server 2005 to help protect and manage your company's data—whether automating tasks; creating indexes and views; performing backups and recovery; replicating transactions; tuning performance; managing server activity; importing and exporting data; or performing other key tasks. Featuring quick-reference tables, lists, and step-by-step instructions, this handy, one-stop guide provides fast, accurate answers on the spot, whether you're at your desk or in the field!

Microsoft SQL Server 2005 Administrator's Companion

Marci Frohock Garcia, Edward Whalen, and Mitchell Schroeter ● ISBN 0-7356-2198-5

Microsoft SQL Server 2005 Administrator's Companion is the comprehensive, in-depth guide that saves time by providing all the technical information you need to deploy, administer, optimize, and support SQL Server 2005. Using a hands-on, example-rich approach, this authoritative, one-volume reference book provides expert advice, product information, detailed solutions, procedures, and real-world troubleshooting tips from experienced SQL Server 2005 professionals. This expert guide shows you how to design high-availability database systems, prepare for installation, install and configure SQL Server 2005, administer services and features, and maintain and troubleshoot your database system. It covers how to configure your system for your I/O system and model and optimize system capacity. The expert authors provide details on how to create and use defaults, constraints, rules, indexes, views, functions, stored procedures, and triggers. This guide shows you how to administer reporting services, analysis services, notification services, and integration services. It also provides a wealth of information on replication and the specifics of snapshot, transactional, and merge replication. Finally, there is expansive coverage of how to manage and tune your SQL Server system, including automating tasks, backup and restoration of databases, and management of users and security.

Microsoft SQL Server 2005 Analysis Services *Step by Step*

Hitachi Consulting Services ● ISBN 0-7356-2199-3

One of the key features of SQL Server 2005 is SQL Server Analysis Services—Microsoft's customizable analysis solution for business data modeling and interpretation. Just compare SQL Server Analysis Services to its competition to understand/grasp the great value of its enhanced features. One of the keys to harnessing the full functionality of SQL Server will be leveraging Analysis Services for the powerful tool that it is—including creating a cube, and deploying, customizing, and extending the basic calculations. This step-by-step tutorial discusses how to get started, how to build scalable analytical applications, and how to use and administer advanced features. Interactivity (which is enhanced in SQL Server 2005), data translation, and security are also covered in detail.

Microsoft SQL Server 2005 Express Edition
Step by Step
Jackie Goldstein ● ISBN 0-7356-2184-5

Inside Microsoft SQL Server 2005:
The Storage Engine
Kalen Delaney ● ISBN 0-7356-2105-5

Inside Microsoft SQL Server 2005:
T-SQL Programming
Itzik Ben-Gan ● ISBN 0-7356-2197-7

Inside Microsoft SQL Server 2005:
Query Processing and Optimization
Kalen Delaney ● ISBN 0-7356-2196-9

For more information about Microsoft Press® books and other learning products, visit: **www.microsoft.com/mspress** *and* **www.microsoft.com/learning**

Additional Windows (R2) Resources for Administrators

Published and Forthcoming Titles from Microsoft Press

Microsoft® Windows Server™ 2003 Administrator's Pocket Consultant, Second Edition

William R. Stanek ● ISBN 0-7356-2245-0

Here's the practical, pocket-sized reference for IT professionals supporting Microsoft Windows Server 2003—fully updated for Service Pack 1 and Release 2. Designed for quick referencing, this portable guide covers all the essentials for performing everyday system administration tasks. Topics include managing workstations and servers, using Active Directory® directory service, creating and administering user and group accounts, managing files and directories, performing data security and auditing tasks, handling data back-up and recovery, and administering networks using TCP/IP, WINS, and DNS, and more.

MCSE Self-Paced Training Kit (Exams 70-290, 70-291, 70-293, 70-294): Microsoft Windows Server 2003 Core Requirements, Second Edition

Holme, Thomas, Mackin, McLean, Zacker, Spealman, Hudson, and Craft ● ISBN 0-7356-2290-6

The Microsoft Certified Systems Engineer (MCSE) credential is the premier certification for professionals who analyze the business requirements and design and implement the infrastructure for business solutions based on the Microsoft Windows Server 2003 platform and Microsoft Windows Server System—now updated for Windows Server 2003 Service Pack 1 and R2. This all-in-one set provides in-depth preparation for the four required networking system exams. Work at your own pace through the lessons, hands-on exercises, troubleshooting labs, and review questions. You get expert exam tips plus a full review section covering all objectives and sub-objectives in each study guide. Then use the Microsoft Practice Tests on the CD to challenge yourself with more than 1500 questions for self-assessment and practice!

Microsoft Windows® Small Business Server 2003 R2 Administrator's Companion

Charlie Russel, Sharon Crawford, and Jason Gerend ● ISBN 0-7356-2280-9

Get your small-business network, messaging, and collaboration systems up and running quickly with the essential guide to administering Windows Small Business Server 2003 R2. This reference details the features, capabilities, and technologies for both the standard and premium editions—including Microsoft Windows Server 2003 R2, Exchange Server 2003 with Service Pack 1, Windows SharePoint® Services, SQL Server™ 2005 Workgroup Edition, and Internet Information Services. Discover how to install, upgrade, or migrate to Windows Small Business Server 2003 R2; plan and implement your network, Internet access, and security services; customize Microsoft Exchange Server for your e-mail needs; and administer user rights, shares, permissions, and Group Policy.

Microsoft Windows Small Business Server 2003 R2 Administrator's Companion

Charlie Russel, Sharon Crawford, and Jason Gerend ● ISBN 0-7356-2280-9

Here's the ideal one-volume guide for the IT professional administering Windows Server 2003. Now fully updated for Windows Server 2003 Service Pack 1 and R2, this *Administrator's Companion* offers up-to-date information on core system administration topics for Microsoft Windows, including Active Directory services, security, scripting, disaster planning and recovery, and interoperability with UNIX. It also includes all-new sections on Service Pack 1 security updates and new features for R2. Featuring easy-to-use procedures and handy work-arounds, this book provides ready answers for on-the-job results.

MCSA/MCSE Self-Paced Training Kit (Exam 70-290): Managing and Maintaining a Microsoft Windows Server 2003 Environment, Second Edition
Dan Holme and Orin Thomas ● ISBN 0-7356-2289-2

MCSA/MCSE Self-Paced Training Kit (Exam 70-291): Implementing, Managing, and Maintaining a Microsoft Windows Server 2003 Network Infrastructure, Second Edition
J.C. Mackin and Ian McLean ● ISBN 0-7356-2288-4

MCSE Self-Paced Training Kit (Exam 70-293): Planning and Maintaining a Microsoft Windows Server 2003 Network Infrastructure, Second Edition
Craig Zacker ● ISBN 0-7356-2287-6

MCSE Self-Paced Training Kit (Exam 70-294): Planning, Implementing, and Maintaining a Microsoft Windows Server 2003 Active Directory® Infrastructure, Second Ed.
Jill Spealman, Kurt Hudson, and Melissa Craft ● ISBN 0-7356-2286-8

For more information about Microsoft Press® books and other learning products, visit: **www.microsoft.com/mspress** *and* **www.microsoft.com/learning**

Prepare for Certification with Self-Paced Training Kits

Official Exam Prep Guides—
Plus Practice Tests

Ace your preparation for the skills measured by the MCP exams—and on the job. With official *Self-Paced Training Kits* from Microsoft, you'll work at your own pace through a system of lessons, hands-on exercises, troubleshooting labs, and review questions. Then test yourself with the Readiness Review Suite on CD, which provides hundreds of challenging questions for in-depth self-assessment and practice.

- **MCSE Self-Paced Training Kit (Exams 70-290, 70-291, 70-293, 70-294): Microsoft® Windows Server™ 2003 Core Requirements.** 4-Volume Boxed Set. ISBN: 0-7356-1953-0. (Individual volumes are available separately.)

- **MCSA/MCSE Self-Paced Training Kit (Exam 70-270): Installing, Configuring, and Administering Microsoft Windows® XP Professional, Second Edition.** ISBN: 0-7356-2152-7.

- **MCSE Self-Paced Training Kit (Exam 70-298): Designing Security for a Microsoft Windows Server 2003 Network.** ISBN: 0-7356-1969-7.

- **MCSA/MCSE Self-Paced Training Kit (Exam 70-350): Implementing Microsoft Internet Security and Acceleration Server 2004.** ISBN: 0-7356-2169-1.

- **MCSA/MCSE Self-Paced Training Kit (Exam 70-284): Implementing and Managing Microsoft Exchange Server 2003.** ISBN: 0-7356-1899-2.

For more information about Microsoft Press® books, visit: **www.microsoft.com/mspress**

For more information about learning tools such as online assessments, e-learning, and certification, visit: **www.microsoft.com/mspress** *and* **www.microsoft.com/learning**

Microsoft Windows Server 2003 Resource Kit
The *definitive* resource
for Windows Server 2003!

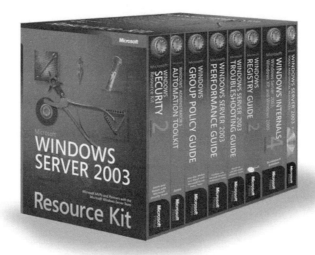

Get the in-depth technical information and tools you need to manage and optimize Microsoft® Windows Server™ 2003—with expert guidance and best practices from Microsoft MVPs, leading industry consultants, and the Microsoft Windows Server team. This official *Resource Kit* delivers seven comprehensive volumes, including:

- **Microsoft Windows® Security Resource Kit, Second Edition**
- **Microsoft Windows Administrator's Automation Toolkit**
- **Microsoft Windows Group Policy Guide**
- **Microsoft Windows Server 2003 Performance Guide**
- **Microsoft Windows Server 2003 Troubleshooting Guide**
- **Microsoft Windows Registry Guide, Second Edition**
- **Microsoft Windows Internals, Fourth Edition**

You'll find 300+ timesaving tools and scripts, an eBook of the entire *Resource Kit*, plus five bonus eBooks. It's everything you need to help maximize system performance and reliability—and help reduce ownership and support costs.

Microsoft Windows Server 2003 Resource Kit
Microsoft MVPs and Partners with the Microsoft Windows Server Team
ISBN: 0-7356-2232-9

For more information about Microsoft Press® books, visit: **www.microsoft.com/mspress**

For more information about learning tools such as online assessments, e-learning, and certification, visit: **www.microsoft.com/learning**

Additional Resources for Business and Home Users
Published and Forthcoming Titles from Microsoft Press

Beyond Bullet Points: Using Microsoft® PowerPoint® to Create Presentations That Inform, Motivate, and Inspire
Cliff Atkinson • ISBN 0-7356-2052-0

Improve your presentations—and increase your impact—with 50 powerful, practical, and easy-to-apply techniques for Microsoft PowerPoint. With *Beyond Bullet Points*, you'll take your presentation skills to the next level—learning innovative ways to design and deliver your message. Organized into five sections, including Distill Your Ideas, Structure Your Story, Visualize Your Message, Create a Conversation, and Maintain Engagement—the book uses clear, concise language and just the right visuals to help you understand concepts and start getting better results.

Take Back Your Life! Special Edition: Using Microsoft Outlook® to Get Organized and Stay Organized
Sally McGhee • ISBN 0-7356-2215-9

Unrelenting e-mail. Conflicting commitments. Endless interruptions. In this book, productivity expert Sally McGhee shows you how to take control and reclaim something that you thought you'd lost forever—your work-life balance. Now you can benefit from Sally's popular and highly regarded corporate education programs, learning simple but powerful techniques for rebalancing your personal and professional commitments using the productivity features in Outlook. When you change your approach, you can change your results. So learn what thousands of Sally's clients worldwide have discovered about taking control of their everyday productivity—and start transforming your own life today!

On Time! On Track! On Target! Managing Your Projects Successfully with Microsoft Project
Bonnie Biafore • ISBN 0-7356-2256-6

This book focuses on the core skills you need to successfully manage any project, giving you a practical education in project management and how-to instruction for using Microsoft Office Project Professional 2003 and other Microsoft Office Professional Edition 2003 programs, such as Excel® 2003, Outlook 2003, and Word 2003. Learn the essentials of project management, including creating successful project plans, tracking and evaluating performance, and controlling project costs. Whether you're a beginner just learning how to manage projects or a project manager already working on a project, this book has something for you. Includes a companion CD with sample Project templates.

Design to Sell: Using Microsoft Publisher to Inform, Motivate, and Persuade
Roger C. Parker • ISBN 0-7356-2260-4

Design to Sell relates the basics of effective message creation and formatting to the specific capabilities built into Microsoft Publisher—the powerful page layout program found on hundreds of thousands of computers around the world. Many Microsoft Office users already have Publisher on their computers but don't use it because they don't think of themselves as writers or designers. Here is a one-stop guide to marketing that even those without big budgets or previous design or writing experience can use to create compelling, easy-to-read marketing materials. Each chapter has an interactive exercise as well as questions with answers on the author's Web site. Also on the Web site are downloadable worksheets and templates, book updates, more illustrations of the projects in the book, and additional before-and-after project makeovers.

Microsoft Windows® XP Networking and Security Inside Out: Also Covers Windows 2000
Ed Bott and Carl Siechert • ISBN 0-7356-2042-3

Configure and manage your PC network—and help combat privacy and security threats—from the inside out! Written by the authors of the immensely popular *Microsoft Windows XP Inside Out*, this book packs hundreds of timesaving solutions, troubleshooting tips, and work-arounds for networking and security topics—all in concise, fast-answer format.

Dig into the tools and techniques for configuring workgroup, domain, Internet, and remote networking, and all the network components and features in between. Get the answers you need to use Windows XP Service Pack 2 and other tools, tactics, and features to help defend your personal computer and network against spyware, pop-up ads, viruses, hackers, spam, denial-of-service attacks, and other threats. Learn how to help secure your Virtual Private Networks (VPNs), remote access, and wireless networking services, and take ultimate control with advanced solutions such as file encryption, port blocking, IPSec, group policies, and tamper-proofing tactics for the registry. Get up to date on hot topics such as peer-to-peer networks, public wireless access points, smart cards, handheld computers, wireless LANs, and more. Plus, the CD includes bonus resources that make it easy for you to share your new security and networking expertise with your colleagues, friends, and family.

What do you think of this book?
We want to hear from you!

Do you have a few minutes to participate in a brief online survey? Microsoft is interested in hearing your feedback about this publication so that we can continually improve our books and learning resources for you.

To participate in our survey, please visit:
www.microsoft.com/learning/booksurvey

And enter this book's ISBN, 0-7356-0535-1. As a thank-you to survey participants in the United States and Canada, each month we'll randomly select five respondents to win one of five $100 gift certificates from a leading online merchant.* At the conclusion of the survey, you can enter the drawing by providing your e-mail address, which will be used for prize notification *only*.

Thanks in advance for your input. Your opinion counts!

Sincerely,

Microsoft Learning

Learn More. Go Further.